The Nature Handbook

THE NATURE HANDBOOK

A Guide to Observing the Great Outdoors

Ernest H. Williams, Jr.

OXFORD
UNIVERSITY PRESS
2005

OXFORD
UNIVERSITY PRESS

Oxford University Press, Inc., publishes works that further
Oxford University's objective of excellence
in research, scholarship, and education.

Oxford New York
Auckland Cape Town Dar es Salaam Hong Kong Karachi
Kuala Lumpur Madrid Melbourne Mexico City Nairobi
New Delhi Shanghai Taipei Toronto

With offices in
Argentina Austria Brazil Chile Czech Republic France Greece
Guatemala Hungary Italy Japan Poland Portugal Singapore
South Korea Switzerland Thailand Turkey Ukraine Vietnam

Published by Oxford University Press, Inc.
198 Madison Avenue, New York, New York 10016
www.oup.com

Library of Congress Cataloging-in-Publication Data
Williams, Ernest Herbert, 1946–
The nature handbook : A guide to observing the great outdoors / Ernest H. Williams, Jr.
   p. cm.   Includes bibliographical references and index.
ISBN-13: 978-0-19-517194-5 (pbk)
ISBN-10: 0-19-517194-2 (pbk)
ISBN-13: 978-0-19-517929-3 (cl)
ISBN-10: 0-19-517929-3 (cl)
1. Natural history. 2. Nature. I. Title.
QH45.2.W55 2004
508—dc22   2004052065

Book design by Susan Day

9 8 7 6 5 4 3 2 1
Printed in China
on acid-free paper

For Sharon and Anne

Acknowledgments

This book demonstrates the collaborative nature of learning. I have benefited greatly from discussing topics in nature with many different people over the past several decades. For times together in the field, I wish to acknowledge Karolis Bagdonas, Mike Beck, Noreen Beck, Bill Bonini, Sandy Bonnano, Deane Bowers, Betsy Flint, Bob Geigengack, Marsha Guzewich, Henry Horn, Chris Norment, Beth Painter, Doug Pens, Matt Perry, Bill Pfitsch, Bob Pyle, Art Shapiro, Randy Shull, Don Stokes, and Meg Thompson. I learned a great deal about teaching from Erling Dorf, with whom I first taught out in the field. For comments on parts of the manuscript, I thank Chris Norment, Bill Pfitsch, Dudley Raynal, Pat Reynolds, Ron Rutowski, and Brian Scholtens. I am especially indebted to Linda Fink and Conley McMullen for their detailed reviews of the manuscript and the challenging questions they posed; the book is much better because of their thoroughness, though I am responsible for any errors. I have appreciated discussing features of the book with Lincoln Brower, Jeff Glassberg, John Nichols, and Bob Pyle. For kindly responding to my questions, I thank Mark Bertness, Bruce Cutler, Don Despain, Bob Dirig, Nick Donnelly, John Dupre, David Gapp, Terry Hawkridge, Tim McCabe, Peter Millet, Daniel Otte, Bob Rothman, George Shields, Paul Thomas, Toni Thomas, Niklas Wahlberg, and Dana York. I thank all the photographers listed in the photo credits for their contributions; their professional skill shows clearly in the photographs. For help in obtaining reference material, I thank the staff of Hamilton College's interlibrary loan department.

For her continuous support and the use of her home over many years as a way station to the field, I thank my mother, Anne Williams. For help in all these ways and many more, I am deeply indebted to my wife, Sharon Williams. These two people have helped me bring this book together. Hamilton College has given me the freedom to pursue my interests in understanding nature and teaching about it, and I thank David Paris for his support. I have been challenged to explain patterns of nature to many, many people, and along the way I learned more myself: more than twenty-five years of field trips with ecology students, high school teachers, Elderhostel groups, graduate students in environmental studies, participants in Princeton University alumni colleges, members of the Utica Marsh Council and the Nature Conservancy, third graders, more than a hundred undergraduates collaborating in biological research, and many friends. For nursing the project from development through refinement and finally to publication, I thank Kirk Jensen, Peter Prescott, Helen Mules, and others at Oxford University Press for their thorough professional efforts. They have made my ideas come to life.

Contents

Introduction

Nature is full of fascinating stories, stories that intrigue those of us who enjoy the outdoors. The basis for this attraction is a deeply ingrained love of nature (biophilia, as described by the biologist E. O. Wilson). As a collection of observations that spur our curiosity, this book explores patterns we can easily see in nature and find pleasure in understanding.

The audience for this book is everyone interested in nature, including birders, gardeners, hikers, butterfliers, tree-huggers, photographers, naturalists of all kinds, wildflower enthusiasts, students, Scouts, and those whose interest is just beginning to develop—in short, anyone who finds learning more about nature interesting, worthwhile, or helpful. People such as birders who are already well versed with one group of organisms will find some new explanations about their favorite group, even if they're already familiar with the general patterns of those organisms, and they'll also find many new patterns in nature around them that they had overlooked.

The general themes of these descriptions are:

- *Relationship of size and shape.* Because function is intertwined with structure, one can often interpret the lifestyle or activity of an organism from its form.
- *Adaptations.* Alternative structures and behaviors exist for different lifestyles.
- *Distributional patterns.* Climate and substrate differences from one site to another set limits to the distributions of living things.
- *Behavior.* Many of the most appealing and intriguing observations in nature are behavioral responses and interactions.
- *Diversity of life.* A first lesson for every observer is the remarkable diversity of nature; there is so much to see and learn!

The observations are arranged in three main sections: plants, animals, and habitats. The descriptions are then organized into chapters based on their primary associations; sometimes that grouping is with certain kinds of organisms (e.g., mechanisms of seed dispersal are associated with plants) and sometimes with a habitat (e.g., elevational zonation of montane forests is associated with mountains). The difference between plant and animal topics is usually straightforward, but the decision to assign a pattern to an organism or a habitat is not always as easy. Still, the assignments should make sense. Although leaf shape, treelines, and fall colors all have to do with trees, leaf shape is most closely associated with trees as organisms, so its description is found in Chapter 2, "Trees"; treelines are most associated with mountains, so their description is in Chapter 8, "Mountains"; and fall colors apply more broadly to forests than just to individual trees, so that description is in Chapter 9, "Forests." Other tree-related topics may be found elsewhere, as with stored nuts (Chapter 1), lenticels (Chapter 3), field succession (Chapter 10), and sculptured forests (Chapter 13). Each chapter has cross-references to related topics. The best way to use this book is to skim through it and find what's interesting to you.

With so many patterns to choose from, any collection of this sort is somewhat idiosyncratic. The patterns described here are particularly apparent and thought-provoking, ranging across plant and animal physiology, animal behavior, functional morphology, and ecological relationships. The 227 descriptions that follow include many of the most common features and patterns of living organisms that one is likely to encounter. People are very visual creatures, so the inclusion of approximately 500 color photos helps make the patterns apparent and recognizable.

Many field guides exist to help identify organisms found in nature. Field guides are available for a wide range of individual taxonomic groups, and I have many dozens of such books on my own shelves. Among the best-known are those in several fine series: the Peterson Field Guide series (Houghton Mifflin), Audubon Society Field Guides (Chanticleer Press), Golden Guides (Golden Press), Stokes Nature Guides (Little, Brown), and the Butterflies through Binoculars series (Oxford University Press). These guides are excellent for the purposes of identification and providing information about the species encountered (behavior, distribution, etc.), but they usually fall short in explaining patterns of nature because that is not their purpose. It *is* the purpose of this book.

There are hazards, of course, in extrapolating the results from studies of single species or single places to many species and many places. Nature is complex, and generalizations may be applied too broadly. Different species live independently, isolated reproductively and adapted to different foods, habitat, climate, and other environmental features that surround them. But the extrapolations in this text are mostly appropriate, though, because closely related species share similar physiology, structure, and ecological requirements. Further study of related species, however, will undoubtedly show variations in these patterns.

When multiple causes are possible, I've tried to refer to all explanations yet highlight the one or ones that seem most likely. Why do forest seed-producing trees switch between years of heavy seed production and years without (masting)? Is it to satiate seed predators or to enhance pollination through flowering synchrony? Often two or more ideas may be correct simultaneously. Many of the patterns described here are well understood (e.g., ring structure of trees), whereas others are quite speculative (e.g., retained leaves). Continuing study of these phenomena will add new ideas and enhance our understanding.

Curiosity about the world around us is the basis of human learning. We investigate what we don't understand, and that curiosity has generated the entire scientific process. *The Nature Handbook: A Guide to Observing the Great Outdoors* serves to aid the process of learning more about the living things we see. In writing it, I've made extensive use of primary as well as secondary scientific literature to interpret observable patterns of nature, and the written explanations include the best current understandings of the phenomena described. Use the brief list of the sources that accompanies each description and then the full bibliographic information on the book's Web page (given at the end, in "References"). These sources connect to the scientific and popular literature.

In sum, *The Nature Handbook* has a number of features intended to make it useful:

- A focus on what one sees when looking at nature
- An emphasis on patterns rather than individual species
- Easy access to a wide range of observations of nature
- A brief, scientifically current explanation about each observation
- Color photos that illustrate each pattern
- References to further information

I hope you find it handy and helpful.

Species Names

All described living species have been assigned unique scientific names both to promote the understanding of their evolutionary relationships and to enhance precise communication about them. The names are part of an enormous filing system for all the living things on earth, providing an internationally recognized reference. For standardization and accuracy, I've included the scientific names in the figure legends of the subjects shown in the photographs so that you can find more information elsewhere about them.

Scientific names include two parts: a genus name (capitalized) for a group of closely related species, and a species name (lowercase) for the members of an interbreeding group. The potential to reproduce successfully is the most common definition of a single species, though that description must be modified to apply to asexual organisms and those isolated in space or time. Some people view scientific names as foreign and difficult and resist using them. Though the words do come from Greek and Latin, they are hardly more complicated than common names. More importantly, they help one find more information about each kind of organism. Scientific names aren't always necessary—for example, the birds of North America have a formalized list of common names—but I've chosen to be consistent in the use, when possible, of scientific names for all organisms.

Common names vary from one locality to another (most of the common names we think of are actually English common names). The butterfly *Nymphalis antiopa* (Fig. 7.8a) is known in North America as the mourning cloak, while in Britain it is the Camberwell beauty, and in Germany it is *Trauermantel* (which translates to "robe of sorrow"). On the other hand, one common name may be used to describe two different species, as is the case with the robin in North America, *Turdus migratorius* (Fig. 6.18), and the robin in Britain, *Erithacus rubecula*. For some species, the scientific name is widely accepted as the common name, as for aster (Fig. 3.1c), geranium (Fig. 1.11c), rhododendron (Fig. 3.15a), delphinium (Fig. 8.10b), and trillium (Fig. 1.6a). Scientific names aren't all drudgery; they may be descriptive of the organism (e.g., *Acer saccharum*, sugar maple, Fig. 2.5c), named after a person (e.g., *Sylvilagus auduboni*, a rabbit named for John James Audubon, Fig. 4.6a), or simply provide humor (e.g., *Heerz tooya* and *Lalapa lusa*, both wasps).

Photograph Credits

Because this book is based on patterns one can see, the photographs included herein are vitally important for illustrating those patterns and thus for supporting the goals of the book. Most of the approximately five hundred photographs are by the author, but the photographers listed below made superb contributions. I thank them all. The photographers retain copyright to their own images. Locations of the photographs seem particularly important for views of habitats, so I've included this information for all broader views, though not for photos of single species.

John Alcock: Figures 7.4 (pipevine swallowtail), 11.4b (ocotillo stem), 11.4c (paloverde stem), 11.5b (paloverde trunk), 11.8a (creosote flat), 11.8b (bajada),11.9a, b (desert flowers), 11.10a (paloverde nurse), 11.10b (bursage nurse)

A. and S. Carey/VIREO: 6.18 (robin with worm)

Lang Elliot/Cornell Lab Ornithology: 6.2a (common tern), 6.16a (redpoll)

C. H. Greenewalt/VIREO: 6.3a (swallow)

S. Greer/VIREO: 5.10b (black-backed gulls), 6.6b (plover young)

John Himmelman: 4.5a (tuliptree beauty moth), 4.10b (underwing moth), 4.12a (banded hairstreak), 4.15a (katydid), 4.16b (white-ribboned carpet moth), 7.8b (spring azure), 7.9a (grasshopper nymph), 7.11a (cecropia cocoon), 12.4a (spring peeper)

Mike Hopiak/Cornell Lab Ornithology: 6.5a (oriole nest)

Rick Kline/Cornell Lab Ornithology: 5.1a (goshawk)

S. J. Lang/VIREO: 4.2c (albino robin)

Michael Leski: 7.3b (tiger swallowtail)

David Liebman: 1.11c (geranium pods), 3.11a (poison ivy), 3.14 (mimosa), 4.3c (iridescent beetle), 4.4 (glowworm), 4.7a (yellow perch), 4.8b (raccoon), 4.12b (spicebush caterpillar), 4.13a (milkweed bugs), 4.13c (saddleback caterpillar), 4.14c (tiger swallowtail), 4.14e (black swallowtail), 4.16a (giant swallowtail caterpillar), 5.4b (jackrabbit), 5.17b (opossum), 6.1b (evening grosbeak), 6.6a (robin nest), 6.12 (V-formation), 6.19a (blue jay), 7.1b (damselflies), 7.7 (monarchs), 7.10a, b (geometrid caterpillars), 7.12a (cicada molting), 7.15a (moths at light), 7.16b (firefly), 7.19 (velvet ant), 9.1c (sugar pine), 9.11a (slippery elm bark beetle), 10.6a, b (crab spiders), 10.10 (fairy ring), 12.11a (water strider)

James Lloyd: 7.16a (firefly field)

A. Morris/VIREO: 4.7b (sanderling)

Richard Nickson: 4.11b (butterflyfish), 5.8b (bald eagle), 5.14 (squirrel), 6.1c (pelican), 6.1d (willet), 6.1e (mallard), 6.3b (bluejay), 6.9 (pileated woodpecker), 6.21b (snowy egret), 13.6b (sanderling)

William Pfitsch: 3.7a (trail plant)

Roger Rageot: 3.9d (Venus flytrap), 4.1b (Canada warbler), 4.8a (white-tailed deer fawn), 4.9a (copperhead), 4.15b (thorn bugs), 5.6b (pygmy shrew), 6.4b (wood duck), 12.8b (red-winged blackbird)

James D. Ronan, Jr.: 5.5b (brown bear)

Edward Ross: 4.17b (robber fly), 7.2 (midge swarm), 7.20e (paper wasp)

Leonard Lee Rue III: 4.19b (long-tailed weasel), 5.18 (white-tailed deer)

Len Rue, Jr.: 4.13b (skunk), 4.19a (snowshoe hare), 5.3a (Alaskan moose), 5.4a (arctic fox), 5.11b (deer at mineral lick)

Ron Rutowski: 7.3a (Empress Leilia)

Frank Schleicher/Cornell Lab Ornithology: 6.2b (red-tailed hawk)

Allan Sheldon: 4.2b (albino frog), 4.3b (Karner blue), 4.14a (hover fly), 4.14d (red-spotted purple), 5.2a (elk), 5.3b (Shira's moose), 5.6a (hummingbird), 5.7 (indigo snake), 5.17a (killdeer), 5.17c (hognose snake), 6.7 (meadowlark), 6.15b (turkey vultures), 6.15c (red-winged blackbird), 6.16b (snowy owl), 7.12b (stonefly exoskeleton), 12.5b (tadpole), 12.8a (yellow-headed blackbird)

Dennis Sheridan: 4.6a (cottontail), 5.8a (mountain lion), 6.13 (peregrine falcon), 6.19b (acorn woodpecker), 7.21 (cricket), 13.14 (sea otter)

Leroy Simon: 4.11a (io moth), 4.14b (pipevine swallowtail), 4.14f (spicebush swallowtail), 6.22 (long-billed curlew)

Hugh Smith: 4.17a (zone-tailed hawk), 5.1b (Cooper's hawk), 5.1c (sharp-shinned hawk), 5.12a (cedar waxwings), 6.5b (cliff swallow nests), 6.10 (mobbing), 6.11a (redtail hawk), 6.15a (cliff swallows), 6.21a (red-necked phalarope), 9.14a (sapsucker)

N. G. Smith/VIREO: 6.11b (hawk kettle)

M. Stubblefield/VIREO: 6.8 (honking goose)

T. Veso/VIREO: 6.4a (cardinals), 6.14 (snow geese)

Tom Veso/Cornell Lab Ornithology: 6.4c (painted bunting)

Nellie Watson: 3.4a (burdock)

D. Wechsler/VIREO: 6.17 (feeding waders), 12.8c (Brewer's blackbird)

Jenny Winkelman: 1.12a, b (needlegrass), 2.22b (walnut trees)

The Nature Handbook

I. FLOWERS AND SEEDS

The central theme in this chapter on the reproduction of flowering plants is the tremendous diversity of reproductive mechanisms both to achieve pollination and to disperse seeds. The floral features that attract visual pollinators such as bees, butterflies, and hummingbirds are appealing to the human eye, too, though for several reasons not all flowers are visually attractive. For many, wind is an alternative mechanism for the transfer of pollen; for some, odor is more important than appearance; and for those that open at night, visual patterns are decidedly secondary. Further steps are needed after pollen has been transported from one flower to another and each egg in the flower's ovary has been fertilized by one of the two sperm nuclei from each pollen grain. Reproduction isn't complete until the developed seeds have been dispersed to germinate and grow, and plants offer a surprising array of mechanisms to achieve that goal.

Additional discussion of flowers, fruits, and seeds is found in:

1.1 Showy Flowers

Few things represent the beauty of nature as well as a bouquet of wildflowers. The profusion of floral shapes and colors we see serves to attract diverse animals that carry pollen from plant to plant. The process of pollen transfer effects the genetic exchange that is the essence of sexual reproduction. To avoid wasting pollen on flowers of different species, a plant may specialize in only one kind of pollinator, which visits only other flowers of the same species. Although colorful petals and sweet fragrances are general attractants, pollinators come in different sizes and sensory capacities and respond to different floral characteristics.

Bees are attracted to pink, yellow, blue, and distinctly marked flowers, many of which also reflect ultraviolet light, sometimes in a bull's-eye pattern; bees are also relatively large and strong enough to enter flowers that are closed or oddly shaped. Flies are weaker and have limited color vision, so they visit flowers that are saucer-shaped and brightly white or yellow. Butterflies must land to feed with their strawlike mouthparts; upright composite inflorescences with thin, tubular flowers are particularly attractive to them. Night-feeding moths are attracted to heavy fragrance, but because colors aren't visible at night, moth-pollinated flowers are usually pale green or white. Bats visit large, pale, heavily scented flowers, while beetles are also attracted to strong odors and bright flowers. Hummingbirds often choose red, tubular, hanging flowers with abundant nectar. This matching of floral traits to potential pollinators illustrates how the specificity of pollinators can be strengthened, and one consequence is the tremendous floral diversity we find so attractive.

REFERENCES: FAEGRI & VAN DER PIJL 1979; RAVEN ET AL. 1999

Fig. 1.1.   Diverse floral shapes and colors: (a) windflower, *Anemone multifida*; (b) larkspur, *Delphinium nuttallianum*; (c) glacier lily, *Erythronium grandiflorum*; (d) Indian paintbrush, *Castilleja* sp.; (e) fairyslipper orchid, *Calypso bulbosa*; (f) blue penstemon, *Penstemon cyaneus*; (g) hibiscus, *Hibiscus* sp.; (h) wild passionflower, *Passiflora incarnata*.

a

b

c

d

e

f

g

h

1.2 Ray and Disk Flowers

The structure of most colorful flowers is readily recognizable, with the standard four floral whorls, seen in order from the outside to the middle: (1) sepals, green flaps that serve as bud covers early in the flower's development and, in some species, add color later on; (2) petals, expanded colorful straps that collectively form the corolla and make the flower conspicuous to pollinating insects and birds; (3) pollen-bearing stamens, the male reproductive structures; and finally (4) a pistil, the female reproductive structure in the middle, where egg cells in the ovary develop into seed embryos. The flowering structures of one very common and diverse family of plants, the composites or aster family, have evolved from a clustering of many small flowers with this same basic structure. Disk flowers (or florets) fill the middle, but for them the corollas are very short and inconspicuous, and the sepals have been modi-

Fig. 1.2. Flowers of composites: (a) fleabane, *Erigeron* sp.; (b) arrowleaf balsamroot, *Balsamorhiza sagittata*; (c) dandelion, *Taraxacum officinale*; (d) hoary chaenactis, *Chaenactis douglasii*.

a

b

c

d

fied into hairs or bristles. Around the outside of the inflorescence are ray flowers, whose corollas are greatly expanded on one side to form the large, projecting straps that many people think are the petals of a single large flower. Ray flowers often lack internal reproductive structures.

Asters and sunflowers display the full structure of a composite inflorescence, with central disk florets surrounded by a ring of ray florets (Fig. 1.2a, b). But composites don't have to have both kinds; dandelions are clusters of ray florets only (Fig. 1.2c), whereas flowers in the genus *Chaenactis* have disk florets only (Fig. 1.2d). Why should this clustered form have evolved? The composite structure produces large, conspicuous inflorescences that are colorful and easily visible to pollinators, which is the reason for the attractiveness of flowers in the first place.

REFERENCE: RAVEN ET AL. 1999

1.3   Inconspicuous Flowers

Plants in open, dry habitats or those that grow in dense numbers of the same species can cross-fertilize passively by taking advantage of the wind blowing pollen from one plant to another. The pollen must be small and light to be borne by the wind, and because wind pollination is less efficient than animal pollination (pollen typically carries no more than 100 yards and is not targeted toward other flowers), a large amount must be released. The yellow clouds of pollen that one sees wafting in spring breezes and causing human allergies are from wind-pollinated plants such as pines and poplars. These plants don't need to attract pollinating insects, so their flowers are small and inconspicuous and often overlooked. Wind-pollinated flowers have exposed anthers (male parts) to release pollen easily and expanded feathery stigmas (female parts) to catch it, but the petals and sepals are greatly reduced or missing entirely. To promote genetic exchange, male and female parts of wind-pollinated plants are often found in separate flowers, as with oaks and birches, or even on separate plants, as with willows, cottonwoods, and boxelder.

Wind-pollinated trees flower before their leaves unfold and block the movement of air. Western prairies are windy habitats, so sagebrush is evolving from insect to wind pollination (Fig. 1.3d); the retention of small yellowish petals reflects the intermediate status of their form. One can be surrounded by wind-pollinated plants in full bloom and never even notice their inconspicuous flowers.

REFERENCES: FAEGRI & VAN DER PIJL 1979; RAVEN ET AL. 1999; CULLEY ET AL. 2002

Fig. 1.3.   Wind-pollinated flowers: (a) smooth brome grass, *Bromus inermis*; (b) maple, *Acer* sp.; (c) meadow rue, *Thalictrum venulosum*; (d) sagebrush, *Artemesia tridentata*.

1.4   Hot Flowers

Through the crust of late winter snows, buttercups and skunk cabbage push their way up to light, forming welcome signs of spring. That they are able to emerge so early is surprising, but the plants become active as they trap whatever sunlight penetrates the snow, and their growth surges in the lengthening spring days. Carbohydrates stored the previous year in rhizomes, bulbs, and other root structures fuel their resumed growth.

Skunk cabbage is remarkable in another way, too: even when the air temperature hovers near a cool 40°F, a plant can generate enough heat to maintain a temperature of nearly 70°F in its flowers. The flowers become warm enough to melt pockets in the snows of early spring, although heat production ceases when the air temperature drops close to freezing. The advantage of heat is easy to see: floral warmth attracts flies, beetles, and early-appearing bees, the insects that actively pollinate the flowers. Increased warmth may accelerate seed development, too. Tropical relatives of skunk cabbage use warmth to help volatilize attractant chemicals.

Why flower so early? With few plants in bloom at this time, competition for available pollinators is reduced. Furthermore, many early-flowering plants grow where the time for reproduction is short because of either an abbreviated growing season in a cold climate or imminent coverage by a dense canopy overhead. Either way, the energetic costs of producing early, hot flowers are paid back by reproductive gains.

REFERENCES: KEVAN 1989; SEYMOUR 1997; SEYMOUR & BLAYLOCK 1999; MARCHAND 2000

Fig. 1.4.   Skunk cabbage, *Symplocarpus foetidus*, in flower, having melted a cylindrical hole in early spring snow.

1.5 Flowering Phenology

The times at which different plant species come into flower appear to be spread evenly throughout the growing season, as if each were assigned its own place in the spring-to-fall sequence. A common hypothesis for this gradual unfolding is that in flower-rich habitats, plants benefit by spreading out their flowering times so that they don't compete too strongly for limited pollinators. There may be some truth to this reason for divergence, particularly when pollinators are floral generalists or when different plants rely on the same group of pollinators (e.g., hummingbirds). But a plant's flowering time depends on other factors, too, including the seasonal timing of herbivory and seed predation that beset it, with the result that sometimes pollinator competition is not the most important determinant. When multiple factors affect flowering phenology, staggered flowering times result anyway. Of course, plants of the same species vary in their flowering times due to genetic differences and local conditions of moisture, soil nutrients, and solar warming. All factors combined produce the pattern we see of displaced flowering times.

REFERENCES: HEINRICH 1976; MOTTEN 1986; OLLERTON & LACK 1992; BRODY 1997; LEBUHN 1997

a

b

c

Fig. 1.5. Seasonal change in flowering in a montane meadow (Wyoming): (a) June 27 (mostly spring beauties, *Claytonia lanceolata*); (b) July 27 (mostly sticky geranium, *Geranium viscosissimum*, and lupine, *Lupinus* spp.); (c) September 6 (mostly yampah, *Perideridia gairdneri*; (d) a graph showing the duration of flowering of all thirty-nine flowering species (non-graminoids) in an alpine meadow (unpublished data).

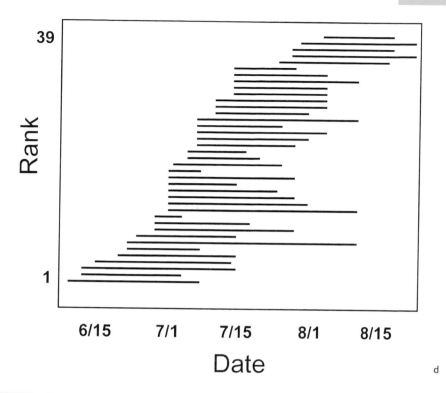

d

1.6 Forest Wildflowers

Wildflowers bloom on the floor of a deciduous forest as soon as spring bursts forth. Flowering can't take place until rising temperatures are ensured or until sufficient warmth has accumulated (daily temperatures added together to total what is known as degree-days), yet flowering must precede the closing of the canopy above. An additional problem is the limited abundance and diversity of pollinators early in the growing season. So how do forest-floor herbaceous plants successfully achieve the genetic benefits of pollen exchange? One answer is that their flowers aren't specialized for particular pollinators; many are open, bowl-shaped, and white-colored to attract any of the flies and solitary bees that happen to be present. Rather than divide up the pollinator resources, they converge in form. Anemones, trillium (Fig. 1.6a), spring beauties (Fig. 1.6b), hepatica (Fig. 1.6c), and bloodroot (Fig. 1.6d) are examples, although other early spring flowers such as trout lilies (Fig. 1.6e) and Dutchman's breeches (Fig. 1.6f) do have specialized shapes. Some wildflowers also remain receptive to incoming pollen for a long time. Furthermore, those that are more specialized in form, such as irises and Dutchman's breeches, reproduce asexually by rhizomes or bulblets as well. The first opening of forest wildflowers is shifting to earlier dates in some parts of North America because of global warming, but the same features of the wildflower community may be observed apart from when flowering begins. The rewards for flowering early include sufficient moisture and high sunlight intensity through the leafless trees above.

REFERENCES: MOTTEN 1986; GARLAND 1997; VASSEUR ET AL. 2001

Fig. 1.6.   Flowers of the eastern forest floor (New York): (a) large white trillium, *Trillium grandiflorum;* (b) spring beauty, *Claytonia virginica;* (c) round-leaved hepatica, *Hepatica americana;* (d) bloodroot, *Sanguinaria canadensis;* (e) trout lily, *Erythronium americanum;* (f) Dutchman's breeches, *Dicentra cucullaria.*

1.7 Winged Seeds

Newly matured seeds are scattered, most noticeably in the autumn, to find new places to germinate the following year. Wind is a reliable mechanism of dispersal in open habitats, but to be blown from one place to another, the seeds must achieve buoyancy by either being small or having structures that catch the wind. There are several possible designs to catch the wind: (1) Seeds that are small enough, such as those of many orchids, are carried directly by the wind. These seeds are so small that they are not easily seen. (2) In contrast, feathery-plumed seeds

Fig. 1.7. Seeds and fruits blown by wind:
(a) common milkweed, *Asclepias syriaca*;
(b) goatsbeard, *Tragopogon pratensis*; (c) bull
thistle, *Cirsium vulgare*; (d) red maple, *Acer rubrum*.

float in the air after a breeze blows through a ripened seed head. The plumed seeds of milk-weeds (Fig. 1.7a) and plumed fruits of dandelions and their relatives (Fig. 1.7b, c) are familiar to all. (3) Cottonwoods produce seeds covered with long, thin hairs, and when shed, seed-bearing bits of cotton waft about in the air. (4) Especially for seeds that are larger, the seed-containing fruits have single wings, such as those of maple (Fig. 1.7d) and ash seeds, that promote floating in the wind; the wings produce a helicopterlike spinning motion that slows their descent. Most designs for wind dispersal increase the surface area of the seed with little change in weight, producing sails that catch the wind.

Plumed seeds are carried farther by wind than are larger, single-winged seeds, but large seeds survive and germinate better (and are also collected more by seed-feeding animals). Thus, every wind-dispersed plant must achieve some balance in seed size. Dispersal distance increases with the square of the wind speed, so most seed dispersal occurs as a result of occasional strong gusts. Even for seeds that are wind-dispersed, most drop near the parent plant.

REFERENCES: MCEVOY 1984; HENSEN & MUELLER 1997; RAVEN ET AL. 1999; NATHAN ET AL. 2002

1.8 Burs and Stickseeds

During a walk through a field in late summer, a person's socks collect burs and seeds that represent a range of attachment devices. Because plants produce more surviving offspring when their seeds disperse to open spaces, many plants have evolved seeds with hooks, burs, spines, and adhesives that attach to the fur coats or feathers of passing animals. By wallow-ing in or scraping the ground, animals create disturbances in the vegetation that open up new sites for the dispersed seeds to germinate and grow. A good example is the common weed burdock, whose ripened flower heads have curved hooks that are highly effective in reversibly grabbing the fibers of human clothing (Fig. 1.8a); as the hooked structures are carried away from the plant that produced them, seeds shake out and are dispersed. The strong attachment of hooked burs to the threads of clothing is what spurred the Swiss outdoorsman George de Mestral to use the same design in creating Velcro, which uses hooks and loops for reversible attachment. Burdock may be called nature's Velcro, but more accu-rately, Velcro is really people's burdock. Other plants have seeds with hooks and spines that are durable and attach well, too. The herbaceous plant aptly named stickseed (Fig. 1.8b) produces ridges of small hooks along the margins of its seeds, and if you've ever stepped barefoot on the burs of sandbur (Fig. 1.8c), a grass of sandy soils, you know just how strong and sharp (and painful) a seed's attachment device may be.

REFERENCES: BROWN 1979; JOHNSON & NICHOLS 1982; RAVEN ET AL. 1999; VELCRO USA INC. 2003

1.9 Fleshy Fruits

One way for a plant to disperse its seeds is to embed them in a nutritious and tasty pulp that attracts fruit-eating birds and mammals. Animals that feed on such fruits then transport the seeds some distance away from the parent plant and regurgitate them or, after the seeds have passed through the digestive tract, drop them in a pile of fresh fertilizer. The fruits may even have a laxative effect to promote rapid passage and easy dispersal.

a

b

c

Fig. 1.8. Seeds in floral structures that attach: (a) burdock, *Arctium minus*; (b) many-flowered stickseed, *Hackelia floribunda*; (c) sandbur, *Cenchrus longispinus*

Despite the seeming complexity of this design, seeds originate within plant ovaries, and making the ovary wall sweet and fleshy has been accomplished many times in the evolution of modern plants. Fruits are simply matured plant ovaries. To survive ingestion, the fruit-embedded seeds must possess a strong covering so that they are neither crushed nor digested in the animal's gut; many seeds actually require abrasion of the seed coat from passage through an animal in order to germinate. As they ripen, fruits become sweeter and soften from the break-down of their tissues, and brightening colors signal their maturation. Ripened fruit may ferment, too; sometimes cedar waxwings appear intoxicated after eating fermented berries.

Red and black are the most frequent colors for animal-dispersed fruits, while yellow, blue, and white are less common, and green and brown the least frequent. Red is especially common against the green vegetation of summer, while black fruits are more apparent against the changing colors of fall foliage. Furthermore, red fruits are apparent to red-sensitive birds and mammals, which disperse the seeds, but not to insects, which don't. But because red is also a warning color of distasteful insects (see 4.13), birds must use context to distinguish a red signal as food or something to be avoided.

REFERENCES: WILLSON & WHELAN 1990; RAVEN ET AL. 1999; ALTSHULER 2001; BLEHER & BOHNING-GAESE 2001; GAMBERALE-STILLE & TULLBERG 2001; BURNS & DALEN 2002

a

b

c

Fig. 1.9. Seeds in fleshy fruits: (a) American mountain-ash, *Sorbus americana*; (b) honeysuckle, *Lonicera* sp., and raspberry, *Rubus* sp.; (c) winterberry holly, *Ilex verticellata*.

1.10   Stored Nuts

Seed dispersal away from a parent plant leads to reduced competition among seedlings, lessened mortality, and greater genetic exchange within the plant population. Jays and squirrels are very effective agents of seed dispersal because these animals can carry many seeds over long distances and bury or hide them selectively in good locations (see 6.19). The costs to the plant, of course, are that some seeds are consumed instead of being moved about, and the seeds must be rich enough as food to attract animal dispersers.

For seed eaters, nuts are good foods to store for winter consumption because they are dormant, surrounded by a protective cover, and energy-rich (hickory nuts have particularly high energy content). Animals that store food may scatter-hoard, which is spreading the food items out in numerous hidden places, or larder-hoard, which is caching many nuts together in a single location. Scatter hoarding is typical of gray squirrels and jays, which have remarkably good memories for hundreds or thousands of cache locations, but they don't recover all the stored seeds, and the ones forgotten can grow into new plants. Larder hoarding is limited to those animals, such as chipmunks and kangaroo rats, that can defend or hide their larders from others. Larder hoarding is more common at higher latitudes, where greater environmental variation increases the availability of food at one time and the need for it at another.

Caching behavior can affect tree distribution. Whitebark pine often grows in clumps because of the germination of several seeds cached together and forgotten. As a result of their carrying acorns more than a mile from their source, jays are largely responsible for the range expansion of oaks following the last ice age. Even the Great Basin bristlecone pine, which has winged seeds for wind dispersal, grows predominantly at high elevations because its seeds are cached there by Clark's nutcrackers.

REFERENCES: HAVERA & SMITH 1979; DARLEY-HILL & JOHNSON 1981; SORK 1983; SMITH & REICHMAN 1984; JOHNSON & ADKISSON 1986; LANNER 1988; JACOBS 1989; TOMBACK ET AL. 1993; WENNY 2001; WANG & SMITH 2002

a

b

Fig. 1.10.   Nuts stored by small mammals: (a) acorns of northern red oak, *Quercus rubra*; (b) nuts of bitternut hickory, *Carya cordiformis*.

1.11   Ballistic Seeds

Some plants develop so much tension in the walls of their seed pods that when fully ripe, the pods spring open with enough force to fling the seeds outward. This process, known as explosive dehiscence, propels the seeds several feet away from the parent plant. Dispersal is built into the pods themselves. The ballistic mechanism usually involves the ripening and hardening of the ovary walls under tension. To enhance dispersal, only a few seeds are found in each pod, the seeds are dense and small or streamlined in shape, and surrounding structures such as sepals and bracts either drop off or fold back before the pods ripen. Once thrown from the parent plant, the seeds may be carried farther away by secondary dispersal agents such as water, ants, or rodents.

A common example of explosive seed dispersal is jewelweed (also called touch-me-not, native *Impatiens* spp.), which is named for its plump, spring-loaded pods (Figs. 1.11a, b). When triggered by the slight touch of a wind-blown leaf, ripened capsules explode as the walls snap quickly backward, tossing the seeds into the air. If you see a swollen pod on one of these plants, try pinching the bottom. There are other examples, too. The capsules of the small tree witch hazel spring open in the fall, tossing their seeds 10 feet or more. Dwarf mistletoes, which are parasites on conifers, also have explosive dehiscence that uses the pressure built up in their fruits to fling seeds up to 15 yards away, with an initial velocity of an astonishing 60 miles per hour. Geraniums (Fig. 1.11c), violets, and phlox are other seed tossers.

REFERENCES: STOKES 1981; ARMBRUSTER 1982; STAMP & LUCAS 1983; ZAGT & WERGER 1997; RAVEN ET AL. 1999

a

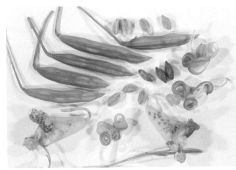

b

c

Fig. 1.11. Flower pods with ballistic seeds: (a) orange jewelweed, *Impatiens capensis*; (b) orange jewelweed with exploded and unexploded pods and seeds; (c) wild geranium, *Geranium maculatum*.

1.12 Twisting Seeds

Once dispersed from a parent plant by wind, water, or the movement of animals, seeds must lodge in the ground to germinate and root. A number of plant species have a seed shape that actively promotes burial. Some grasses and geraniums produce hairy or barbed seeds connected to long, visibly twisted tails. Lying on the ground and moistened by rain, the tail of a seed slowly untwists, driving the seed forward. When the seed dries, the process reverses, and the tail twists tightly back again, increasing tension, but at the same time hairs and barbs around the seed keep it from sliding backward. This process is repeated daily and through wet-dry cycles, so that gradually the seed drills itself down through the leaf litter or into cracks in the soil. Self-burial is most effective in silty or sandy soil. The advantages in accelerating burial lie in escaping the higher temperatures and roaming seed predators of the soil surface, as well as in aiding penetration by the seedling's developing root.

REFERENCES: STAMP 1984; HOU & SIMPSON 1992

a   b

Fig. 1.12. Twisting seeds of needlegrass, *Stipa spartea*: (a) seed and awn; (b) seedhead.

2. TREES

Dwarfing human beings and dominating most landscapes, trees are the most conspicuous and majestic living organisms around us. Despite their fundamentally simple structure, they dramatically alter the landscape and draw our attention. Due to tree immobility and the wide range of environmental features found on land, each tree species grows within a limited geographic range and under only certain conditions. Individuals of the same species as well as different parts of the same tree vary in form because of differences in the conditions they encounter as they develop. Trees' varied growth patterns and their dominant visual presence yield many easy-to-make observations about size, shape, growth patterns, leaves, and reproductive structures.

This chapter describes features one can observe in individual trees. Features seen in forests, both those of groups of trees and the effects of other living things found in forests, are described in Chapter 9, "Forests." For additional discussion of features of trees, see:

2.1 Woody Habit

Without the strength provided by wood, plants would reach heights no greater than about 6 feet, would be unable to stand up to the stresses of strong winds and gravity, and could be overshaded. The strength of wood comes from chemicals known as lignins that are added to the plant's cell walls. Lignins bind together the strong, light fibrils of cellulose and add stiffness to plant stems and the strength to resist gravity. Lignins are highly complex polymers, chains of molecules with ringlike molecular structure (following cellulose, lignin is the second most abundant kind of organic molecule on earth). Three different kinds of units are strung together in lignins, although the actual structure varies from plant to plant and from tissue to tissue within a plant. Lignins allow plants to branch extensively, exposing many leaves to sunlight, and to transport water and minerals upward to great heights. Lignin is also commonly found in the vascular cell walls of many herbaceous plants. Joshua trees of southern California (Fig. 2.1c), palms, and cycads lack true wood but have lignin-fortified, strongly fibrous trunks that allow them to grow to treelike sizes.

In addition, being hydrophobic, lignins add waterproofing to a plant's cells. They are typically found in water transport (xylem) tissues because of their strength to withstand the tensile stresses that develop within stems and their water resistance to retard the sideways

a

b

Fig. 2.1. Trees showing the woody habit: (a) mixed deciduous forest (Virginia); (b) longleaf pine, *Pinus palustris* (South Carolina); (c) Joshua tree, *Yucca brevifolia* (California).

c

movement of water. The toughness of lignified tissues can deter herbivores, too. Strength is also important in responding to injury; lignification of tissues at a wound site gives resistance to further damage. Because it is gluelike and produces a brownish color, lignin must be removed from wood pulp to make paper products.

To see the importance of lignin, look at a forest and then imagine what would remain if you removed every woody stem and every leaf supported by a lignin-reinforced stem. With only mosslike plants left behind, that world would look very strange indeed.

REFERENCES: RAVEN ET AL. 1999; BROWN 1999; COLLINS 2001

2.2 Deciduous or Evergreen

The best photosynthetic design for a tree is to have broad leaves for intercepting the most light and to retain the leaves year round. Sure enough, many tropical trees have broad evergreen leaves. When part of the year is clearly unfavorable for growth due to low temperatures or lack of water, however, the next best choice is the deciduous habit: drop the leaves during the poor season and then regrow new ones for the next good season. The extensive forests of eastern North America are deciduous because of the cold winters that occur here. But the regrowth of a full complement of leaves requires nutrients and water, resources scarce in sandy soils and western mountains. In these environments, a better solution is to have evergreen, needlelike leaves because they can better withstand the drought of wintertime cold and needn't be replaced all at once at the start of the growing season. With only about 20 percent of their leaves developing new each year, conifers don't require as high an influx of nutrients in early spring, so they dominate on poorer soils and in stressed habitats.

Fig. 2.2.   The contrast between deciduous and evergreen trees: (a) maple, *Acer* sp., and ash, *Fraxinus* sp. (New York) and (b) spruce, *Picea* sp. (Alberta).

a

b

Needles are better than broad leaves in tolerating severe winters because they are structurally stronger, have a thicker and more watertight protective layer (cuticle), and conceal the openings for gas exchange (stomates) in sunken pits away from exposed leaf surfaces. Despite lower rates of photosynthesis, conifers have a larger total leaf area and can capture light throughout the canopy for photosynthesis on mild winter days, which adds to the yearly carbon gain of the trees. These advantages are why tenacious evergreens are found in very cold and dry habitats. Evergreens also dominate in the poor conditions of continuously saturated soils. Even needlelike leaves can't endure extreme cold, however, so the most severe environments support larches, trees whose leaves are needle-shaped (the most resistant design) but also deciduous.

REFERENCES: MARCHAND 1987; SPRUGEL 1989; GOWER & RICHARDS 1990; SMITH 1993; AERTS 1995; ANTUNEZ ET AL. 2001

2.3 Tall or Broad

Choose an oak or other broad-leaved deciduous tree to find the broadest noontime shade, but choose a conifer to find the tallest tree. The density of wood in broad-leaved trees, aptly known as hardwoods, provides greater support of horizontal branches, and this increased strength explains the success of deciduous trees in canopy diameter.

The success of conifers in height is likely due to the way they transport water up to the treetop. The water transport tissue of conifers, the xylem, consists of dead spindle-shaped cells that collectively resemble overlapping perforated straws. Evaporative losses pull water under tension up through the xylem to the highest leaves, creating tiny, upward-flowing streams; a large tree may lose as much as 100 gallons each day. The water in these continuous

a

b

Fig. 2.3. The shapes of coniferous and hardwood (flowering) trees: (a) swamp white oak, *Quercus bicolor*; (b) ponderosa pine, *Pinus ponderosa*.

Table 2.3.   The tallest and broadest species of North American trees based on living specimens (from American Forests 2004). All twelve of the tallest trees are conifers; eleven of the twelve broadest trees are hardwoods (angiosperms).

Rank	Height (ft.)	Species	Crown diam. (ft.)	Species
1	321	Coast redwood	156	Southern red oak
2	301	Coast Douglas-fir	142	White willow
3	274	Giant sequoia	140	Live oak
4	272	Noble fir	140	Black walnut
5	257	Grand fir	138	American beech
6	241	Western hemlock	136	Cherrybark oak
7	229	Port-Orford-cedar	136	Willow oak
8	227	Ponderosa pine	134	Darlington oak
9	218	Pacific silver fir	131	Crack willow
10	217	California white fir	130	Torrey pine
11	209	Sugar pine	128	Siberian elm
12	204	Sitka spruce	127	Black maple

columns is held together by the attraction of water molecules for each other. Water molecules have positive and negative ends (they are called dipoles), and ends with opposite polarity attract each other (the special attraction between water dipoles is known as hydrogen bonding). Higher above the ground, the tension in the water column increases because of the downward pull of gravity, and the column can become blocked if an air bubble develops from gases dissolved in the xylem sap. A gas embolism in the xylem is known as cavitation. The xylem of conifers cannot transport water as efficiently in bulk flow as the larger, strawlike xylem vessels of broad-leafed trees, which are more open-ended, but conifer xylem is better at resisting tension in the water column, reducing the likelihood of cavitation. Of course, trees of all designs risk cavitation at great heights, so tall trees lessen the risk of damage by reducing the amount of canopy leaves relative to the amount of xylem.

By their design, conifers generally win the contest to be tallest, but no one structural design is best for all outcomes, and hardwoods win the race to be broadest. (Australian eucalyptus, hardwoods, are something of an anomaly; measured in the 1800s at over 400 feet, one of these is the tallest tree ever reported.) The difference in the growth of conifers and hardwoods is borne out in records of the largest trees in North America (Table 2.3).

REFERENCES: AMERICAN FORESTRY ASSOCIATION 1988, 1994; RYAN & YODER 1997; GUINNESS 1999; RAVEN ET AL. 1999; ZIMMER 2000; HACKE ET AL. 2001; MCDOWELL ET AL. 2002

2.4 Old Trees

Trees increase in size as they age: trunks thicken, branches elongate, and new branches are added. It may seem that they can keep growing forever. But there are challenges with greater size: more and more energy must be allocated to producing new wood, and transport of water to greater heights is more difficult. As new branches sprout and new layers of wood are added, an aging tree may gradually use up its food reserves. It may skip a year of growth, or a limb may die. Infections start to invade the dead inner wood. As the tree suffers the accumulated insults of disease, drought, and fire, parts of it die at a rate faster than they are replaced, and with weakened physiology, the tree approaches the end of its life.

The maximum age ranges widely among different species. Fast-growing trees such as aspen and cottonwoods reach their largest size in about fifty years, whereas the largest trees, giant sequoias and coastal redwoods, attain their majestic form by growing for two thousand to three thousand years. The record for old age, however, belongs to bristlecone pines. These modestly sized trees with antlerlike dead branches poking upward are the oldest living things on earth, reaching nearly five thousand years of age. Groves of bristlecone pines live near 12,000 feet elevation in the White Mountains of California, where it is cold and dry and the soils are nutrient-poor and rocky. The trees grow very slowly, twisted and pruned by severe environmental conditions, with only a few surviving branches remaining among many dead ones and roots just below the surface in shallow soils. Because of slow growth (one hundred rings per inch), their size remains relatively small, like giant bonsai trees, and their wood is dense and resinous, transporting water inefficiently but resisting decay. Slow growth in such a harsh growing environment makes possible living to such extraordinary ages.

REFERENCES: BEASLEY & KLEMMEDSON 1980; HITCH 1982; BOLEN 1998; THOMAS 2000B

a

b

Fig. 2.4. The shapes of old trees: (a) bristlecone pine, *Pinus longaera*, one of the oldest known trees; (b) sugar maple, *Acer saccharum*.

2.5   Tree Shape

As trees grow larger, they spread according to species specific branching patterns to expose more and more leaves to solar radiation. Greater size improves a tree's competitive ability, but the shape of each tree is a compromise among three factors: (1) leaves must be arrayed outward so they don't overshade each other, (2) branches can't be so long that they generate

a

b

c

d

Fig. 2.5.   Branching patterns of trees as seen in winter: (a) American elm, *Ulmus americana*; (b) swamp white oak, *Quercus bicolor*; (c) sugar maple, *Acer saccharum*; (d) paper birch, *Betula papyrifera*.

severe mechanical stresses, and (3) transport of water and sugars among different parts of the tree cannot be impeded. Different tree species have evolved alternative solutions to these architectural and ecological constraints, varying mostly in the frequency of branching and the angular separation between branches. Small divergent angles separate the branches of elms (Fig. 2.5a), giving a characteristic and majestic vaselike shape to these trees. Apples and oaks (Fig. 2.5b), on the other hand, branch with larger angles, giving rounded crowns with tangled branches. Sugar maples (Fig. 2.5c) send out branches that spread and ascend to produce an overall egg shape. The branching patterns of trees resemble fractals because of their repeated, irregular forms (fractals are patterns that are independent of scale; trees resemble fractals when the branching pattern of a twig repeats that of the whole tree, giving the same pattern at different scales). When lateral branches grow faster than the central trunk, then crowns broaden, and when the tree is intolerant of shade, it grows upward more rapidly and sheds its lower branches.

Additional factors affect the final shape of a tree. Growth of a sapling repeats the characteristic branching pattern of its species, but branches expand more toward light gaps in the canopy. The general direction of solar radiation also has an effect. The sun is always overhead at low latitudes, so many tropical trees have horizontally flattened crowns; in contrast, most trees in the angled light of high latitudes are vertically narrow and pointed. Disturbance and injury during development further affect shape, with more branching after the loss of growing tips from storms and animal feeding. And trees growing in well-lit open areas are typically fuller in form than those in dense forests. The differences among species are seen most clearly when observing wintertime skeletal outlines of deciduous trees.

REFERENCES: HORN 1971; TOMLINSON 1983; NIKLAS & KERCHNER 1984; NIKLAS 1986; KUULUVAINEN 1992; GREEN 1995; KOZLOWSKI & PALLARDY 1997; SUMIDA & KOMIYAMA 1997

2.6   Tree Rings

Each year, trees add a tapering cylinder of wood, made of cells of water-transport tissue (xylem), just underneath their bark (we're more used to thinking of trees in cross section, in which these nested cylinders appear as rings). During the prime growing conditions of spring and early summer, large, light-colored, thin-walled cells (earlywood) are produced, but as growth slows later in summer, smaller, more compact, darker, thicker-walled cells (latewood) appear. The change within a growing season is gradual, but the transition from latewood of one year to earlywood of the next is more abrupt. Normally a single ring is added each year, but extreme fluctuations in water availability may lead to the production of false annual rings, while a very dry year might limit photosynthesis and allow no growth at all. As a tree ages, its rings usually become narrower as the trunk diameter increases. A quick transition to wider rings in an older tree means that the tree's growth accelerated suddenly, as might happen after the removal of surrounding trees by death, storm, or timber harvesting.

Tree rings provide a record of past growing conditions because warmer and wetter years, which are favorable for growth, lead to wider rings. Dating backward from the present and correlating growth patterns from many different trees, both living and dead, dendrochronologists (the scientists who study these things) have used ring widths to determine detailed climate records for the past eight thousand years in the American Southwest. Because of

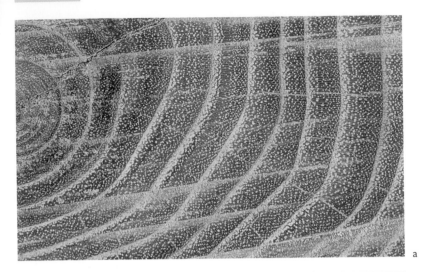

a

b

Fig. 2.6. Tree rings: (a) black locust, *Robinia pseudoacacia*, showing the abrupt transition from dark latewood of one year to light earlywood of the next; (b) weathered lodgepole pine, *Pinus contorta*, showing the greater resistance of the denser, darker summer wood to abrasion.

their ring structure and longevity, oaks and Douglas-firs are particularly good record keepers. Trees at higher elevations and latitudes (e.g., those in Alaska) are more sensitive to changes in temperature, whereas those in arid regions are more sensitive to changes in precipitation. The best climate records are found in the rings of water-stressed trees.

REFERENCES: FRITTS 1972; HITCH 1982; LABORATORY OF TREE-RING RESEARCH 2001

2.7 Heartwood

Cylindrical shells of wood that appear in cross section as rings are added annually to the outside of a tree, just underneath the bark (see 2.6). This new wood is xylem: layers of cells specialized to transport water from the roots upward. A large tree must transport and store a greater amount of water to support its additional leaves, so its trunk widens to accommodate the addition of more water-conducting xylem. The oldest xylem, nearest the middle of the trunk, ceases to function for storage or conduction; its cells fill with resins and oils instead, making them darker and occasionally aromatic. This is the heartwood, while the still-functioning xylem is known as sapwood. The ratio of sapwood to heartwood varies among tree species; sapwood is thick in maples and birches, thin in locusts and yews, and not easily distinguished in poplars and firs. The greatest water flow in all cases, however, is through the newest sapwood.

Heartwood provides structural support for a tree, but despite the protection by lignin in the cell walls (see 2.1), heartwood is completely dead and so is subject to fungal attack. As a result of decaying heartwood, many older trees have cavities in the middle. Heartwood may also serve for the storage of toxic compounds moved from living parts of the tree, and sometimes these chemicals slow the rotting process, but they do not stop it entirely.

REFERENCES: KOZLOWSKI & PALLARDY 1997; NIKLAS 1997; RAVEN ET AL. 1999; SCHULTZ & NICHOLAS 2000; WULLSCHLEGER & KING 2000; WLOCH ET AL. 2002

a

b

c

Fig. 2.7. Heartwood as seen in cross section: (a) sugar maple, *Acer saccharum*, with the heartwood of the main stem having rotted away; (b) black walnut, *Juglans nigra*, showing beautiful dark heartwood; (c) recently cut eastern white pine, *Pinus strobus*, with sap oozing from the rings of the functional sapwood but not from the central, darker heartwood.

2.8 Spiral Grain

When stripped of bark, some conifers show an upward spiral in the grain of the wood. The most common pattern is a left-handed spiral when young, switching to a right-handed spiral in the outer rings when larger and older. Some trees simply keep a left-handed spiral. The grain of the wood changes angle because of unequal cell division in the cambium, the wood-producing layer. It may seem odd that a tree should spiral rather than grow straight upward, but there are two hypotheses to account for this growth pattern. The less well supported idea is that spiral growth distributes sap more uniformly from roots to branches.

The more supported hypothesis has a geographic basis. Trees in the Northern Hemisphere spiral mostly to the right, while those in the Southern Hemisphere spiral mostly to the left, and therein lies a clue. With more sunlight coming from southern directions, southward-pointing branches of North American trees are usually longer and leafier, so prevailing winds, coming mostly from the west, act on the asymmetry of branch length to produce a torque or twisting force on the tree trunk. The trunk then spirals to the right as it grows upward. While there is an environmental influence on spiraling, the right-handed tendency is built into the genetic code of the trees; North American trees grown in the Southern Hemisphere retain their tendency to right-handedness. The constant angle of the spiral also suggests genetic control. Although the underlying cause is uncertain, an adaptive advantage is that spiral grain adds mechanical strength to the trunks that helps in resisting fiber breakage from the torsion of wind blowing on an irregular crown.

REFERENCES: MINORSKY 1998; SKATTER & KUCERA 1998; EKLUND & SALL 2000; GJERDRUM ET AL. 2002

a b

Fig. 2.8.   Spiral grain in western conifers: (a) Douglas fir, *Pseudotsuga menziesii*; (b) lodgepole pine, *Pinus contorta*.

2.9 Burls

Burls are large spherical growths that appear on the trunks of maples, spruce, birch, and numerous other trees, but the causes of these structures can't always be identified. Most burls begin as galls, abnormal growths that result from the penetration of the plant's epidermis (outer layer) by a fungus, bacterium, or egg-laying insect (see 3.5). Chemical signals from the invading organism alter the growth pattern of the plant, which produces tumorlike tissue around the injured site. Burls grow in size along with the tree trunk they're on, but they grow faster, as shown by the greater width of their annual rings. Faster growth also makes burl wood a little softer. A clustered occurrence of burls in a forest suggests that they were caused by pathogens spread by insects with penetrating mouthparts. Some people have suggested that burls are more likely to be found on trees already under environmental stress. Although burls don't kill trees, they may weaken the structure of the trunk. Because of their unusual patterns and the beauty of their grain, burls are often harvested to cut and polish for making furniture.

After being burned, woody plants may regrow from buds on the root crown just below ground level. Repeated regrowth through multiple fire cycles leads to enlarged woody platforms, and these are also known as burls. With age, these burls may rot away in the middle but still support new sprouts around their edges.

REFERENCES: DAVIS 1979; BOLEN 1998

a

b

Fig. 2.9. Burls: (a) sugar maple, *Acer saccharum*, and (b) white spruce, *Picea glauca*.

2.10   Bark Patterns

More complex in structure than the wood inside, bark is the skin of a tree, and the appearance of that skin depends on the tree's pattern of cell growth and the diameter of the trunk. It helps to look at bark structure to understand how this patterning arises. Several tissues make up bark, forming both outer and inner bark layers. Outer bark is made of (1) cork, the protective outer part we see, which consists of dead cells embedded with waxes and oils to prevent water loss and to protect against injury; (2) cork cambium, a layer of dividing cells that produces cork cells to the outside and other cells to the inside; and (3) phelloderm, the layer of cells formed by the cork cambium to the inside. Continuing toward the center of the trunk is the inner bark, which includes (4) cortex, a layer of basic trunk tissue, and (5) phloem, the tubes of living cells through which sugars made by photosynthesis are transported. Next to the inside is (6) vascular cambium, another layer of dividing cells, which every year produces phloem to the outside and (7) xylem, water transport tissues that make up wood, to the inside. When pulled from a tree trunk, bark separates from the wood at the vascular cambium.

a

A tree with smooth bark has a mostly uniform layer of outer bark (cork, cork cambium, and phelloderm) present on the surface of the trunk, but in a tree with scaly or fissured bark, additional layers of these tissues, known collectively as periderm, form repeatedly underneath as the tree increases in diameter. Stacks of periderm build up and are stretched and crack with a periodicity that depends on the width of the patches, the number of layers, how extensively the layers overlap, and the amount of strengthening fibers within. The result is a range of bark appearances—smooth, ridged, scaly, fissured, and peeling. Beech (Fig. 2.10a) produces little cork, so its bark is smooth; oak, in contrast, has faster-growing bark than beech, and its bark is thicker and fissured with multiple layers of periderm. Deeply furrowed barks, such as that of black locust (Fig. 2.10b), contain many tough fibers, which harden the bark and keep the layers together. The patterning is distinct enough on many trees to allow you to recognize the species from just the bark.

REFERENCES: WHITMORE 1962; KOZLOWSKI & PALLARDY 1997; RAVEN ET AL. 1999

b

c

d

e

f

Fig. 2.10. Diverse bark patterns: (a) American beech, *Fagus grandifolia*; (b) black locust, *Robinia pseudoacacia*; (c) shagbark hickory, *Carya ovata*; (d) yellow birch, *Betula alleghaniensis*; (e) ponderosa pine, *Pinus ponderosa*; (f) Engelman spruce, *Picea engelmannii*.

2.11   Green Bark

Why do some trees have greenish-colored bark? Green tissue anywhere on a plant suggests photosynthesis, and that's exactly what takes place in green bark. This phenomenon has been studied most in quaking aspen, in which chlorophyll-containing tissue within the bark adds to the photosynthetic gain of the tree. Although a large proportion of the tree's chlorophyll (15–40 percent) is in the bark, the rate of photosynthesis there is less than half that in the leaves. Photosynthesis requires carbon dioxide, and some of what's needed is obtained from the normal metabolism of interior cells, but light is limited to what penetrates the outer bark: 20–30 percent of blue light and 50–60 percent of red light. As a result, bark chlorophyll shows the same characteristics as those of shade-adapted leaves (see 2.15).

Perhaps the most significant contribution of bark photosynthesis to the tree's overall carbon budget is during a long winter without leaves (although photosynthesis ceases when the air temperature falls below 27°F). An additional benefit, though, is that the oxygen released reduces the occurrence of anaerobic conditions within the tree's trunk. Bark photosynthesis takes place in more species of trees than is generally recognized, and it appears more frequently in younger stems and trunks.

REFERENCES: FOOTE & SCHAEDLE 1976, 1978; KHAROUK ET AL. 1995; PFANZ 1999; ASCHAN ET AL. 2001; CERNUSAK ET AL. 2001; PFANZ ET AL. 2002

a   b

Fig. 2.11.   Photosynthetic bark: (a) quaking aspen, *Populus tremuloides* (outer layer stripped away) and (b) striped maple, *Acer pensylvanicum.*

2.12 Buttresses

Buttresses are exposed, vertically flared projections from the base of tree trunks that connect to roots and provide stabilizing support. Because trees grow toward light gaps in the canopy, an asymmetric gravitational load can form within the trunk. It is during critical stages of tree development when loads are shifting that buttresses form. The greatest support is typically found on the side opposite the leaning direction, which means that the wood in a buttress is being stretched rather than compressed. Buttresses on the stretched (tension) side grow larger. As trees grow in size, so do the buttresses, usually with several flared buttresses per tree. After the trees reach large sizes, the buttresses provide support against torque from strong winds. Buttresses are characteristic of large trees at low elevations and in wet soils, which is why they are known particularly from the tropics; in North America they are broadest on baldcypresses (Fig. 2.12a) and water tupelo growing on flooded grounds.

REFERENCES: COLLINGWOOD & BRUSH 1984; RICHTER 1984; KAUFMAN 1988; WARREN ET AL. 1988; KOZLOWSKI & PALLARDY 1997; TER STEEGE ET AL. 1997; CHAPMAN ET AL. 1998; WALKER 1998

a

b

c

Fig. 2.12. Buttressed trunks:
(a) baldcypress, *Taxodium distichum*;
(b) sandbox tree, *Hura crepitans*;
(c) American beech, *Fagus grandifolia*, with roots producing the appearance of buttresses.

2.13   Extra Roots

Roots must have oxygen to remain alive, which is why plant growth is limited in oxygen-poor, permanently saturated soils. One solution to the problem of poor gas exchange is to grow accessory roots with internal openings that allow the downward diffusion of oxygen. Mangroves tolerate submersion in salt water by growing air roots known as pneumatophores upward through the water, just like snorkels, to provide aeration to submerged tissues. With less oxygen in the sediments, more pneumatophores are produced. Baldcypresses in southern swamps are known for their "knees," upwardly pointed root projections also called pneumatophores (Fig. 2.13a), and baldcypresses in deeper water have taller knees.

Other trees have flexible roots that grow from their stems and branches down through the air, branch outward, and penetrate the soil. Also known as prop or stilt roots, these aerial roots provide support and take in nutrients and water. The spectacular prop roots of red mangroves (Fig. 2.13b) give added support against wave action and facilitate gas exchange for the tree; the larger the mangrove trunk, the more prop roots that develop. Thickets of mangrove prop roots retard water movement, too, allowing silt to collect and form small mangrove islands.

REFERENCES: MALL ET AL.1987; BOLEN 1998; MATSUI 1998; WALKER 1998; RAVEN ET AL. 1999

a   b

Fig. 2.13.   Extra root structures: (a) the "knees" (pneumatophores) of baldcypress, *Taxodium distichum*; (b) prop roots of red mangrove, *Rhizophora mangle*.

2.14   Leaf Shape

In contrast to the smooth margins of leaves in the tropics, leaves of North American trees commonly have teeth or lobes. Several factors give rise to this difference. Deciduous leaves in temperate zones are retained for only one growing season, so they can be thinner than evergreen leaves; thinness reduces the costs of production and accelerates gas exchange for photosynthesis. A membranous layer doesn't hold up as well as a thicker one, however, so the area of the leaf blade is reduced between the larger veins, and as a result, lobed leaves are common among the thin deciduous leaves of temperate forests. A second reason is that as buds break, photosynthesis can begin immediately in leaf tips if the tips are exposed before the main parts of the leaves are able to expand. Quick onset of photosynthesis can give an advantageous surge of energy for deciduous trees in a cool climate with a short growing season. A third reason is that toothed and lobed leaves offer less drag in wind. Fourth, smaller leaves are subject to less heat load under intense light, and deep lobing reduces effective leaf size. Compound leaves take lobing to the extreme; the separate leaflets of a compound leaf are functionally similar to a lobed leaf with deeply indented margins. Finally, it has been proposed that complex leaf shapes may retard insect herbivory by their marginal indentations and the weblike orientation of their veins, which make them hard to chew through. While North American leaves usually have complex toothed or lobed margins, with the exception of birches, they rarely display a feature commonly seen in tropical rainforests: a drip tip, an extended point at the tip of the leaf to facilitate water running off.

REFERENCES: GIVNISH 1978; WHITE 1983; BROWN & LAWTON 1991; BAKER-BROSH & PEET 1997; THOMAS 2000A

Fig. 2.14. Variations in leaf shape: (a) a collection of leaves, showing (counterclockwise from the bottom) entire (lilac, *Syringa* sp.), toothed (American beech, *Fagus grandifolia*), palmately lobed (red maple, *Acer rubrum*), pinnately lobed (northern red oak, *Quercus rubra*), and compound (white ash, *Fraxinus americana*) leaves; (b) Devil's walking-stick, *Aralia spinosa*, a small tree with doubly compound leaves (several large leaves are apparent in this photo); (c) seedling of sassafras, *Sassafras albidum*, a tree that produces mitten-shaped leaves with 3 and sometimes 2 lobes as well as unlobed leaves.

2.15   Sun and Shade Leaves

Conditions for growth differ from higher to lower in a forest mostly because of decreasing light intensity. Leaves near the tops of trees are exposed to more sunlight and greater wind, so these sun leaves are smaller, more deeply notched between the lobes, thicker, and hairier; they also have a deeper epidermal (skin) layer and additional internal transport tissues. The temperature of broad leaves in full sun may exceed air temperature by up to 20°F, so the dissipation of added heat is important. The smaller size and deeper lobing of sun leaves ensure that all parts of the leaf surface are near an edge, from which air currents can remove heat by convection.

Leaves low in the forest are more shaded and experience less damage by wind. It is advantageous for trees to unfurl wide leaves with less lobing in such circumstances to collect the diffuse light and sunflecks that penetrate the canopy. Shade leaves are thinner as well and have fewer openings (stomates) for gas exchange and less chlorophyll per unit area. Shade leaves also have a rapid photosynthetic response to increased light at low levels, but if exposed to intense light, shade leaves photosynthesize less efficiently than sun leaves due to light-induced chemical inhibition. Developmental flexibility, with the amount of light received during leaf growth being important, leads to the different forms. Even plant architecture can be affected; stems in low light branch to minimize self-shading of their leaves. The visible differences between sun and shade leaves are easily seen by comparing leaves from the canopy of trees such as oaks and maples with those of saplings underneath.

REFERENCES: VOGEL 1968; LEI & LECHOWICZ 1990; MOORE 1991; KOZLOWSKI & PALLARDY 1997; RAVEN ET AL. 1999

a   b

Fig. 2.15. Sun and shade leaves: (a) sun leaves of sugar maple, *Acer saccharum* on top, intermediate leaves in the middle, and shade leaves on the bottom (the largest); (b) a sun leaf of white ash, *Fraxinus americana*, on the left, an intermediate leaf in the middle, and a shade leaf on the right.

2.16 Leaf Retention

We think of deciduous leaves as dropping off trees as soon as the leaves have died, so it's surprising when they don't. The deciduous habit evolved to circumvent a season of severe cold or drought; deciduous leaves senesce at the end of the growing season, lose their green color as chlorophyll degrades, turn yellow and brown, and drop from the trees, giving a good reason for us to call October a fall month. But dead brown leaves remain on the branches of many oaks and beeches for several months, as if the trees are reluctant to be deciduous. One explanation for the retention of dead leaves far into the winter is that by dropping their

b

Fig. 2.16. Wintertime retained leaves: northern red oak, *Quercus rubra*, (a) tree and (b) branch.

a

leaves slowly, the trees gradually return nutrients to the soil around them for reuse. If all their leaves fell at once, then a single pulse of soluble nutrients would be released through simultaneous decomposition, and most would be leached away and lost. In contrast, gradual leaf drop can serve as a timed-release process for continuous replenishment of the nutrient pool. Oaks typically grow in well-drained soils that don't retain nutrients for long, so dry leaves on a tree's branches are an oak's best nutrient reservoir. Leaves stay mostly on lower branches, possibly because they are the leaves that would drop and decay near the tree's roots. Little evidence actually supports this nutrient hypothesis, but it's an intriguing idea nevertheless.

Generally, leaf retention may be prolonged by heat or frost during the fall, which slows the forming of a separation layer (an abscission zone) at the base of the dying leaves. Furthermore, trees that leaf out early (see 9.5) senesce late and retain their leaves longer into the fall.

REFERENCES: OTTO & NILSSON 1981; COLLINGWOOD ET AL. 1984; WANG ET AL. 1992

2.17 Quaking Leaves

The sound of leaves rustling in the wind is familiar to all of us, but the leaves of quaking aspen tremble in even the lightest breezes and shake more readily than those of other trees. The mechanical reason for such ready movement is easily seen. The leaf stalk or petiole of each aspen leaf is conspicuously flattened side to side where it attaches to the flat part (blade) of the leaf, and the leaves flop back and forth at the flattened zone. From a simple engineering perspective, for the leaves to be held more firmly, the petioles should be round or cylindrical, as they are on most plants. Quaking aspen is worthy of its scientific name, *Populus tremuloides*, because its leaves tremble so easily.

Why the tree benefits from leaves that tremble is a different question. Most plants can still photosynthesize at a maximal rate on bright cloudy days or when leaves are partially shaded. Quaking aspen grows in open, sunny habitats, and its branches retain leaves through-out the volume of the tree such that some leaves are almost always directly above others. If the leaves were held firmly, upper leaves might overshade lower leaves and reduce their photosynthetic gain. But the shaking of the leaves transmits significant light through to lower leaves by serving as a neutral-density filter of full sunlight; it also allows bright sunflecks through the canopy in a shifting pattern. Leaf flutter does not increase the uptake of CO_2, but it does increase the amount of usable light available to lower leaves, and it may reduce leaf temperature by promoting convective heat losses. There are good reasons for all the shaking goin' on.

REFERENCES: HORN 1971; RODEN & PEARCY 1993A, 1993B

a

b

Fig. 2.17. Leaves of quaking aspen, *Populus tremuloides*: (a) leaves showing a flattened petiole near the attachment with the blade (flat part); (b) leaves trembling in a slight breeze.

2.18 Needle Drop

Spruce, firs, and pines are evergreen because they maintain a set of functional leaves year round. That does not mean, however, that each needlelike leaf is retained for the life of the tree; many leaves die and drop each year. The new needles produced each spring last two to five years—or longer in colder, northern latitudes—before being shed. The tree remains green and photosynthetic because some younger needles always stay behind when older ones are dropped. Each tree supports several years' crops of needles.

Needles have a natural life cycle that influences how long they last. Pines in moist, mod-erate conditions grow quickly and produce soft needles that are retained only two or three years; in contrast, species in stressed, nutrient-poor habitats grow slowly and retain their needles for five years or more. The long-lived needles have lower photosynthetic rates but

Fig. 2.18. Dead needles of eastern white pine, *Pinus strobus*, being shed.

are structurally stronger. Growing in a very harsh, slow-growing environment, the ancient bristlecone pines of the American Southwest (see 2.4) retain their needles for up to forty years, the record age for leaves. But needle longevity is reduced by damage from accumulated injury; being functional for more than a single year, needles are exposed to more freeze, drought, and air pollution than are deciduous leaves.

REFERENCES: RAVEN ET AL. 1999; COLLINGWOOD ET AL. 1984; WARREN & ADAMS 2000

2.19   Cone Distribution

Most people recognize only one kind of cone on each coniferous tree, but actually there are two. Large, woody, conspicuous cones are female structures in which ovules—sacks containing egg cells—develop into seeds. But there's another kind of cone, small and paler in color, that appears in clusters at branch tips. These are the male cones (Fig. 2.19a), where sperm-bearing pollen grains are produced. Pollen cones are small and papery in texture and disintegrate readily when spent. Wind transports pollen from male cones of one tree to female (seed) cones of the same or another tree; to counter the inefficiency of wind pollination, pollen grains are very light and winged. Furthermore, pollen is released in huge amounts by abundant male cones, so in spring and early summer pine branches release dense puffs of yellow pollen when bumped or blown by wind gusts (Fig. 2.19b). The buoyancy of pollen also shows in the dense pollen layers that collect on the surfaces of ponds and puddles and on automobile windshields.

Male cones grow throughout the trees to generate the large amounts of pollen needed, but seed cones grow mostly near the tops of the trees on young twigs (Figs. 2.19c, d). The age and species of the conifer have some effect on where the cones grow. This distributional pattern promotes the exchange of genetic information because the seed cones are less likely to receive pollen that falls from male cones on the same tree (most pollen cones are below them) and more likely to receive pollen blown upward by the wind from distant trees.

REFERENCES: KOZLOWSKI & PALLARDY 1997; STAGER 1998; RAVEN ET AL. 1999

Fig. 2.19.　Cones on conifers: (a) male cones on eastern white pine, *Pinus strobus*; (b) pollen being shed from the male cones of pitch pine, *Pinus rigida*; (c) clustering of female cones high on white spruce, *Picea glauca*; (d) female cones at the top of limber pine, *Pinus flexilis*.

2.20　Cone Variation

Some of the variation in the sizes and shapes of pine cones is due to what eats the seeds and how they are dispersed. Pines such as eastern white, loblolly, and shortleaf pines produce winged seeds that are dispersed hundreds of yards by wind. For these trees, seed-eating animals such as squirrels are harmful, so the trees have evolved mechanisms to deter seed predators: thick cone scales, few seeds per cone, sharp spines on the scales, small seeds, less palatable seeds, and gummy resin on the cones. All these features lessen the food value of the cones because they increase the time required for an animal to extract the seeds. The longer that seed-bearing cones are retained on the trees, the more elaborate the spines. The aptly named bristlecone pine is an example of a species with sharp, protective spines. Trees in drier habitats, such as digger, Coulter, and table mountain pines, produce heavy cones with strong woody protection to guard against the increased attention of seed eaters in these less-productive environments.

Other pines produce seeds adapted for animal dispersal. Pinyon and whitebark pines have plump, unwinged, nutlike seeds that are collected and cached by birds such as western Clark's nutcrackers (and are tasty to people, too). It is hard for tree squirrels to cut the gummy, clustered cones of these species from their branches, but the cones open wide, lack spines, and grow on upswept branches to promote harvesting by the birds that disperse and cache the seeds.

These and complex other factors lead to the remarkable variation within North American pine cones. Those of sugar pine may reach 21 inches in length, the longest cones in North America, while at 4 to 5 pounds each, the cones of Coulter pine are the heaviest.

REFERENCES: SMITH 1970; MCCUNE 1988; TOMBACK & LINHART 1990; TOMBACK ET AL. 1993; BENKMAN 1995; COFFEY ET AL. 1999

Fig 2.20   Variation in the size and shape of pine cones; from the left these include: digger pine, *Pinus sabiniana*; eastern white pine, *P. strobus*; longleaf pine, *P. palustris*; lodgepole pine, *P. contorta*; ponderosa pine, *P. ponderosa*; limber pine, *P. flexilis*; table mountain pine, *P. pungens*; and sugar pine, *P. lambertiana*.

2.21   Closed Cones

The cones that characterize pines are female reproductive structures in which seeds develop under woody scales. After seed maturation, usually late in the second year after fertilization, the cones open and release their seeds for dispersal by wind or seed-feeding birds and rodents. Pines in habitats that burn regularly, however, produce closed or serotinous cones, ones whose scales are sealed shut with resin. Serotiny (the term is from a Latin word meaning "late-developing") is correlated with a high frequency of forest fires. The heat of a fire scorches the closed cones on a burning tree, volatilizing the high-melting-point resins inside. This process forces the scales open and releases the seeds for germination in the fire-scorched, nutrient-rich, newly opened habitat below.

Pines differ genetically in the proportion of closed cones they produce; the more frequent fires have been historically, the higher the percentage of cones that are closed. Closed cones may remain on the trees for up to forty years, keeping seeds available, and the seeds may remain viable for another ten or twenty years after that. There is a trade-off, however:

a
b

Fig. 2.21. Closed cones: (a) lodgepole pine, *Pinus contorta*; (b) pitch pine, *P. rigida*.

because of greater investment in the woody, resinous structures that hold them, fewer seeds are produced in closed cones than in open ones. Fire-adapted trees have other features as well to withstand fires, including thick bark, self-pruning branches, and flammable foliage, but closed cones are their most noticeable characteristic. Fire-adapted pitch pine of the East, jack pine of the upper Midwest, lodgepole pine of the West, and giant sequoias all produce closed cones.

REFERENCES: GIVNISH 1981; MUIR & LOTAN 1985; GAUTHIER ET AL. 1993; SCHWILK & ACKERLY 2001; SMITH & SMITH 2001; TURNER ET AL. 2003

2.22   Walnut Inhibition

It was first noted long ago (by Pliny in A.D. 1) that garden plants don't grow well under walnut trees. These trees engage in chemical warfare for the control of growing space by secreting a chemical, juglone, that inhibits the germination and growth of other plants. Juglone is one of the best-studied allelochemicals, which are natural compounds made by one organism to harm another. It is synthesized in the leaves and then transported through the phloem to other tissues, especially to the husks around the developing seeds. Juglone is also released by the roots. Even at a very low concentration (one described chemically as 10^{-6} molar),

a
b

Fig. 2.22.   Black walnut, *Juglans nigra*, inhibition: (a) fallen black walnuts with their husks; (b) a grove of black walnut trees, with different vegetation under the trees than nearby.

juglone reduces plant growth and photosynthetic rates. In affected plants, the function of both chloroplasts and mitochondria—organelles found in plant cells—is disrupted, and mineral uptake is inhibited. Juglone produces noticeable effects around walnut trees as it accumulates in the soil; it concentrates especially in poorly drained soils, where degradation by microbial activity is reduced. Walnuts, pecans, and related trees that release this chemical gain another benefit, too, because as a toxin, juglone inhibits the growth of fungi that could harm the trees.

REFERENCES: RIETVELD 1983; RICE 1984; BORAZJANI ET AL. 1985; EINHELLIG 1986; SCHMIDT 1988; NEAVE & DAWSON 1989; PRASAD & GUELZ 1990; HEIJL ET AL. 1993; JOSE & GILLESPIE 1998

3. PLANT FEATURES

The diversity in size, shape, and growth requirements of different plants produces an astonishing array of features to see, from hairs, thorns, and waxes to tilting responses toward sunlight (phototaxis) and rapid responses to touch. Widely differing growth forms also occur, including those associated with photosynthetic, parasitic, and carnivorous lifestyles, as well as the mining and galling effects of insects. This chapter describes a few of the many interesting features of plants.

Additional discussions of plant characteristics are given in the other two chapters on plants, Chapter 1, "Flowers and Seeds," and Chapter 2, "Trees," as well as in a number of different descriptions scattered throughout the book. They include:

3.1   Leaf Hairs

The diversity of plant hairs is enormous, generating a hundred different technical terms to describe their varied forms. Hairs may be dense and tangled (tomentose), short and bristly (hispid), starlike with radiating branches (stellate), or filled with volatile secretions (glandular). Leaf hairs, properly known as trichomes, are simply outgrowths from the outer cell layer of the leaves, the epidermis. In the dryness of deserts and on windblown mountain tops, leaves are often furry with long, thick hairs that reflect light, reducing leaf temperature and retarding water loss; in bright and warm environments, a silvery mat of leaf hairs can reflect enough of the sun's intense radiation to lessen heat stress (see 11.3). Glandular hairs impart a sticky feel to leaves and, with the chemicals they release, produce a distinctive fragrance.

Often, leaf hairs reduce herbivory. Hooked trichomes catch and impale tiny insects, while branched trichomes can create a nearly impenetrable tiny forest that prevents herbivorous insects from reaching the leaf surface. It has been shown, for example, that hairy varieties of potatoes and beans suffer less damage by leaf hopper insects than do smoother varieties. Wherever you look, the hairiest leaves are often fed on less by insects than are smoother leaves.

REFERENCES: RAVEN ET AL. 1999; BEGON ET AL. 1996; BARLOW 2001

Fig. 3.1.   Leaf hairs: (a) branched hairs of common mullein, *Verbascum thapsus*; (b) stiff hairs of blazing star, *Mentzelia* sp.; (c) filamentous hairs of New England aster, *Aster novae-angliae*.

3.2   Spines, Thorns, and Prickles

When walking through a field, people avoid plants with sharp, poking points that tear at and damage clothing and skin. Thorns and their allies are defensive structures that deter feeding by vertebrates such as deer and rabbits through slowing the rate of consumption and reducing bite size to fewer leaves at a time, both of which make the plants less valuable as food. Confirming the beneficial effect of thorns is the fact that some trees have been shown to grow less well after their thorns have been removed experimentally. But because of their relatively large size, these structures don't deter small herbivorous insects, which the plants must combat in other ways, such as chemical defenses or small hooked hairs (trichomes) that act like tiny thorns (see 3.1).

Spines, thorns, and prickles are all sharp and hurt our skin, but they originate in different ways. Spines are modified leaves or leaf margins attached to stems. When you look at a cactus, you can recognize the green parts as enlarged, water-retaining stems, with spines

a

c

b

d

Fig. 3.2.   Sharp, protective structures: (a) spines of cactus, *Opuntia polyacantha*; (b) thorns of hawthorn, *Crateagus* sp.; (c) branched thorns of honeylocust, *Gleditsia triacanthos*; (d) prickles of multiflora rose, *Rosa multiflora*.

emerging directly from the expanded stems (Fig. 3.2a). Thorns, on the other hand, are modified branches that grow from leaf axils, which is where each leaf attaches to a branch, or from stems (Fig. 3.2b). Thorns may even be branched; the astonishingly complex thorns of honeylocusts (Fig. 3.2c) don't deter living North American mammals from stripping the trees of their leaves, so a popular hypothesis is that these thorns originated many thousands of years ago as protection against the feeding of mastodons. Prickles are various sharp outgrowths from the epidermis or outer layer of the plant, and they include the "thorns" of roses (Fig. 3.2d). All three kinds of structures couple sharpness with a hardened exterior of dense cell walls, sometimes strengthened with silica or organic crystals. It doesn't take much to convince large vertebrates, including people, to avoid plants with these sharp points.

REFERENCES: COOPER & OWEN-SMITH 1986; MILEWSKI ET AL. 1991; ARMS & CAMP 1995; RAVEN ET AL. 1999; LUCAS ET AL. 2000; SMITH & SMITH 2001

3.3 Resins and Waxes

A distinctive fragrance is part of the sensory experience of walking through a pine forest. The pungent aroma comes from volatile chemicals called terpenes that are found in the resins that make pine branches gummy to the touch. Plants secrete gluelike resins to seal wounds and to protect against the invasion of beetles and pathogenic fungi. The resins may also deter rabbits and squirrels from chewing on stems. Resins are produced in broad-leafed trees, too, but are more abundant in conifers, which is where we think of finding them. Similar terpene-bearing compounds are made and released by the glandular hairs of a number of herbaceous plants as well.

Many plants secrete surface waxes instead of resins. Long-chain lipids that are solid at normal temperatures, waxes are the most water-repellent materials a plant can make. Waxes are secreted on the surface of a leaf, stem, or fruit to protect against the loss of water and the uptake of pollutants, and they form irregular microscopic patterns on the plant's surface. You become aware of their presence when you rub an apple to polish it; the apple is prewaxed, and all you have to do is buff it! Waxes are difficult to transport, however, so they are made and secreted by cells right at the plant surface. They give a white or blue appearance (bloom) to leaves, especially those in deserts where the reflectance of light away from the plant provides protection against heat stress and water loss (waxes reflect both ultraviolet and visible radiation). Waxes may be fragrant, too, like those of bayberry, which are used in making candles. As surface chemicals, both resins and waxes are protective, but in different ways.

REFERENCES: ARMS & CAMP 1995; KOZLOWSKI & PALLARDY 1997; STAGER 1998; RAVEN ET AL. 1999; HOLMES & KEILLER 2002

Fig. 3.3. Resins and waxes: (a) pine resin dripping from lodgepole pine, *Pinus contorta*, scraped by the horns of bison; (b) resinous receptacles of gumweed flowers, *Grindelia squarrosa;* (c) wax-coated needles of blue spruce, *Picea pungens;* (d) wax-coated fruit of juniper, *Juniperus communis*.

a

b

c

d

3.4   Variegated Leaves

If leaves are green so that they can harvest energy from the sun, why then are some leaves only partly green? Variegated leaves, those with photosynthetic pigments in only part of the leaf blades, are caused by recessive mutations in the plant's DNA. Sometimes the chloroplasts, the cellular components that contain chlorophyll, are missing entirely, and sometimes the chloroplasts are present but cannot manufacture functional chlorophyll. The insertion of a magnesium ion into the chlorophyll molecule may be blocked, for example. Partial formation of chlorophyll can leave a yellow color, while the production of anthocyanin pigments can create a pink tinge in a pale leaf. A related color pattern that appears occasionally is that of nongreen veins, which results when the cells above and below the conducting tissue of the leaf lack the photosynthetic apparatus.

Variegated leaves have a reduced ability to manufacture the sugar products of photosynthesis, so the leaves grow slowly and may be smaller than fully green leaves on the same plant. Furthermore, sugars must be transported from the green areas to the nongreen areas for maintenance. Because slowed growth is disadvantageous, plants with variegated leaves are uncommon, although their repeated occurrence in tropical areas suggests the possibility of a counterbalancing benefit under some conditions. The high frequency of variegation among ornamental plants is a result of human appreciation and propagation of these natural rarities.

REFERENCES: WEISBERG ET AL. 1988; MASUDA ET AL. 1996; MATHIAS BOTANICAL GARDEN 2002

a   b

Fig. 3.4.   Variegated leaves: (a) common burdock, *Arctium minus*; (b) Norway maple, *Acer platanoides*.

3.5   Galls

Swellings on stems, thick leaf clusters, odd surface projections, and other abnormal structures on plant parts are usually galls, which are the active growth responses of plants to the presence of insect eggs and feeding larvae. The distinctiveness of size and shape of each kind of gall results from the characteristic chemical stimulus of the insect and the specific reaction of the plant. Galls range in appearance from simple stem swellings to ornate structures entirely different from the rest of the plant. A gall forms as each wound made by an insect generates a new growth center that interacts with the plant's normal growth pattern. As the gall enlarges, plant tissue encapsulates the insect larva, sealing it off from the external environment. Hidden in its protected home, the larva then feeds on sugary plant fluids. Growth of the plant above the gall is often reduced because of the loss of photosynthetic products to the gall insect and the partial blockage of transport tissues.

Galls are most noticeable on leaves and stems. The presence of an insect larva invites other organisms, including predators, parasitic wasps, and just plain roommates, to invade the gall, so the insect that emerges from a gall may not be the one that caused it to form. Although more kinds of galls are found on plants in the oak family than in any other, goldenrods have more than fifty species of gall-making insects attacking them, making them excellent places to look for galls (Figs. 3.5a, b). Because the adult insects lay their eggs near the growing points of stems, the height of a gall above the ground shows the height of the goldenrod plant when the egg was placed there. Especially in the winter, woodpeckers and chickadees peck at goldenrod galls to eat the insects inside; even hard-walled galls can't provide complete protection from the outside world.

REFERENCES: HUTCHINS 1969; PRICE ET AL. 1987; TSCHARNTKE 1989; SHORTHOUSE & ROHFRITSCH 1992

a

b

c

d

Fig. 3.5.　Galls: (a) ball gall on tall goldenrod, *Solidago altissima*; (b) opened goldenrod ball gall, revealing the fly larva, *Eurosta solidaginis*, inside; (c) aphid galls (unidentified species) on wild grape, *Vitis labrusca*; (d) wool sower gall on white oak, *Quercus alba,* from the wasp *Callirhytes* sp.; (e) gall on white spruce, *Picea glauca,* from eastern spruce gall adelgid, *Adelges abietis.*

e

3.6   Leaf Mines

Blotches or serpentine trails within a leaf reveal the presence of leaf-mining larval insects. Mines are pale in color because the leaf miners have consumed the nutritious, chlorophyll-bearing leaf tissue between the upper and lower leaf surfaces, often leaving a blackened trail of frass (larval fecal pellets) in the middle of the trail. Linear mines are narrow at their onset, where an insect hatched from an egg, and then visibly wider where the growing larva moved and fed. Leaf mines are made by the larvae of tiny moths, flies, beetles, and sawflies, and the vertical confinement of the space requires the larvae to have a flattened body, reduced appendages, and protruding mouthparts. The larvae pupate either inside the leaf or after dropping to the ground, and by the time you see the mine, the insect may have already departed.

Leaf mining is an effective way to feed. Sheltered between the leaf surfaces, the insect finds a moist environment, reduced incidence of disease, protection against ultraviolet radiation, and avoidance of morphological plant defenses against herbivory. But there are costs, too, including a high incidence of attack by parasitic wasps due to constraints on mobility, mortality from premature leaf fall resulting from a plant's response to damage, and limited egg production because only small larval sizes fit within a leaf, and larval size constrains adult size. A plant with many leaf mines will be harmed, experiencing reduced growth and fruit production, but over time, plant species subject to attack may evolve leaf surfaces that are difficult to puncture or chemicals that deter the egg-laying insects.

REFERENCES: HUTCHINS 1969; PRITCHARD & JAMES 1984; STILING 1988; SCOBLE 1995; CONNOR & TAVERNER 1997

a

b

c

Fig. 3.6.   Leaf mines of insects of three different orders: (a) blotch mine on blue vervain, *Verbena hastate*, likely from *Liriomyza* sp., leafminer fly; (b) trail mines on raspberry, *Rubus* sp., from blackberry leafminer sawfly, *Metallus rubi,*; (c) trail mine on quaking aspen, *Populus tremuloides,* from poplar serpentine leafminer moth, *Phyllocnistes populiella.*

3.7 Plant Spirals

We often see spirals when looking at the leaves of a stem, flowers of an inflorescence, and scales of a cone. Spiral-like patterns result from a physical process that minimizes the overlap of new structures added around a central point or the amount of space needed to pack a number of plant parts together. Additional features of the plant's developmental design determine details of the pattern: the distance between successive structures, the number of structures in a single spiral, and the number of spirals.

The spiral patterns of plants are related to the Fibonacci numbers, numbers that lead to the most efficient packing of separate units around a point (the Fibonacci numbers form an infinite series in which each successive number is the sum of the two previous numbers; beginning with 1, the series is 1, 1, 2, 3, 5, 8, 13, ...). To understand the advantage of spirals, consider what would happen if successive leaves on an upright stem were separated by 180°: the third and fourth leaves would overshade the first and second completely, lessening their photosynthetic gain. In contrast, a divergence angle of 137.51° between successive struc-

tures around a central point minimizes overlap and maximizes their exposure to the sun (Fig. 3.7a). This optimal angle is produced by the golden ratio (also known as phi, the golden section or number), a number closely related to the Fibonacci series (the ratio of any number in the Fibonacci series to the next number in the series converges to the golden ratio: 0.618...). The golden proportion 0.618 of 360° gives the complementary angle 137.51°.

For the seeds of a ripened sunflower, the problem is not overlap but the need to fit as many seeds as possible on the base of a developing inflorescence. To be packed optimally on the seed head, seed arrangement is also related to the optimal divergence

Fig. 3.7. Plant spirals: (a) leaves on a stem of trail plant, *Adenocaulon bicolor*; (b) disk flowers of giant sunflower, *Helianthus annuus*, within a surrounding circle of ray flowers; (c) cone scales of ponderosa pine, *Pinus ponderosa*.

a

b

c

angle, and spirals are visible in each direction outward from the center (Fig. 3.7b). The number of spirals is a Fibonacci number, too. Spirals and Fibonacci numbers are surprisingly widespread in plant growth and provide many examples of geometric beauty in nature.

REFERENCES: MITCHISON 1977; KIRCHOFF 1984; WILLIAMS & BRITTAIN 1984; ABBOTT & SCHMITT 1985; RIDLEY 1986; GREEN & BAXTER 1987; GREEN 1999; RAVEN ET AL. 1999; KNOTT 2002

3.8   Lenticels

Raised dots, ovals, and lines contribute a rough texture to the uniform surface of bark that would otherwise be smooth, as well as to the skin of fruits such as apples and pears. These marks are lenticels, small breaks in the outer impermeable layers of the plant; they develop

a

b

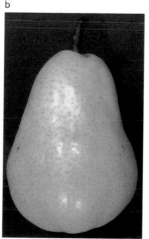

c

Fig. 3.8.   Lenticels: (a) horizontal lenticels of pin cherry, *Prunus pensylvanica*; (b) spot-shaped lenticels on the skin of a pear, *Pyrus* sp.; (c) elongate lenticels of paper birch, *Betula papyrifera*.

to allow the exchange of oxygen and carbon dioxide between the living cells within the stem or fruit and the surrounding air. The outer tissue layers of most plant parts are so protective against the outside environment and so impermeable that specialized passageways are needed for the gas exchange required by all living cells. Often, the lenticels appear as raised dots, but they stretch out as horizontal lines on the bark of birches, cherries, and roses. Roots also develop lenticels for gas exchange within air pockets in the soil. As passageways, lenticels may allow for some uptake of water and minerals as well as gases, but they also have a cost by sometimes permitting the entry of unwanted intruders such as fungal infections.

REFERENCES: GARREC & BARROIS 1992; KOZLOWSKI & PALLARDY 1997; RAVEN ET AL. 1999

3.9 Carnivorous Plants

As a rule, plants absorb energy from the sun and nutrients from the ground, so it seems perverse that some green plants also prey on animals. Where carnivorous plants are found, however, gives a clue to the advantages of carnivory: they grow in habitats—bogs, ponds, and sandy soils—that are well lit but nutrient-poor, especially in the nitrogen needed to make proteins. Nitrogen-based compounds leach out of these saturated and acidic soils, and nitrogen-fixing bacteria don't grow there. As a result, carnivorous plants are small-rooted perennials that gain nitrogen and other minerals from animal prey, and those that trap more prey grow bigger and produce more seeds. Those that fail shed leaves. Carnivory, therefore, is an adaptive response to a habitat well provided with light and water but impoverished in nutrients.

Carnivorous plants lure insects with red coloration and nectarlike, sweet-smelling secretions, and they catch their prey using several different mechanisms. Pitcher plants produce pitfall traps, which are tube-shaped leaves with downward-pointing hairs that encourage insects to slip down into a digestive soup of enzymes in rainwater at the leaf bottom (Figs. 3.9a, b). Sundews produce adhesive traps, using small leaves with glandular hairs that stick to small insects (Fig. 3.9c); just like Brer Rabbit's tar baby, the more an insect struggles, the more it becomes entangled (though sometimes ants steal a sundew's catches). Venus flytraps (Fig. 3.9d) clamp their jawlike, snap-trap leaves shut within a fraction of a second when triggered by an insect. After the prey has been trapped, the plant secretes digestive enzymes that break down the insect tissues for absorption. Most of the prey of carnivorous plants are flying insects, but pitcher plants occasionally trap spiders, slugs, and small frogs, too. The flowers of these plants are tall or open at a different time of year to avoid catching their own pollinators.

Like other green plants, carnivorous plants use energy from the sun for photosynthesis, but they use carnivory to supplement their nutrient supply, the nitrogen of which would otherwise come only from precipitation. But where humans have increased the concentration of nitrates in rainwater, pitcher plants grow smaller leaves and are less carnivorous.

REFERENCES: GIVNISH ET AL. 1984; SCHULZE & SCHULZE 1990; GIBSON 1991; KRAFFT & HANDEL 1991; RAVEN ET AL. 1999; ELLISON & GOTELLI 2001, 2002; GOTELLI & ELLISON 2002; SCHNELL 2002

Fig. 3.9. Carnivorous plants: (a) purple pitcher plant, *Sarracenia purpurea*; (b) yellow pitcher plant, *Sarracenia flava*; (c) round-leaved sundew, *Drosera rotundifolia*; (d) Venus flytrap, *Dionaea muscipula*.

3.10 Parasitic Plants

Most plants collect light energy from the sun and nutrients from the soil to grow, but an alternative way to obtain the essentials of life is to take them from other living things. A parasitic plant connects its own transport system to that of another plant through a modified root called a haustorium, whose development follows chemical cues to attach and penetrate the tissues of the host plant. With this physiological bridge, the parasite may appropriate water, nutrients, and sugars from its host. Parasites lose water more rapidly than their hosts, which creates a gradient that draws water from the host into the parasite, bringing nitrogen and even carbon compounds with it. The host plant may wilt or show other signs of stress as it loses carbohydrates.

Some plants, such as Indian paintbrushes, may be facultative hemiparasites (Fig. 3.10a); they are green and photosynthesize but benefit from tapping into the roots of nearby host plants. Paintbrushes also take in defensive chemicals from their hosts, such as alkaloids from

a

b

c

Fig. 3.10. Parasitic plants: (a) white paintbrush, *Castilleja longispica;* (b) clustered broomrape, *Orobanche fasciculata*, on larkspur, *Delphinium nuttallianum;* (c) Indian pipe, *Monotropa uniflora.*

lupines, that subsequently deter their own herbivores. Others, such as broomrape (Fig. 3.10b), are obligate parasites that lack chlorophyll or the ability to photosynthesize; they appear oddly brown or purple, sometimes have a waxy texture (Fig. 3.10c), and look less like plants than mushrooms. Still others, including mistletoe (see 9.17) and dodder, connect to their hosts through stems rather than roots. The harmful effects on the host plant are the same in all cases.

Parasitic plants develop as a result of a complex interplay among the host, parasite, and local environment, so they are very difficult to transplant to a garden. They pop up as surprising reminders of the diversity of plant lifestyles.

REFERENCES: EHLERINGER ET AL. 1986; MILLER 1994; ADLER 2002; MATHIAS BOTANICAL GARDEN 2002

3.11 Poison Plants

Poison ivy and its relatives poison oak and poison sumac cause more cases of allergic dermatitis and sales of calamine lotion in the United States than any other source. Whenever people recognize the shiny, trifoliate leaves of poison ivy—"leaves of three, let it be"—they should avoid contact. These plants release a poisonous oil-bearing sap that gives us a rash with a characteristic streaklike appearance and red swelling from dilated blood vessels. The chemicals in the sap likely deter browsing by many, though not all, herbivores. Even the scientific name of poison ivy, *Toxicodendron radicans* (the genus name means "poison tree"), says to stay away, so it is surprising to discover that the poison plants are related to edible cashews, all of which are in the plant family Anacardiaceae.

The source of our distress is the group of nonvolatile organic alcohols known as urushiols, which we must touch directly to be affected. Then, within fifteen minutes, the chemicals form strong bonds with proteins in our skin. Quickly rinsing the affected skin may lessen the rash, but the urushiol oils are not water-soluble, and if one is not careful, rinsing with plain water may actually spread the oils over the skin. You're not apt to suffer too much from a healthy plant touched lightly because the sap is inside the cells, but the plants are fragile and release urushiols easily, even to wind and insect damage. Most poisoning takes place in the spring when the plants are young and easily bruised. Penetration by the oils occurs most easily where our skin is thin, such as between the fingers or on the neck, and the itching and swelling peak one to three days after exposure. One should never burn the plants because urushiol-coated smoke particles could then enter the lungs, where the reaction may be severe.

Poison ivy is very toxic; one doctor has estimated that 1 ounce of urushiol could give a rash to everyone on earth. But nothing is completely bad; deer eat poison ivy leaves, and birds such as robins and catbirds eat the berries.

REFERENCES: KINGSBURY 1968; RAVEN ET AL. 1999; DUNN ET AL. 1986; DUNPHY 1999

a

b

Fig. 3.11. Poison plants: (a) leaves and (b) berries of poison ivy, *Toxicodendron radicans*.

3.12 Solar-Tracking Leaves

More light means greater warmth and higher photosynthetic rates, so some plants increase their uptake of solar energy by tilting their leaves to keep them perpendicular to the sun's rays. Solar tracking is well known in some legumes and arctic-alpine plants. But when solar radiation is too strong and causes heat stress, the plants rotate their leaves to be parallel to incoming sun instead. This sun-avoidance response—solar tracking but for the opposite reason—minimizes heat load and water loss by exposing less surface area. Sun avoidance is best seen in dry habitats, where it provides a clear benefit. There's a cost to reducing water loss, however; vertical leaves in midday sun photosynthesize at a slower rate because they intercept less light.

Short-term changes in leaf orientation are produced within a thickening, known as a pulvinus, at the base of each leaf. Here, potassium ions are actively transported into and out of cells that surround a cylinder of vascular tissue; when pumped into cells on one side, that side takes up water osmotically, expands, and becomes more turgid, thus tilting the leaf toward the opposite side. This reversible mechanism is similar to muscle flexors and extensors in animals. Leaves that solar-track receive nearly 40 percent more light than do continuously horizontal leaves, so unless light and heat are excessive, a solar-tracking plant receives clear benefits from its active movement.

REFERENCES: MOONEY & EHLERINGER 1978; EHLERINGER & FORSETH 1980; BERG & HSIAO 1986; PRICHARD & FORSETH 1988; RAVEN ET AL. 1999

Fig. 3.12. Solar-tracking leaves of wild blue lupine, *Lupinus perennis*.

3.13   Solar-Tracking Flowers

Aptly named sunflowers point eastward to intercept morning sun (Fig. 3.13a), while butter-cups and their relatives track the sun across the sky (Fig. 3.13b). This movement, known as heliotropism, gives a thermal advantage because by facing the sun, flowers gain additional warmth. In cold arctic and alpine environments, where solar tracking is more common, saucer-shaped flowers absorb solar energy to create a microenvironment that may be up to 14°F warmer than the surrounding air. The warmth is an added lure for pollinating insects, such as bees and flies, which are inactive at low temperatures; the flowers become alpine saunas for these insects. The attractiveness of warm flowers is apparent when you see alpine flies congregating on sun-facing buttercups. While warming up and feeding on the nectar found there, the insects become more efficient pollinators that need less time for sun bask-ing, so the plants produce a greater number of viable seeds. Of course, the plants may benefit directly, too, since added warmth accelerates seed development.

The mechanism that orients flowers toward the sun differs from that causing leaves to move. In snow buttercups, sensors in the stem just below each flower respond to blue wave-lengths of light, and the plant growth hormone auxin then moves away from the sunlit side. Auxin causes cells on the shaded side to take in water and elongate, which bends the stem toward the sun. This is the same growth response that causes developing plants to grow toward the light.

REFERENCES: KEVAN 1972; REESE & BARROWS 1980; STANTON & GALEN 1989; SHERRY & GALEN 1998; GALEN 1999; LUZAR & GOTTSBERGER 2001

a   b

Fig. 3.13.   Solar-tracking flowers: (a) a meadow of little sunflowers, *Helianthella uniflora*; (b) subalpine buttercups, *Ranunculus eschscholtzii*.

3.14   Sensitive Plants

Most people think animals react quickly and plants very slowly to outside stimuli, but see-ing the response of the sensitive mimosa might lead one to change that opinion. When heated or touched, this plant collapses its leaves and drops its stems with surprising rapidity as if it had a simple nervous system. In fact, the folding response takes only a second or so, and the

Fig. 3.14. Open and folded leaves of sensitive plant, *Mimosa pudica*.

parallels of how it works to the functioning of an animal's nerve network are astonishing. When a mimosa leaf is stimulated, potassium ions move out of its cells through potassium ion channels; the rapid change in voltage differential across the membrane that follows ion flow then leads to a wave of depolarization across the leaf through a conduction pathway of phloem cells. The change in ion distribution causes a reversible loss of water and a shrinking of movement-control cells, the pulvini, at the base of the leaves and leaflets (see 3.12). Muscle-like actin proteins are found in these cells, and some people have suggested that the rapidity of water movement and leaf response are promoted by the contraction of these filaments. Afterward, sugars are unloaded from the phloem into the pulvini, and the ion gradients are reestablished. Slower, daily movement rhythms occur as well, regulated with different chemicals and controlled by a biological clock.

Why should a plant evolve such a remarkable response? The cost is reduced photosynthesis when the leaves have collapsed, but there must be some counterbalancing advantage. One idea is that folding might reduce the leaching of nutrients to raindrops, but there is no evidence to support this. Some have suggested that the folding response of sensitive plants is defensive because, in many species, leaf folding exposes thorns to would-be herbivores, and the movement itself may frighten insects away. Whatever the reason, the movement is real, and its speed is impressive.

REFERENCES: SANBERG 1976; CAMPBELL & THOMSON 1977; EISNER 1981; WALLACE ET AL. 1987; FROMM 1991; FLEURAT ET AL. 1993; HOLLINS & JAFFE 1997; MOSHELION & MORAN 2000

3.15   Rhododendron Leaves

On frigid mornings, the leaves of most rhododendrons roll downward and droop in the cold, dry air. For a long time, people thought this temperature-sensitive movement took place to prevent water loss from the stomates, the pores for gas exchange; curling keeps the stomates closed by compressing the lower epidermis of the leaf, and it also traps still air near the leaf, lessening the diffusion gradient and therefore slowing the loss of water vapor. But leathery rhododendron leaves have a thick protective cuticle to reduce midwinter water loss, and the stomates are already tightly sealed in dry conditions.

It now appears that curling is advantageous for a different reason. High light intensities combined with low temperatures damage the photosynthetic machinery of the leaves in a process known as photoinhibition. Especially under the leafless canopy of a winter deciduous forest, rhododendron shrubs are hit with a combination of deep cold and bright light. Tight curling of the leaves in such conditions exposes only a minimum of surface area to incident radiation. Drooping the leaves serves another purpose; it slows the thawing of leaves each morning to lessen the freeze-thaw oscillation that damages leaves by repeatedly forming internal ice crystals.

Temperature determines the extent of curling, but leaf curl has limited use as a natural thermometer. Curling starts just below freezing and reaches its maximum around 20°F, only 10° lower. Rolling and drooping serve simply to minimize the exposure of leaf surfaces to winter sun.

REFERENCES: STOKES 1981; BAO & NILSEN 1988; NILSEN 1990

Fig. 3.15.   Leaves of the same rhododendron shrub: (a) open in midsummer (70°F); (b) curled in midwinter (16°F); and (c) graph of the relationship of leaf curling to temperature (unpublished data).

3.16 Plant Patches

Fields and meadows never seem to be homogenous. Plants grow in patches wherever one walks, from a clump of goldenrods here to a stand of Queen-Anne's-lace there, from a cluster of asters in one place to a thicket of brambles in another. Environmental factors help produce some of this spatial structure; slightly higher mounds of soil are drier and more exposed to sunlight, while soil depth, nutrients, and moisture vary among sites only yards apart. Other factors have to do with the plants themselves. The shade from one plant may promote or deter the growth of others near it, and some plants release chemicals (allelopathic compounds) that retard the germination and growth of other plants competing for the same space (see 2.22). Reproduction may be through roots or slender surface stems (runners) that produce dense clonal growth, as with goldenrods, or from seeds that disperse only short distances. Herbivores may completely clear their favored food from patches where they feed, and the presence of herbivores varies greatly from place to place. A final factor is that a new species may colonize a newly disturbed site, and disturbance—an event such as fire, overgrazing, or storm that disrupts the soil or vegetation—usually occurs in one patch at a time. It is apparent wherever you look and at whatever scale, from that of neighboring plants to meadows and forests spread across the landscape, that vegetation resembles a patchwork quilt far better than it does a homogeneous cover.

REFERENCES: BAZZAZ 1996; KREBS 2001; SMITH & SMITH 2001

Fig. 3.16.   The clumped distribution of plants near a wetland, showing patches of sedges, cattails, giant reed (*Phragmites australis*), grasses, and trees (New York).

4. COLOR AND PATTERN

To us, the most conspicuous feature of an animal is its appearance because, as visually oriented creatures, we perceive and respond quickly to different colors and patterns. This chapter includes descriptions of animal colors and patterns, including physiological explanations of what produces the colors we see and ideas about the evolution of these patterns. Some colors and patterns are not very common in nature (e.g., bioluminescence, false heads, and aggressive mimicry), but they are spectacular to see. Others (e.g., seasonal forms, countershading) are common but subtle, and those having to do with deception (e.g., eyespots, camouflage) can be remarkable. Taken together, these appearances suggest that people aren't the only living creatures responding strongly to what can be seen; vision is clearly important to many animals.

Other discussions of the appearance of animals are found in:

4.1 Pigment Groups

Nature displays a full rainbow of rich colors, most of which result from specific wavelengths of sunlight being reflected from small pigment molecules. A molecule absorbs light only when its electrons resonate with the frequency of the incoming wavelengths; other wavelengths are reflected back, and they produce the colors we see. With three different color receptors (red, blue, and green cones), we humans see colors throughout the visible spectrum. But the palette of visible colors varies among groups of animals; birds add a fourth receptor in the ultraviolet, and honeybee vision also extends into the ultraviolet but lacks a red receptor. Thus, birds, bees, and humans perceive different but overlapping color spectra.

Distinct groups of pigments are common in living organisms. Plant colors are characterized by the greens of chlorophylls, the yellows and reddish oranges of carotenoids, and the reds and blues of anthocyanins. Green-reflecting chlorophylls are the most abundant pigments on earth (see 14.1). Oil-soluble carotenoid pigments absorb energy from blue and green light, which they pass on to chlorophyll; to imagine the color of a carotenoid, just think of a carrot. Water-soluble anthocyanins, on the other hand, block ultraviolet radiation and give a range of colors to plants, from reds when cell sap is acidic to blues when the sap is alkaline. Anthocyanins are most noticeable in beets, roses, purple grapes, and blue flowers (Fig. 4.1a).

Pigment groups in animals include the blacks and browns of melanins, the yellows and reddish oranges of carotenoids, the whites of guanine, and the reds of hemoglobin (in highly vascularized patches of skin). Melanins are the most abundant surface pigments of animals and so create a high frequency of dark coloration (see 4.6). Sometimes animals absorb pigments from the plants they eat rather than manufacture all their pigments themselves. Carotenoids that have been ingested are found in lobsters, shrimp, and flamingoes, which lose their pink color if deprived of their crustacean food. The reddish flush of house finches is also derived from ingested carotenoids, as is the pink of salmon flesh and the yellow of warbler feathers (Fig. 4.1b). Insects make use of additional pigments, including pterins (red, yellow, white) and ommochromes (red, yellow, brown). Pigments for blues and greens are rare in animals, however, and cannot be obtained from consuming blue plants, so these colors usually result from the interaction of light waves (see 4.3). Exceptions include the bluish blood of some invertebrate animals, which have the pigment hemocyanin instead of hemoglobin, and the blue of living lobsters, which is produced by a protein bound to a carotenoid. In cooking, heat splits the protein away, leaving the red-reflecting carotenoid. These pigment groups all contribute to the diverse and fascinating beauty of nature.

REFERENCES: BURTT 1981; WILLIAMSON & CUMMINS 1983; ROMOSER & STOFFOLANO 1994; HILTON 1996; RAVEN ET AL. 1999; ANDERSON 2000; *COLUMBIA ENCYCLOPEDIA* 2001

Fig. 4.1. Some of the pigment colors seen in nature:
(a) lupine, likely *Lupinus argenteus* (blue pigments are common
in plants but rare in animals); (b) Canada warbler, *Wilsonia
canadensis*; (c) Milbert's tortoiseshell butterfly, *Nymphalis
milberti*; (d) painted turtle, *Chrysemys picta*.

a

b

c

d

4.2 Albinos

Everyone recognizes human albinos by their very pale skin, white hair, and pinkish eyes, but the same lack of pigmentation appears occasionally in nearly all animal species, including mice, squirrels, deer, birds, snakes, fish, insects, and even sea cucumbers. The skin, fur, or feathers of albinos appear white because they lack pigments, and the eyes of many albinos appear pink because blood in the retina at the back reflects light through their pale irises. Lacking the protection of pigmented skin, human albinos burn rather than tan when exposed to the sun's ultraviolet light. They may also suffer from associated eye problems. Lacking camouflage, albino animals are never abundant in nature.

The dark pigment melanin is produced by a series of biochemical transformations that begins with the amino acid tyrosine, one of the basic building blocks of proteins. The first chemical change, which limits the rate at which melanin is made, is catalyzed by the copper-containing enzyme tyrosinase. Albinos have an inherited genetic mutation that makes this enzyme nonfunctional, and without a functioning enzyme, no melanin is produced. Partial albinos and less common forms of albinism result from other genetic flaws, some of which affect different enzymes and others of which alter the melanocytes, the cells in the skin that make melanin. But faulty tyrosinase is the cause of most albinism. Diets deficient in either tyrosine or copper can also lead to a reduction in melanin.

The genetic defect is recessive, which means that albinos have duplicate copies of the defective gene. One in seventeen thousand humans has some form of albinism. If pigments

a

b

Fig. 4.2.   Albinos: (a) white house or lab mouse, *Mus musculus*; (b) northern leopard frog, *Rana pipiens*; (c) American robin, *Turdus migratorius*.

c

other than melanin are also produced in an animal's coat, a mutant tyrosinase may leave a yellowish hue rather than a pure white. The starkly contrasting appearance of albinos makes it obvious how much melanin the rest of us possess.

REFERENCES: GRIFFITHS ET AL. 2000; KING ET AL. 2002

4.3 Iridescence

The most brilliant, shifting colors and metallic sheens found in nature originate from the interaction of reflected light waves rather than from the solid colors of pigments. These iridescent sheens change in shimmering hue with the angle at which light is reflected, from sparkling and flashy to unexpectedly dark and drab. Iridescence develops when light is reflected such that some light waves are added to others (constructive interference), reinforcing the color given by that wavelength. The colors become brilliant in strong light because when waves are added together, the color intensity increases with the square of the amplitude. Colors diminish when the combined reflected waves are out of phase and cancel each other (destructive interference).

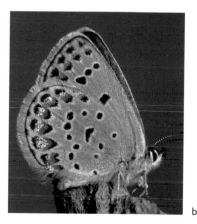

a

b

Fig. 4.3. Iridescence: (a) shell of abalone, *Haliotis* sp.; (b) iridescent metallic spots on the wings of a Karner blue butterfly, *Plebejus melissa samuelis*; (c) bark-gnawing beetle, *Temnochila virescens*.

c

Two structural patterns create the colors of iridescence. An oil slick, a soap bubble, and mother-of-pearl are iridescent because light reflects from extremely thin, close-lying layers of a translucent material. The microscopic distance between layers, less than a wavelength apart, determines which colors of reflected light are added together and which are canceled out. The second structural design is typified by the microscopic texture of the chitinous scales on a butterfly's wing; the scales are structured so complexly and precisely that they look as though each had been formed in a microscopic waffle iron. Each is composed of a grid with dozens of ridges, each ridge with dozens of ribs that are uniformly spaced less than a wavelength apart. Diffraction from delicate frameworks such as this gives rise to the iridescence of many butterfly wings and the brilliance of some bird feathers. The color produced depends on the spacing of the ribs and the angle of light reflectance.

The two structural patterns may act simultaneously, which is how the strongest iridescence is produced. Butterfly wings can create thin-film interference from the different cuticular layers of their scales in addition to diffraction grating, while the iridescence of an abalone shell develops from the reflection of light from regular layers of calcium carbonate separated by thin organic films as well as diffraction from the edges of rows of calcium carbonate crystals. The final color of a structure, as well as its ultraviolet reflectance, may depend on both pigmentation and iridescence, as with the greens of bird feathers. It is a little unexpected that the most sparkling colors in nature are produced not by pigments but by reflectance patterns from structured surfaces.

REFERENCES: WILLIAMSON & CUMMINS 1983; PETERSON 1995; KEMP 2002; ORSORIO & HAM 2002; SHUICHI ET AL. 2002

4.4   Bioluminescence

The luminescence of fireflies on a summer evening and of plankton in an ocean swell at night are among the more astonishing visual effects in nature. Bioluminescence is spoken of

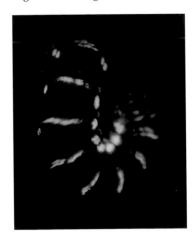

as cold light because the conversion of energy from a chemical state into light is efficient, with little energy lost as heat. Light results from the reaction of oxygen with a protein known as luciferin (from the Latin *lucifer*, for "light-bearing"), catalyzed by an enzyme known as luciferase. The luciferin becomes chemically excited from oxidation and releases a photon of light as it drops back to its normal energy state. The hue of the light is determined by the emitted wavelength.

Bioluminescence is frequently seen in marine organisms, particularly in the deep ocean, although it has been best studied in fireflies. In some species, light is produced by the organisms' own chemistry (e.g., fireflies), while in others, luminescent bacteria are maintained symbiotically within the animal's tissues (e.g., fish, mollusks). Luminescence is activated by the nervous system in fireflies and by disturbance in ocean bacteria and algae.

Fig. 4.4.   Bioluminescence of a female glowworm beetle, *Phengodes plumose,* a relative of fireflies.

Why living things should luminesce is another question. Fireflies signal to attract mates (see 7.16); their glowworm larvae luminesce to advertise themselves as unpalatable to predators such as toads; and some fish luminesce to attract prey. But for many species, including some fungi, the advantage of light production is unclear. Bioluminescence can be as puzzling as it is pretty.

REFERENCES: WILLIAMSON & CUMMINS 1983; ROMOSER & STOFFOLANO 1994; DECOCK & MATTHYSEN 2001, 2003

4.5   Cryptic Coloration

Like beauty, visibility is skin deep. For most animals, the primary defense against predators is blending into the background. Camouflage or cryptic coloration—hiding in plain sight— is achieved by matching color and pattern to the substrate: the speckled green of a frog perched in the grass, the mottled brown of a moth resting on tree bark, and the gravel color of a bottom-resting flounder. Only the ventral surface of some butterflies' wings is exposed at rest, so only that side is camouflaged. Cryptic coloration is enhanced by cryptic behavior, including the seeking out of an appropriate resting spot and remaining motionless.

Predators of camouflaged prey, such as blue jays that feed on moths, form highly specific search images to find their targets against the background shading. But moths, in turn, have evolved many different color patterns, and a few species have been shown to choose appropriately matching resting spots for themselves. The chrysalids of some butterflies, immobile and with few defenses, are environmentally cued to turn green or brown to match their different pupation sites, green stem or brown bark. Sometimes, when the adults have other defenses, only the young of a species are cryptically colored. Camouflage can also help a predator remain concealed from prey, as when crab spiders turn white, pink, or yellow to match the color of the flower they sit on and thus remain unseen to unsuspecting insects that land to feed on nectar (see 10.6). With matches to a wide variety of backgrounds, the frequency of camouflage in nature is a testament to the importance of vision in so many animals, including humans.

REFERENCES: WICKLER 1968; SARGENT 1976; ENDLER 1980; WILLIAMSON & CUMMINS 1983; ALCOCK 1993; ARMS & CAMP 1995; JOHNSEN 2002

a   b

Fig. 4.5.   Examples of cryptic coloration: (a) tulip-tree beauty moth, *Epimecis hortaria*, on tree bark; (b) pika, *Ochotona princeps*, among rocks.

4.6 Light versus Dark

How light or dark an animal appears is determined by the need for camouflage, the absorbing and reflecting of sunlight to regulate warmth, and limiting ultraviolet exposure. Because hiding from predators or prey is advantageous, birds and mammals living in a snowy environment are often white (e.g., polar bears, arctic foxes, snowy owls, ptarmigans; see 4.19) even though they would warm up more quickly if they were darker and absorbed more solar radiation. In deserts, where the soils are pale and the vegetation sparse, animals such as hares and coyotes are light-colored, making them cryptic and reducing the heat load in these hot habitats by reflecting sunlight (Fig. 4.6a). Matching the background to help them avoid owl predators in the American Southwest, rock pocket mice on light-colored rocks are sandy-colored, but those that live on lava fields are darker.

Insects are often darker at higher altitudes and latitudes, a pattern known as alpine melanism. Because small invertebrates in cold climates gain warmth solely from their surround-

a

b

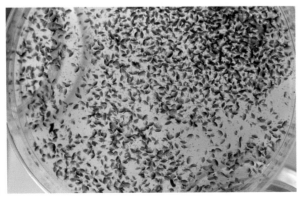

c

Fig. 4.6. Light and dark patterns: (a) pale appearance of a desert cottontail rabbit, *Sylvilagus auduboni*; (b) sulphur butterflies: (top to bottom) a darker alpine species (*Colias meadii*), a lighter low elevation species (*Colias philodice*), and a darker northern species (*Colias nastes*); (c) melanistic zooplankton from high-elevation shallow ponds (mostly *Daphnia middendorffiana* and *Diaptomus shoshone*) in a petri dish.

ings, the contribution of darker wings to thermal gain is important in their overall appearance (Fig. 4.6b). The black forewings of one butterfly have been found to absorb almost all incident light, for example, whereas the white wings of another absorb less than 20 percent. Darker alpine butterflies have been shown to fly longer and farther under cool conditions. The parts of the wings next to the body provide the greatest influence on core temperature, so those are often the darkest. Industrial melanism is another process that produces darker insects. Dark-form moths are better concealed wherever pollution has darkened the tree bark on which they rest. Over the past two centuries, dark moths have increased in frequency in industrialized areas, although lighter forms have rebounded in abundance after the enactment of clean air legislation.

Among the forested shadows of humid climates, animals are better concealed by being darker, in accord with an old observation known as Gloger's rule. Dark pigments have another effect, too: they block harmful ultraviolet radiation, which is intense in the tropics and at high elevations. This protection is illustrated by the deep pigmentation of crustacea and frog eggs in alpine ponds (Fig. 4.6c). Repeated exposure to the sun increases the manufacture of the dark pigment melanin in human skin, giving us a tanned appearance that reduces by tenfold how much light penetrates our skin; it's a telling point that dark-skinned humans evolved in parts of the globe (low latitudes) where UV levels are high. These examples show that there's more to an animal's pigmentation than first meets the eye.

REFERENCES: WICKLER 1968; BURTT 1981; ROLAND 1982; WILLIAMSON & CUMMINS 1983; GUPPY 1986; SCHMITZ 1994; RELETHFORD 1997; BROWN & LOMOLINO 1998; GRANT & WISEMAN 2002; NACHMAN ET AL. 2003

4.7 Countershading

The darker appearance of the dorsal or upper side of an animal, a pattern known as countershading, is thought to make the animal less visible to its predators or prey by either of two mechanisms. The first is obliteration of form through counterillumination. Whether in water or on land, light comes from above, so the back of an animal is better lit while its belly is in shadow. Being darker above counterbalances the natural shadowing effect so that, from a side view, all of the animal, top to bottom, appears to reflect light uniformly. Without a visible shadow, the animal blends in better with the background, and its outline is concealed. The second mechanism, particularly for aquatic organisms, is concealing pigmentation. When looking down on an animal, one sees the darker top against a darker background, whereas when looking from underneath, the lighter ventral surface blends in better with the brighter sky. Countershading increases crypsis of animals viewed from either direction.

Many aquatic animals are countershaded, including perch (Fig. 4.7a), trout, dolphins, tuna, sharks, sea turtles, and even penguins. Octopus, squid, and cuttlefish can quickly darken whichever side is up; when turned partially or completely over, their upper surfaces darken while their lower surfaces blanch, all from nervous system control of pigment-bearing cells that are contracted (becoming less apparent) or expanded to many times their original size. Some shrimp and fish use dim bioluminescence to lighten their undersides, and African catfishes that swim upside down have reverse countershading, with darker bellies and lighter backs.

On land, shadows are stronger, and less concealment can be gained by countershading, but shorebirds on a sandy beach appear to benefit from softened shadows and silhouettes

a

b

Fig. 4.7. Examples of countershading, with darker backs and lighter bellies: (a) yellow perch, *Perca flavescens*; (b) sanderling, *Calidris alba*.

(Fig. 4.7b). And in experimental studies, birds (jays) captured fewer right-side-up countershaded caterpillars than they did those upside down. Alternatively, darker dorsal coloration on land may serve to shield against ultraviolet light rather than to provide crypsis. The effect may differ for different species, but countershading is one of the most common patterns in animal appearance.

REFERENCES: TINBERGEN 1957; WILLOUGHBY 1976; KILTIE 1988; FERGUSON & MESSENGER 1991; EDMUNDS & DEWHIRST 1994; ARMS & CAMP 1995; LINDSAY ET AL. 1999; STAUFFER ET AL. 1999

4.8   Spots and Stripes

Deer fawns and leopards are spotted, while tigers and zebras are striped, all because spots and stripes make the animals wearing them less easily seen. The patterns of a mammal's spots and stripes are quite variable, providing the same individuality as fingerprints for humans. Some general correlations yield strong clues about the benefits of different patterns. Spotted and striped coats give general camouflage by enhancing the match of the animal to the splotchy shadows of its background. Deer fawns can't outrun predators during the first few months of life, for example, so having spots helps them hide in the vegetation; being inconspicuous is the only way they can survive (Fig. 4.8a). Although a tiger's coat is always cryptic, that of a zebra serves at least two purposes, being conspicuous for communication during the day but cryptic in the shadows of twilight (zebras' stripes also seem to deter flies). The direction of stripes normally parallels that of the surrounding vegetation; bitterns point their heads straight up when detected, for example, and that aligns their stripes with marsh grasses. It's a telling point that fish with vertical stripes swim in short grass while some with horizontal stripes rest head down in tall grass beds.

Spots and stripes limited to specific places may serve other purposes. Tail markings facilitate communication among individuals, with ringed tails more common among nocturnal mammals of forest habitats and dark-tipped light tails more common among diurnal mammals of grasslands. Tail marks may also deflect the attention of predators and prey away from the head of the animal. Dark markings near the eyes are more common among mam-

a

b

Fig. 4.8. Spots and stripes: (a) spotted back of a white-tailed deer fawn, *Odocoileus virginianus*; (b) facial mask of a raccoon, *Procyon lotor*.

mals such as raccoons that are active in twilight, and the dark spots reduce the interfering glare of reflected light (Fig. 4.8b). Birds that feed regularly in sunlight often have dark bills. When competing in athletic contests on brightly lit fields, people sometimes add dark stripes under their eyes to minimize glare, making themselves look like raccoons.

REFERENCES: BURTT 1981; GODFREY ET AL. 1987; ORTOLANI 1999; MURRAY 1988; KONDO & ABE 1995; RUXTON 2002; CAMAZINE 2003

4.9 Disruptive Coloration

Animals sometimes hide by concealing their silhouettes. Bold patterns and colors can help achieve this because splotches of color draw attention to the scale of the splotches, not the scale of the whole animal. The patches on a rattlesnake's or copperhead's skin look like dead leaves and so conceal the elongate form of the animal (Fig. 4.9a). Butterfly wings with white or yellow bands across a dark background make the bright pattern more conspicuous than the outline of the wings, so predators are less apt to recognize the wings and see the insects as prey (Fig. 4.9b). In these cases, the animals don't simply match their backgrounds but instead elude detection by distracting observers from recognizing their actual shape or contour. It is a mismatch of outline and pattern. Color patterns that disrupt the margins of the animal, with part of the pattern blending in with the background and part standing out, are especially helpful in avoiding recognition. The camouflage clothing that military forces wear is part cryptic and, with large color blotches, part disruptive. Spots and stripes (see 4.8) can also contribute to disruptive patterning.

REFERENCES: ARMS & CAMP 1995; MERILAITA 1998; SMITH & SMITH 2001

a   b

Fig. 4.9.   Disruptive patterning: (a) northern copperhead snake, *Agkistrodon contortrix*; (b) white admiral butterfly, *Limenitis arthemis arthemis*.

4.10   Flash and Startle

a

b

Fig. 4.10.   Flash coloration of colorful hind wings: (a) a band-winged grasshopper (subfamily Oedipodinae); (b) oldwife underwing moth, *Catocala palaeogama*.

There are flashers in nature. Quickly spreading their wings for flight when disturbed by a bird, some moths and grasshoppers flash patches of bright colors on their hind wings that startle the hungry predator that had just been looking at a very plain-appearing food morsel. The surprising change in appearance can alarm or distract the predator, especially a young or inexperienced one, enough to give the prey a valuable split second to escape. This response explains the red and yellow hind wings of many insects that are cryptically colored when perched with folded wings (Fig. 4.10a). Underwing moths usually have a dark stripe across their colored hind wings as well, making the wing pattern eyecatching as well as surprising (Fig. 4.10b). The diverse designs among different species of moths mean that birds keep encountering novel patterns from one moth to another. Another kind of flash is the conspicuous tail display of a fleeing white-tailed deer, which likely notifies an approaching predator that it has been seen (see 5.18).

After danger has passed, the bright patches are concealed, ready to flash again when needed, and the animals blend in with their backgrounds once more. In all forms of warfare, surprising the enemy is a successful strategy, and it also helps to have a backup plan (a flash) when the primary plan (camouflage) fails.

REFERENCES: SARGENT 1976; SCHLENOFF 1985; ALCOCK 1993; SMITH & SMITH 2001

4.11 Eyespots

It's a startling sight to face a pair of large eyes unexpectedly staring right back at you. Fake eyespots on an animal are conspicuous features; they can deter, misdirect, or even attract another animal, and they range from simple black spots surrounded by light rings to remarkably intricate designs with pupils and light-reflecting glimmers. Not all black spots mimic eyes; some are thought to look like glands with poison droplets, and the spots on some fish look more like air bubbles in turbulent water.

For insects, large paired false eyespots (Fig. 4.11a) usually deter predators by resembling the eyes of a bird or mammal or even a snake (see 4.12). When exposed, they surprise the hunter, giving the prey a moment to escape, just as in flash and startle coloration (see 4.10). Birds in one study were less active when exposed to experimental spots that resembled vertebrate eyes, and the larger the eyespots, the more startled the bird. Doves and crows avoid balloons with eyespots but not those without, while eye patterns deter starlings from feeding. Smaller eyespots, especially those exposed along wing margins of an insect, are thought to misdirect a predator's attack away from the body. The first line of defense for many insects is camouflage to avoid detection, but if they are found, eyespots on the wings may help perplex the predator. Some butterfly fish have stripes that conceal their real eyes along with larger, conspicuous false eyespots on fins away from their heads (Fig. 4.11b).

Eyespots can play a very different role, however, as they do on the tail of a male peacock. Stronger, healthier, and better-fed males are able to grow larger tails with more eyespots, and females are attracted to gaudy tails and choose these grander males as mates. Once again, eyespots fulfill their function by grabbing attention.

REFERENCES: WICKLER 1968; INGLIS ET AL. 1983; POUGH 1988; MINNO & EMMEL 1992B; PETRI & HALLIDAY 1994; ROMOSER & STOFFOLANO 1994; HOLLOWAY ET AL. 2002

a   b

Fig. 4.11. Eyespots: (a) male Io moth, *Automeris io*; (b) foureye butterflyfish, *Chaetodon capistratus*.

4.12 False Heads

Even for an individual animal, two heads may be better than one—especially if one is a false head that diverts the attention of a predator away from the real head. A bird attack aimed at marks on a butterfly's outer wing margin that resemble the insect's head may tear a wing, but a torn wing is survivable, while a damaged head is not. The convincing false head on the hindwings of hairstreak butterflies (Fig. 4.12a) include brightly colored eyespots, thin tails that mimic antennas, bold lines that point toward the false head, outwardly bent wing margins that give three-dimensionality, and even wing movement that draws attention. And the decoys work: when false head markings were drawn on butterflies that don't naturally have them, the attention of blue jay predators was successfully misdirected away from the real heads, and the butterflies were better able to escape the initial attack. Even those that were caught by the birds were more likely to be mishandled and escape. Observations of several species of butterflies captured in the field show more bite marks near the false heads than elsewhere on the wings.

Other kinds of animals have false heads, too. Some fish have posterior eyespots that divert the attention of predatory fish toward the back. Even caterpillars may have false head patterns that make them appear daunting (Fig. 4.12b). Snakes are especially good models because so many animals avoid them, and the deterrence is so strong that only the head need be mimicked. The brightly colored tails of some lizards, though they don't look like fake heads, serve a similar function by drawing attention from the animals' heads to their tails. For a visual predator, it's not always easy to get a head in life.

REFERENCES: WICKLER 1968; ROBBINS 1980, 1981; WOURMS & WASSERMAN 1985; MINNO & EMMEL 1992B; ALCOCK 1993; TONNER ET AL. 1993; KRIZEK 1998; CORDERO 2001

Fig. 4.12. False heads: (a) banded hairstreak, *Satyrium calanus*; (b) caterpillar of spicebush swallowtail, *Papilio troilus*.

a   b

4.13   Warning Coloration

Bold patterns on an animal, especially with vivid shades of red, orange, yellow, or white contrasted against a black background, usually indicate some kind of noxiousness. Such patterns are easily learned signals that draw attention in nature and say "leave me alone." Animals with these colors are said to be warningly colored or aposematic (from Greek, *apo-,* "away"; *-sematic,* "signal"), and predators instinctively avoid or learn to avoid such patterns.

We stay away from buzzing insects with alternating black and yellow stripes, for example, because yellow jackets and bees can sting. Dragonflies avoid them, too. Another form of noxiousness directed at predators is unpalatability. Some bad-tasting insects make their own distasteful chemicals, while others ingest plant toxins from their food and then store the unpalatable compounds in their own tissues. The effectiveness of chemical defense was illustrated years ago when monarch butterflies that had incorporated plant cardenolide compounds from their milkweed host plants were fed to hungry blue jays; the birds ate the butterflies but then vomited, learning to leave monarchs alone. Studies of some organisms have shown that warning coloration of unpalatable insects yields higher survivorship because it actively discourages attack.

Warning signals are more conspicuous when the patterns have greater contrast or the animals are individually larger or grouped together, so warningly colored insects are often

gregarious (Fig. 4.13a). Insects aren't the only animals with aposematic coloration: the black-and-white stripes of skunks effectively advertise their presence (Fig. 4.13b), as do the red-yellow-black-yellow bands of poisonous coral snakes and the conspicuous colors of toxic-skinned red-spotted newts.

REFERENCES: WICKLER 1968; BROWER 1969; HARVEY & GREENWOOD 1978; SILLEN-TULLBERG 1985; ALCOCK 1993; BEGON ET AL. 1996; ARMS & CAMP 1995; MALLET & JORON 1999; ROWE & GUILFORD 2000; SHERRATT 2001; NILSSON & FORSMAN 2003

Fig. 4.13.   Warning coloration: (a) milkweed bugs, *Oncopeltus fasciatus;* (b) striped skunk, *Mephitis mephitis;* (c) saddleback caterpillar, *Acharia stimulea,* which has a distinctive bold pattern rather than a red color.

a

b

c

4.14   Mimicry

Nature is a masquerade ball, full of deception. To avoid predators, some animals appear to be dangerous or inedible; in this form of defense, one species, the mimic, resembles an unpalatable species, the model, so much that predators confuse the two and leave the mimic alone (the resemblance of a harmless mimic species to a noxious model is known as Batesian mimicry, named for the English naturalist H. W. Bates, who described this phenomenon from his observations of tropical butterflies in the 1800s). The animal resembled may be a related species or something very different: black swallowtail butterflies mimic unpalatable pipevine swallowtail butterflies, hover flies mimic stinging bees, and lizards mimic poison-laden millipedes. Mimicry may be of something dangerous rather than inedible: caterpillars with eyespots on swollen ends mimic small snakes (see 4.12). People, too, are often deceived by this kind of mimicry: a black-and-yellow striped flying insect may appear to be a wasp when sometimes it's just a fly (Fig. 4.14a). The resemblance of the mimic doesn't have to be perfect for mimicry to work, and highly repellent models may have numerous mimic species (Figs. 4.14b–f). Social wasps are strongly deterrent models, for example, so any similar appearance can be beneficial. Mimicry is scarce in larger animals because details of form are so apparent with them, but it is common in insects. Mimicry may include sound and behavior as well as appearance.

a

When several unpalatable or noxious species resemble each other, the phenomenon is known as Mullerian mimicry (named for its naturalist describer, Fritz Muller, who reported this pattern in 1877 after observing Brazilian butterflies). The predators learn that single pattern more rapidly than they would several different warning patterns. Mullerian mimicry is best known from the species-rich tropics, where a predator would be confused if it had to learn a separate pattern for each unpalatable species. A widely described example of mimicry, that of viceroy butterflies mimicking monarch and queen butterflies, actually ranges between Batesian and Mullerian forms because, depending on their diet, some viceroys are palatable mimics but others are distasteful. The pattern of Mullerian mimicry most familiar to North Americans is the black and yellow striping that characterizes many species of bees and wasps.

REFERENCES: WICKLER 1968; RITLAND & BROWER 1991; VITT 1992; ARMS & CAMP 1995; SMITH & SMITH 2001

Fig. 4.14.   Mimicry: (a) America hover fly, *Metasyrphus americanus*, that mimics a wasp; (b) the unpalatable pipevine swallowtail butterfly, *Battus philenor*. The other photographs show palatable mimics of the pipevine swallowtail: (c) female Eastern tiger swallowtail, *Papilio glaucus* (dark form); (d) red-spotted purple, *Limenitis arthemis astyanax*; (e) female black swallowtail, *Papilio polyxenes*; (f) spicebush swallowtail, *Papilio troilus*.

b

c

d

e

f

4.15 Disguise

To hide from predators, some insects resemble objects quite different from themselves—plant parts, for example. Katydid grasshoppers look like leaves (Fig. 4.15a), inchworm caterpillars look like twigs, and plant hoppers look like thorns (Fig. 4.15b), which, as someone has pointed out, is a pretty sharp idea. Is this mimicry, camouflage, or protective resemblance? The label doesn't matter; the result is that the insects escape discovery by animals that could eat them. Butterflies such as the eastern comma, whose folded, jagged-margined wings resemble withered leaves, are both harder to find and, if found, unrecognized for what they really are. But quiet behavior is important, too; the deception doesn't work when the mimicked leaves, twigs, and thorns start walking up and down plant stems. Another factor is that the appearance of an animal depends on the scale and distance from which it is observed. Katydids appear cryptic from a distance, for example, but they resemble a leaf when close by, and this disguise gives them an additional line of defense. Disguise also works for sit-and-wait predators such as praying mantises, which resemble leaves and stems, and crab spiders (see 10.6), which resemble flowers.

REFERENCES: ENDLER 1981; SMITH & SMITH 2001

a

b

Fig. 4.15. Disguise: (a) greater angle-wing katydid, *Microcentrum rhombifolium;* (b) thorn bugs, a species of treehopper (family Membracidae).

4.16 Bird-Dropping Patterns

Neither people nor other animals choose to pick up bird droppings; they are just white and brown messes left on plants and windshields. The distinctive bicolored appearance of the droppings results from birds having digestive waste (dark colors) coated with excretory waste (light colors). Water is conserved by eliminating these two waste products together and by

Fig. 4.16. Appearances resembling bird droppings: (a) caterpillar of giant swallowtail, *Papilio cresphontes*; (b) white-ribboned carpet moth, *Mesoleuca ruficillata*.

the kind of excretory waste formed, which is uric acid, a concentrated nitrogenous waste that differs in chemical form from the dilute urine of mammals. White light reflects from the uric acid salts.

A number of insects escape predators by resembling bird droppings and taking advantage of this avoidance response. Small, dark caterpillars with a white saddle in the middle are characteristic mimics of bird or lizard droppings. In North America, common species using this tactic include several swallowtail butterflies (giant, black, and spicebush) and several admirals (viceroy, red-spotted purple). The resemblance fails as the insects become larger, though, so as they grow, many bird-dropping mimicked caterpillars revert to other color patterns for protection. After all, how large a bird dropping do you see? For those retaining a black-and-white saddle appearance as full-size caterpillars, the pattern likely serves as much for disruptive coloration (see 4.9) as for bird-dropping mimicry. A number of adult moths also resemble bird droppings, but only when at rest. In any case, nature isn't always as it seems, and the bird-dropping pattern aids the survival of small insects.

REFERENCES: EHRLICH ET AL. 1988; FAABORG 1988; MINNO & EMMEL 1992A

4.17 Aggressive Mimicry

An animal that resembles something else usually does so for protection from its enemies. But beware those that deceive. When the deception allows a predator to approach or lure in its prey, then the resemblance is known as aggressive mimicry. One of the most intriguing cases of aggressive mimicry occurs at dusk on summer evenings when the females of one species of

a

b

Fig. 4.17. Possible cases of aggressive mimicry: (a) zone-tailed hawk, *Buteo albonotatus*, a turkey vulture mimic; (b) robber fly, *Laphria maquarti*, a bumblebee mimic.

predatory firefly flash the light patterns of other fireflies to draw in males, which they then grab and eat (see 7.16). Zone-tailed hawks of the American Southwest are purported, by their dark coloration and soaring behavior with tilted wings, to look like the scavenger turkey vultures with which they fly (Fig. 4.17a). This resemblance may let them approach their lizard prey without raising suspicion. Some rapacious robber flies feed on bumblebees and, despite the absence of evidence, it has been widely considered that they resemble bumblebees to approach these insects more closely (Fig. 4.17b). Other robber flies resemble their damselfly prey. (Mimicking robber flies may, instead, be Batesian mimics [see 4.14] for protection from their own predators.) Snapping turtles and some deep sea fish wiggle wormlike appendages near their mouths to attract small fish, which find themselves suddenly engulfed by the fearsome predators. In nature there really are wolves in sheep's clothing.

REFERENCES: WILLIS 1963; WICKLER 1968; BORROR & WHITE 1970; LLOYD 1984; ALCOCK 1990

4.18 Seasonal Forms

The appearance of all organisms develops through an interplay of their genetic heritage and the surrounding conditions, and the final adult form varies around some norm. When survival of short-lived insects depends on appearance but the environmental background differs over time, different generations may benefit from developing appearances specific for the seasons in which they emerge, a response known as seasonal polymorphism ("multiple forms") or polyphenism.

There are two reasons why many butterflies and moths display different forms in spring and summer. In the coolness of spring, bolder patterns with darker coloration increase the absorbance of solar radiation for added warmth. For example, the spring generation of several species of butterflies known as whites emerge with additional dark scales on their wings (Fig. 4.18a), and other butterflies are often darker in the spring, too (Fig. 4.18b). The parts of the wings exposed when basking are those that are more pigmented (additional spots may appear because of genetic correlation with the spots that are important thermally). Experi-

a   b

Fig. 4.18. Seasonal forms: (a) darker spring (top) and lighter summer (lower) forms of the mustard white, *Pieris napi*; (b) lighter summer (top) and darker spring (lower) forms of pearl crescent butterflies, *Phyciodes tharos*.

mentally marked butterflies have survived better in the field when they match the correct pigmentation for the season, dark in spring and light in summer. Dark pupae also develop more quickly than light ones in the cooler fall months. The second reason is that camouflage is determined by how successfully an animal matches its background, but the background may change seasonally. In the well-studied tropical butterfly *Bicyclus anynana*, the wings of butterflies in the green wet season develop with color bands that disrupt their overall appearance and eyespots that deflect the attention of predators, but in the drab dry season they develop brown, less-patterned wings that provide better camouflage. A remarkable North American example is found in the southwestern moth *Nemoria arizonaria*, whose spring generation caterpillars resemble the oak catkins on which they feed, while the summer generation caterpillars resemble oak twigs instead, after the catkins are long gone.

In insects, seasonal forms are determined by hormonal differences that may be cued by temperature, day length, or food quality. Having different forms in different seasons is an overall strategy for thermoregulation and predator avoidance.

REFERENCES: GREENE 1989; BRAKEFIELD & REITSMA 1991; KINGSOLVER & WIERNASZ 1991; KINGSOLVER 1995; NIJHOUT 1997; BRAKEFIELD 1996; BRAKEFIELD & FRENCH 1999; HAZEL 2002

4.19 Winter Whites

For birds and mammals that molt more than once a year, seasonal changes in color between seasons suggest that survival is related to appearance. The most conspicuous coat-changing occurs in mountains and northern regions, where winter cloaks the landscape in a layer of white snow.

Snowshoe hares are known for brown and gray fur in the summer but white fur in the winter (Fig. 4.19a). These animals escape predators—lynx, coyotes, owls, goshawks—by their

a   b

Fig. 4.19.   Winter white coloration: (a) snowshoe hare, *Lepus americanus*; (b) long-tailed weasel, *Mustela frenata*.

cautious behavior and camouflaged appearance. Shortening day length in the fall spurs hormonal control of the growth of white hairs, and gradual replacement of the fur leaves brown and white patches during the changeover times of late fall and early spring. The hairs of their winter coats actually have white tips over tawny to gray shafts. The winter coat is nearly double in insulation value, providing another adaptation for the winter season. Because changing day length, not the immediate weather, is the cue that initiates the changes, white hares are mismatched to their background in years when the first snowfall is unusually late. Short-tailed and long-tailed weasels change coats for camouflage, too, since they are prey of hawks, owls, snakes, and bobcats, but blending in with the background also helps them hunt their small mammal food (Fig. 4.19b). Although the tips of weasels' tails remain black, the brown coats on their backs molt to white in winter (short-tailed weasels are then known as ermines).

The feathers on birds wear out and are replaced by a new set at least once a year, so birds, too, are able to make seasonal changes in appearance. Ptarmigans are known particularly for their winter white and summer brown plumages, with intermediate stages that include a rufous head and neck over a white body. Against the snowy background, camouflage for all these animals requires a white winter wardrobe.

REFERENCES: EHRLICH ET AL. 1988; WALSBERG 1991; WHITAKER & HAMILTON 1998

4.20   Banded Hair

A close look at the hair of a cat, dog, mouse, deer, or almost any other mammal with common gray to brown coloration shows the presence of color bands on each hair, a color pattern known as agouti. The name originates from the South American mammals called agoutis, which display the banded hair pattern; they are large, guinea-pig-like rodents in the genus *Dasyprocta*, Greek for "hairy butt" (related to capybaras, the largest rodents in the world). Hair color is produced by specialized pigment cells called melanocytes that are found in the skin and hair follicles. These cells produce two different colored pigments: eumelanin (Greek for "true black"), which is dark brown or black, and phaeomelanin ("dusty black"), which is pale

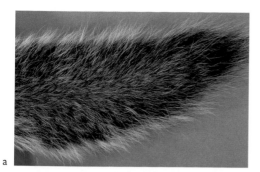

a

b

c

Fig. 4.20. Banded hair: (a) tail of Eastern gray squirrel, *Sciurus carolinensis*; (b) coat of domestic cat, *Felis domesticus*; (c) coat of yellow-bellied marmots, *Marmota flaviventris*.

yellow or red. Production of these two pigments is switched back and forth in a complex way as a hair lengthens. Ultraviolet light and melanocyte-stimulating hormone spur the melanocytes to produce the darker eumelanin, whereas a certain molecule, agouti signal protein, inhibits its formation. The salt-and-pepper wild-type appearance results from an initial period of eumelanin synthesis, then phaeomelanin, and finally back to eumelanin in a single hair. Other alternating light-dark patterns can also be seen. The age and sex of the animal and body location can affect the length of the lighter band. In mice, the agouti pattern is determined by a single gene for coat color that controls the distribution of pigment in hairs. Why have banded hairs? The agouti pattern likely makes an animal's appearance more cryptic.

The same pigments are produced in humans because, after all, we're mammals, too. In us, as in other animals, melanin (eumelanin) protects the skin from ultraviolet radiation, though the pigment ratio is tilted heavily toward phaeomelanin in red-haired individuals, who therefore tan little. Human hair lacks the banded agouti pattern, but as we age, our melanocytes slow their production of melanin, so our hair takes on the natural gray or white of hair protein.

REFERENCES: GALBREATH ET AL. 1980; BOWLING 1988; VALVERDE ET AL. 1995; GRIFFITHS ET AL. 2000; HEARING 2000; ITO ET AL. 2001

4.21   Reflective Eyes

A pair of eyes gleaming brightly in the headlights at night certainly grabs our attention. The eyes of animals active at twilight and night (Figs. 4.21a, b) reflect much more than those of day-active animals for a very good reason. To enhance vision at night when light intensity is low, a deep layer within the retina of a night-active animal reflects light back to give the light receptors above it an additional chance to perceive possible images. Such eyes emit a glow, often yellowish, when seen in the strong beam of light from an automobile headlight. But the cost of that extra light capture is to lose some clarity of vision in brighter conditions—because of the reflected light waves—so the eyes of day-active animals have a darkly pigmented area at the back of the retina to absorb rather than reflect light. Because they don't need to maximize light interception, their retinas aren't as reflective.

a

As every photographer knows, on the other hand, a reddish reflection emanates from day-active human eyes when a light flashes directly at an individual (Fig. 4.21c). The "red eye" effect is produced by illuminated blood vessels at the back of the eye. If the light shines at an angle or if the pupils have already closed down from prior exposure to light, then red eye is reduced.

A good way to find night-active spiders and other arthropods is to search with a flashlight and look for glowing eyes. Whenever you see reflective yellow or green eyes shining back at you in the dark, remember that whatever you're looking at is seeing you better than you're seeing it!

REFERENCE: WILLIAMSON & CUMMINS 1983

b

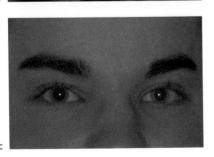

c

Fig. 4.21. Reflective eyes: (a) white-tailed deer, *Odocoileus virginianus*; (b) domestic cat, *Felis domesticus*; (c) human, *Homo sapiens*.

5. ECOLOGY AND BEHAVIOR

Although people encounter mammals and other vertebrates infrequently, most everyone is interested in them. This chapter presents ecological, physiological, and behavioral features of different animals, including vertebrates as well as some invertebrates. Some of these discussions explain extremes in size and shape, while others describe common physiological responses such as panting and shivering. Still others present specific behaviors that are readily observable, including group living and walking on walls. Taken as a group, these pages give a sense of the range of observations one can make.

Related descriptions may be found in:

5.1 Size Sets

When two related species of animals, such as hawks, live in the same habitat, they often differ in size, either overall size or size of their feeding structures. A long-standing hypothesis for this pattern is that divergence in size allows the two species to differ in the food they consume and thus lessen competition for food whenever it is in short supply. An example of size-related feeding is that northern goshawks (Fig. 5.1a) attack ruffed grouse, a large bird, but Cooper's hawks (Fig. 5.1b), their smaller relatives, do not. Sometimes the size difference results from the chance co-occurrence of two species of unequal sizes, but sometimes it reflects an evolved adjustment in size or shape that is known as character displacement. Identifying the actual reason for a size difference can be tricky. Even when food is scarce only occasionally, an advantage accrues to species that differ in their feeding. The linear

Fig. 5.1. Size set of three coexisting species of woodland hawks and their body lengths:
(a) northern goshawk, *Accipiter gentilis*, 19 in.;
(b) Cooper's hawk, *A. cooperii*, 15.5 in.;
(c) sharp-shinned hawk, *A. striatus*, 10.5 in.

a

b   c

ratio of the larger to the smaller species is often near 1.3 (a commonly seen ratio of the lengths of two coexisting species, which is equivalent to a doubling of weight). Of course, animals can minimize their interactions by differing in behavior, too, such as feeding in different habitats (marshes versus forests) or at different times of day (morning versus evening).

Examples of size sequences occur in the bills of seed-feeding finches, the lengths of copepods (small shrimp-like animals found in fresh water), and the body sizes of owls. Size differences may also occur between males and females of the same species, as is seen in several kinds of hawks (see 5.2). With growth constrained by an exoskeleton, the successive stages of caterpillar development also leave behind shed skins that form a size set. Size sequences may be found in sets of nonliving things, too, such as string instruments, musical recorders, children's bicycles, and nested Russian dolls, suggesting that a multitude of factors, both biological and non-biological, can produce patterns of size sets.

REFERENCES: HORN & MAY 1977; WIENS 1977; SCHOENER 1982; MACNALLY 1988; BOSAKOWSKI & SMITH 1992; GANESHAIAH ET AL. 1999; SANDERSON 2000

5.2 Male and Female Size

Because of their different reproductive roles, males and females of many animals diverge in size and shape during development, ending up with different forms (sexual dimorphism). In mammals such as elk and walruses, which have internal fertilization, males can monopolize and inseminate more than one female, so males usually compete for mates by fighting or threatening each other. With larger and stronger males attaining more mates, genetic traits conferring large size are passed on to male offspring. Maturation is typically delayed in male mammals until they have grown to a size more likely to be successful in the mating game. These reasons are why, over time, males of many mammal species have evolved larger sizes than females.

A different size relationship is found in many fish and invertebrates. For them, fertilization is external and mating often promiscuous, so direct competition among males is reduced, and males don't gain an advantage by being larger. Furthermore, a female can leave more offspring if she grows to a larger size and is therefore able to make more eggs. Salmon and lobsters, for example, typically keep growing larger as they age (labeled indeterminate growth), and females of these species are typically larger than males and have delayed maturation, trading energy that could have been allocated to reproducing when young for continued growth instead.

Insects have internal fertilization and reach a standard maximum size (labeled determinate growth), but females of many insects are larger because that enables them to produce more eggs. With greater size, female butterflies also maintain warmth better and spend less time basking in the sun, but their relatively heavier abdomens means that they fly a little differently than males, too. These are just some of the discernable differences between males and females of different kinds of animals.

REFERENCES: GILCHRIST 1990; ALCOCK 1993; BEGON ET AL. 1996; STEARNS & HOEKSTRA 2000; BADYAEV 2002; BERWAERTS ET AL. 2002

a

b

c

Fig. 5.2. Examples of sexual size dimorphism (left to right): (a) male and (smaller) female elk, *Cervus elaphus*; (b) male and (larger) female Baltimore checkerspots, *Euphydryas phaeton*; (c) male and (smaller) female bison, *Bison bison*.

5.3 Size in Cold Climates

Among warm-blooded animals of similar shape, the largest individuals are often found in the coldest climates, thus forming the empirical relationship known as Bergmann's rule. The largest member of the deer family, the Alaskan moose, for example, is the most northern; the largest cat is the Siberian tiger; and the largest bears are the Alaskan brown bear and polar bear (see 5.5). Bergmann's rule applies to many birds, too. The traditional explanation for this pattern is that larger size produces less surface area per unit of weight, and because heat is lost through surfaces, larger animals lose body heat more slowly and can tolerate colder climates better than smaller animals. (Surface area is proportional to the square of body length, whereas volume and weight are proportional to the cube of body length; an animal that keeps the same shape but is twice as long would have four times the surface area but eight times the volume, so the surface-to-volume ratio of the larger animal would be one-half that of the smaller.)

Other factors play a role, too, such as the ability of larger animals to store more food reserves per unit of weight, a trait that is advantageous in a cold and unproductive landscape. Some think that the increased fasting endurance of larger size is more important than heat conservation because heat may be regulated better by alterations in feathers and fur. Some rodents show the same size pattern as Bergmann's rule for the related reason that smaller size, which promotes heat loss, better serves animals that live where the summers are hot. Approximately two-thirds of bird and mammal species follow Bergmann's rule, with greater agreement in sedentary birds than in migratory ones and in larger mammals (over one pound in weight) than in smaller ones. Some have pointed out that the size of large mammals

a
b

Fig. 5.3. An example of latitudinal-based size differences: (a) the largest moose, *Alces alces gigas*, are found in Alaska; (b) Shira's moose, *A. alces shirasi*, from Wyoming are smaller. The antlers of these bull moose reflect the size difference, although antlers also grow to larger sizes on bigger and older animals.

actually declines at the coldest extremes because of low forage. Bergmann's rule is not a natural law; it is a correlation of larger size with lower ambient temperature, and the pattern is surprisingly frequent even if we're not always certain of the mechanisms producing it.

REFERENCES: WOOD 1982; GEIST 1987; BROWN & LOMOLINO 1998; ASHTON 2002A, 2002B; FRECKLETON ET AL. 2003; MEIRI & DAYAN 2003

5.4 Extremities in Cold Climates

Mammals in colder climates often have shorter extremities, such as limbs, ears, and tails, yielding the empirical relationship known as Allen's rule. The shortness of the extremities minimizes heat loss. In cold climates, short ears help conserve needed body heat that would

a

Fig. 5.4. Examples of temperature-based differences in extremities: (a) the small ears of an arctic fox, *Alopex lagopus*, which are smaller than the ears of most foxes; (b) the long ears of a desert-dwelling blacktail jackrabbit, *Lepus californicus*, which are longer than the ears of most rabbits and hares.

b

be lost through the surface area of these organs (Fig. 5.4a), and in hot environments, long ears promote the loss of excess heat (Fig. 5.4b). Alternatively, long ears in hot environments may serve to improve sound detection because sound waves don't travel as far through hot air as through cold. Thus, ears may not need to be as long in cooler climates. Some claim that Allen's rule applies to humans, too, with body shapes ranging from that of stocky Inuit in cold regions to long-limbed, lithe Sudanese in hot areas. Shape changes like these apply to a wide range of mammals, just as one would expect from the influences of temperature on animal physiology, but the generality of Allen's rule has not been well established.

REFERENCES: BROWN & LOMOLINO 1998; STRICKBERGER 2000

5.5 Largest Mammals

Why are some animals so big? Large size provides several clear advantages, such as greater ability to escape predators, defend young, catch prey, and, for herbivores, reach higher up in trees to feed. Less apparent assets of size include better insulation against temperature extremes and less food intake needed per unit of weight (metabolic rate declines with increasing size). On the other hand, there are disadvantages of large size, too: large animals need more time to develop; they cannot climb trees, dig into the ground, or fly (elephants are the only mammals that can't jump); the shape and size of their limbs must be proportionately thicker to support their weight; their population sizes are smaller; and their reproductive rates are lower.

Although North American animals can't match African elephants (more than 5 tons) for size, our browsers and grazers are still large. Based on the average size of large males, bison win the herbivore size contest, topping out at about 2,000 pounds (Fig. 5.5a), with Alaskan moose following behind (1,300 pounds). Among terrestrial carnivores, North America has two of the world's largest, Alaskan brown (Kodiak) bears (Fig. 5.5b) and polar bears. One can argue over which of these two bears is bigger; brown bears average greater weights (1,500 pounds) than polar bears (1,400 pounds), but exceptional polar bears reach giant sizes (the heaviest ever measured weighed 2,200 pounds). Larger still are oceanic mammals, whose massive size is supported by buoyancy in the water (at over 100 tons, the blue whale is the largest animal that has ever lived, larger than all dinosaurs).

The largest animals are usually plant eaters because more food is available to herbivores, even though plants are often of low nitrogen content and overall food quality. Larger geographic areas—continents compared to islands, for example—support larger species, too, because ranges, population sizes, and food supplies can all be greater. No living land animals approach the largest dinosaurs in maximum size, probably because when dinosaurs dominated the landscape during the Cretaceous geological period, the environment was food-rich because of higher temperatures and more carbon dioxide in the air.

REFERENCES: SCHMIDT & GILBERT 1978; BURT & GROSSENHEIDER 1964; CHAPMAN & FELDHAMER 1982; WOOD 1982; MCNAMEE 1984; BURNESS ET AL. 2001; *SCIENTIFIC AMERICAN* 2001; MIDGLEY ET AL. 2002; HUTCHINSON ET AL. 2003

Fig. 5.5. The largest mammals in North America include: (a) herbivorous bison, *Bison bison*; (b) carnivorous Alaskan brown bear, *Ursus arctos* (sometimes placed in their own subspecies, *U. a. middendorffi*, to distinguish them from the rest of the species, which are grizzly bears and Eurasian brown bears).

5.6   Smallest Birds and Mammals

Mammals and birds are warm-blooded (endothermic), using body heat they generate through normal metabolic processes to maintain a near-constant body temperature. The advantage of such a well-regulated physiology is that they can remain active whatever the weather may be around them, but the cost is that they must consume enough food to maintain their body temperature as well as to offset losses of body heat. Smaller animals have more surface area per unit of weight than larger animals (see 5.3), and because heat is lost through body surfaces, smaller animals lose heat more rapidly. Small size gives little room for fat reserves, too. These factors produce a lower size limit below which a bird or mammal cannot take in food fast enough to maintain sufficient body warmth. The limit to small size for warm-blooded animals appears to be a body radius of about 1 inch—not much larger than a bumblebee.

Hummingbirds, the smallest birds (Fig. 5.6a), feed on one of the most energy-rich foods available, nectar, which is essentially sugar water. The bee hummingbird of Cuba is the smallest bird in the world, weighing about as much as a dime (2 grams, or less than 0.1 ounce) and having a full wingspan of only 2.6 inches. Shrews are the smallest mammals and consume their own weight in food each day; the smallest is the pygmy shrew of North America (Fig. 5.6b), which weighs the same as the bee hummingbird. In contrast, insects exist in sizes much smaller than shrews and hummingbirds because, being cold-blooded (ectothermic) and relying on the sun for warmth, they are independent from the same internal energetic constraints.

REFERENCES: WOOD 1982; FAABORG 1988; RANDALL ET AL. 1997; AHLBORN & BLAKE 2001

a

b

Fig. 5.6.   Among the smallest birds and mammals: (a) ruby-throated hummingbird, *Archilochus colubris;* (b) pygmy shrew, *Microsorex hoyi.*

5.7   Largest Reptiles

Lizards and snakes are usually smaller in colder climates, in contrast to the better-known pattern in which mammals are larger (see 5.3). Some of the same factors are important in both cases, however: heat is lost or gained through body surfaces, and larger animals of the same shape have less surface area per unit of volume or weight. But lizards and snakes are ectotherms (cold-blooded animals), which gain heat from the environment around them rather than generate body heat internally. To become active, ectotherms bask in the sun for warmth. Smaller bodies heat up more rapidly than do larger ones, so in cool environments, a small animal basking in sunlight can reach a warm, active state more quickly than a larger one. The largest North American snake is the eastern indigo snake (Fig. 5.7), which can measure over 8 feet in length—large to us but much smaller than the world's largest, all of which are tropical. Among snakes, reticulated pythons are the longest (32 feet), while anacondas are the heaviest (450 pounds), and Komodo dragons are the largest lizards (9 feet, 200

Fig. 5.7. The largest snake in North America (up to 103 in. in length) is the eastern indigo snake, *Drymarchon corais couperi*, followed closely (up to 96 in.) by the eastern diamondback rattlesnake, *Crotalus adamanteus*.

pounds). (Findings of even larger snakes have been announced, including that in 2003 of a 49-foot reticulated python in Indonesia, but these reports haven't been documented.)

In the heat of tropical regions, large reptiles can retain warmth and activity through short, cool periods because of their heavy masses, and like dinosaurs of the past, they can avoid overheating by moving into water, where heat is lost more rapidly than in air. But when the cool periods are longer, then a smaller, quick-warming size is a better solution for an ectotherm.

REFERENCES: CONANT 1958; STEBBINS 1966; WOOD 1982; RUXTON 2001; SMITH & SMITH 2001

5.8   Scarce Predators

Prey such as field mice, doves, and deer are always more abundant than their hawk and wolf predators. As a general rule, species higher in the food web are scarcer than those lower down, with top-level carnivores being the least common. This well-known pattern results from a gradual reduction in available energy at higher levels of a food web. The process begins when the energy from solar radiation is taken up by plants and fixed in organic compounds through photosynthesis. As that chemical energy passes from herbivores feeding on plants to carnivores feeding on herbivores, some of it is used up in the normal metabolic activities that keep an animal alive, and some of it is lost as heat when one form of energy is converted to another. The result is less total energy available to fuel life at the tops of food webs. As high-level carnivores, fierce predators such as mountain lions (Fig. 5.8a), bald eagles (Fig. 5.8b), grizzly bears (Fig. 5.8c), and gray wolves are relatively scarce.

Ecological efficiency represents the proportion of energy at one level of a food web that is fixed into tissue at the next higher level; it measures the overall reduction in available energy. Ecological efficiencies usually range from 2 to 40 percent. Geographic limits of the ecosystem and the relative sizes of individual predators and prey are additional factors that restrict the number of trophic (feeding) levels. The longest food webs, with up to seven levels, are found in surface waters of the open ocean, where productivity is relatively high, the herbivores and lowest-level carnivores are small, and the ecosystem is three-dimensional and huge.

REFERENCES: COLINVAUX 1978; BRIAND & COHEN 1987; SCHOENER 1989; RICKLEFS & MILLER 2000; POST 2002

a

c

b

Fig. 5.8.   Top-level predators are scarce: (a) mountain lion, *Felis concolor*; (b) bald eagle, *Haliaeetus leucocephalus*; (c) grizzly bear, *Ursus arctos horribilis*.

5.9   Shivering

When losing body heat to a cool environment, many animals, including humans, can generate additional warmth through use of their muscles. Shivering is the repeated, rapid contraction of antagonistic muscles (those that have opposite effects) such that there is no overall movement; instead, chemical energy from molecules of ATP, the body's energy currency, is released entirely as heat. Mammals, birds, and even snakes can shiver to warm up.

Some insects shiver, too. Most of the time their body temperature matches that of the surrounding air, but for insects to fly, their wing muscles must exceed 80°F. They can achieve this by shivering. When a large moth is disturbed on a cool evening, the first thing it does is vibrate its wings so that the flight muscles warm up. Bumblebees pump their wing muscles for the same warming effect, but with the wings decoupled from the muscles, the movement

Fig. 5.9.   An example of shivering in the Carolina sphinx (tobacco hornworm), *Manduca sexta*.

is less noticeable. There's a low ambient temperature, however, below which insects become incapable of movement and cannot start activating their flight muscles; called the chill-coma temperature, this limit is just above freezing for most species. Insects from colder climates have adapted to a lower chill-coma temperature. Shivering cannot overcome severe cold, but it can contribute significantly to the ability of an insect to fly or a human to stay warm.

REFERENCES: HARLOW & GRIGG 1984; GOLLER & ESCH 1990; SRYGLEY 1994; RANDALL ET AL. 1997; GIBERT ET AL. 2001; SMITH & SMITH 2001

5.10 Panting

People sweat when overheated because evaporation of water secreted by pores on the skin surface rids the body of significant heat (585 calories per gram of water lost). Animals with fur or feathers don't sweat as easily through their skin, however, so they pant, which is rapid, shallow breathing that expels warm, moist air from highly vascularized passages (Fig. 5.10a). A potential problem in panting is that rapid breathing can lead to an excessive loss of carbon dioxide, changing the acidity of the blood and producing dizziness. To avoid that outcome, panting mammals expel air from dead spaces in their lungs, not from the tiny pockets (alveoli) where gas exchange takes place. In panting, air is channeled in through the nose and directly out the mouth. Panting occurs at a frequency that requires the least muscular effort; at the same time, salivary glands increase their secretions to keep the surfaces moist for evaporation.

Birds have one-way air flow through their respiratory passages, while many large birds, such as pelicans, herons, pigeons, turkeys, and owls, have an additional trick. They flutter their throat (gular) region, a response even more rapid than panting, in which a large internal area is exposed to evaporative loss without interfering with normal respiration (Fig. 5.10b). The rate of gular flutter depends on the resonance frequency of structures in the bird's throat, so it occurs at a constant rate for an individual. A gaping beak and fluttering throat are clear signs of heat stress in a bird. For both panting and gular flutter, the cost of evaporative cooling is water loss at a time when water may be limited.

REFERENCES: FAABORG 1988; SMITH & SMITH 2001; RANDALL ET AL. 2002

a   b

Fig. 5.10. Panting: (a) domestic dogs, *Canis familiaris*; (b) great black-backed gulls, *Larus marinus*. The gulls also experience gular flutter.

5.11 Salt Licks

Wherever they get it, animals require salt. In humans, 0.1 percent of our total body weight is sodium, and our cells pump sodium ions across cell membranes to enable the functioning of our nerves and kidneys. Carnivorous animals obtain the salt they need directly from their animal-tissue food and so are little attracted to salty substances. It's a different story for herbivores, however, because potassium, not sodium, is the primary ion used in active transport across membranes in plants. Except for plants that grow in saline habitats, the concentration of sodium in a plant reflects the limited amount that occurs in its environment, so the sodium/potassium ratio is far lower than in animals.

The feeding patterns of herbivores reveal their need for salt. Moose add less-energy-rich aquatic vegetation to their diet because it may have a hundred times more salt than terrestrial vegetation (Fig. 5.11a). Deer and cattle are lured readily to salt licks (Fig. 5.11b), porcupines chew on ax handles that have accumulated salts from the sweat of heavy use, and mourning doves visit salt sources. Although male deer require an increased intake of sodium in order to grow antlers, adult females need even more for pregnancy and lactation, so females are the most frequent deer visitors to salt licks. Even butterflies visit damp sand to imbibe salty water (see 7.6). In contrast, we humans get all the salt we need—and sometimes too much for our own health—from the diverse foods we eat and the salt shakers on our tables.

REFERENCES: BOTKIN ET AL. 1973; ARMS ET AL. 1974; FRASER 1985; STAMP & HARMON 1991; YU ET AL. 1997; ATWOOD & WEEKS 2002; HAYSLETTE & MIRARCHI 2002

a

b

Fig. 5.11. Herbivores diversify their diets to gain salt: (a) moose, *Alces alces*, feeding on aquatic vegetation; (b) white-tailed deer, *Odocoileus virginianus*, at a mineral lick.

5.12 Group Living

Rather than live solitary lives, many animals remain in groups: flocks of finches and waxwings (Fig. 5.12a), schools of fish, and herds of elk and bison (Fig. 5.12b). Sometimes groups form to find mates, as with swarms of midges (see 7.2), or to live social lives, as with ants and bees. Sometimes living with others increases an individual's chances to feed. When resources are clumped, for example, discovery of rich patches of food is more likely with a group.

a

b

Fig. 5.12. Group living is commonplace: (a) cedar waxwings, *Bombycilla cedrorum;* (b) bison, *Bison bison.*

Birds are more likely to flock when food is less abundant, and tuna swim together to search for schools of small fish. Groups also enable social hunting, as when packs of wolves take down larger moose and elk.

A common reason for group living, however, is that it can provide safety from predators. One reason is that groups provide early detection: more eyes and ears are vigilant for danger. When a hawk approaches, for example, a larger group of pigeons is likely to detect the hawk sooner and take flight, lowering the chances of the hawk making a kill. A second advantage is that only those animals on the outside of the group may be vulnerable, as when bison are attacked by wolves or zebras by a lion. The larger the group, the lower each individual's probability of being caught. When some animals use others as shields against danger, the aggregation is described as a selfish herd, and it is safest to be in the middle of such a group, a location claimed by competitively dominant animals. A related form of protection is that numerous fleeing prey may confuse an unfocused predator. A third reason is that many prey together may be able to deter a predator in ways that a single animal can't: a defensive circle of musk oxen creates a strong barrier against attack, and smaller birds can drive away a hawk or owl (see 6.10). The protective role of groups is illustrated by the more frequent schooling behavior of fish that live in open water, where there are no protective hiding places, as opposed to those that live in streams or along the bottom. Of course, the advantages of group living may be diminished if larger groups also attract predators. For birds, fish, and mammals, full-time group living often serves to reduce predation. From finches to perch to elk, there really is safety in numbers.

REFERENCES: EHRLICH ET AL. 1988; ALCOCK 1993; PHILLIPS 1995; KREBS 2001; JOHNSON ET AL. 2002

5.13   Acorn Preferences

Squirrels scurry about during the fall eating and caching nuts, but the acorns they eat are mostly those from white oaks, whereas the acorns they cache are mostly those from red and black oaks. Acorns from these two groups of oaks differ considerably. Red-oak acorns (Fig. 5.13a) are rich in lipids, a high-energy food source, but they're also bitter with tannins, plant-produced chemicals that slow a herbivore's digestion. Tannins are so named because they are used to tan or preserve leather. A familiar example of their effects is that tannins from grape skins are what give red wine its astringency and lasting power; because the skins are removed to make white wines—the pigments of red and black grapes are in their skins—white wine has neither the astringency nor the endurance of red wine.

Squirrels prefer foods that are low in tannins. But because tannins prevent bacterial and fungal decay, red-oak acorns last for months, germinating after winter has given way to spring. They constitute a food source that lasts through the winter (Fig. 5.13b). White-oak acorns (Fig. 5.13c), on the other hand, contain less lipid and less tannin, and they germinate soon after falling, with nutrients in the seeds moving quickly into unpalatable taproots. With less protection against decay, these seeds don't last as well for winter storage, although they do provide a good source of autumn food. Sometimes squirrels cache white-oak acorns, but first they cut away the seed embryos to prevent germination. Handling time and size of acorn as well as distance to protective cover have less effect on squirrel feeding preferences than the overall difference between these two acorn types. And given a mix of wormy and clean acorns, squirrels will cache the good ones and eat the nutritious infested ones, protein-rich larvae and all.

REFERENCES: FOX 1982; LIMA & VALONE 1986; SMALLWOOD & PETERS 1986; JACOBS 1992; STEELE & SMALLWOOD 1994; HADJ-CHIKH ET AL. 1996; CHUNG-MACCOUBREY ET AL. 1997; BARTHELMES 2001

Fig. 5.13. Acorns consumed by gray squirrels, *Sciurus carolinensis*: (a) acorns of northern red oak, *Quercus rubra*, which are cached for winter consumption; (b) husks of northern red oak acorns that were retrieved from caches in winter and eaten; (c) acorns of white oak, *Quercus alba*, which are low in tannin, begin to germinate in autumn, and are eaten immediately and not cached.

5.14 Finding Caches

Gray squirrels cache nuts for the winter by burying them one by one (a process called scatter hoarding), rather than storing them all together, and the spreading out of many individual caches makes their recovery a daunting challenge. Squirrels are rodents, and because rodents have a

well-developed sense of smell, one might expect squirrels to sniff their way to their buried morsels. But odors are suppressed under soil and the snows of winter, and if a sense of smell were all that was needed to find buried food, then a squirrel wouldn't bother caching its own nuts for winter but instead sniff out the caches of others. To avoid the possibility of odor-aided recovery, squirrels remove the fragrant husks of hickory nuts before burying them.

Gray squirrels are unusual rodents, however, in that they are active during the day, not night, and they live in the three-dimensional habitat of a forest rather than the more two-dimensional habitat of the ground surface. As a result, these animals have well-developed visual abilities in addition to their olfactory skills, along with surprisingly good memories about where they have stored food. Most of the time, they can remember for weeks within inches where they had stored a nut, and they remember cache locations even into winter, when the landscape has changed. They use remembered visual cues to look for food in the right places—the sites where they had cached their food—and then, when possible, their sense of smell to pinpoint the precise location to dig. Surprisingly good memory for cache locations has been demonstrated in various scatter hoarders, including chipmunks, kangaroo rats, jays, Clark's nutcrackers, and chickadees in addition to squirrels.

Fig. 5.14.   Gray squirrels, *Sciurus carolinensis*, use both their sense of smell and their highly developed memory to find cache locations.

REFERENCES: SHETTLEWORTH 1983; MCQUADE ET AL. 1986; JACOBS 1989, 1992; JACOBS & LIMAN 1991; MACDONALD 1997

5.15 Scats

Every animal produces droppings in some form or other, and they are strewn about wherever the animal roams. *Scat* is a word commonly used to refer to animal excrement, and it's a perfectly good word to use in polite company. As signs of animal activity, scats can reveal a lot about the wildlife of an area: which species are present, what they're eating, how long ago they've been living there, and where they like to perch. Bear scats often contain seeds (Fig. 5.15a), showing that berries are part of bear diets. Coyote scats include the bones, teeth, and hair of the small rodents these carnivores have eaten, and one can even use these remnants to identify the species of mice and voles that live nearby. Counts of scats have been used to give an estimate of the density of snowshoe hares as well as of other mammals.

Fig. 5.15. Scats: (a) scat of black bear, *Ursus americanus*; (b) a set of pellet-shaped scats, including (from the smallest to the largest) pika, *Ochotona princeps*; cottontail rabbit, *Sylvilagus* sp.; snowshoe hare, *Lepus americanus*; antelope, *Antilocapra americana*; mule deer, *Odocoileus hemionus*; elk, *Cervus elaphus*; moose, *Alces alces*; piles in the field of (c) moose and (d) rabbit scat.

Curiously, the scats of wild herbivores are often pellet-shaped, ranging from the small droppings of rabbits to the large pellets of moose, and these are the scats seen most often (Fig. 5.15b-d). Pellet producers consume large amounts of hard-to-digest cellulose (animals don't have the enzymes to break down cellulose, although bacteria in their digestive tracts do), and they are typically browsers (animals such as rabbits, deer, and moose, which eat twigs with leaves) rather than grazers (animals such as cattle, bison, and horses, which eat grasses and produce the familiar cow pies, buffalo chips, and horse muffins). Alternating contraction and relaxation of smooth muscles that encircle the intestinal walls produce waves of contraction (peristalsis) that segment and pack the gut contents into pellet form while pushing the pellets down the intestine. The pellets are softer when formed from fresh, spring vegetation and firmer and more fibrous when produced from winter twigs. Rabbits and hares release both hard and soft pellets; the soft ones are reingested later on (coprophagy) to extract additional nutrients. Scat happens, and one can learn much about its producer from what is left behind.

REFERENCES: MURIE 1975; STOKES & STOKES 1986; KREBS ET AL. 1987; STEVENS & HUME 1993; SMITH & SMITH 2001; RANDALL ET AL. 2002

5.16 Antlers and Horns

Antlers and horns on the heads of large hooved mammals are the most conspicuous features of these animals. Horns grow slowly as hollow cones of nonliving keratin, the same protein that forms hooves and fingernails, shaped around a bony core. Horns are characteristic of sheep, goats, and antelope, and except for those of pronghorn antelope, horns are permanent. Antlers, in contrast, grow as bony structures: shells of hard, compact bone surrounding cores of spongy bone, covered with a hairy, highly vascularized skin called the velvet. Antlers are shed

a

b

c

d

Fig. 5.16.   Antlers: (a) elk, *Cervus elaphus*, and (b) moose, *Alces alces*. Horns: (c) mountain goat, *Oreamnos americanus*; (d) big-horned sheep, *Ovis canadensis*.

each winter after the fall mating season and regrow the next spring, creating a strong nutritional need each summer for calcium. As an individual deer, elk, or moose ages, its antlers become larger, reaching maximum size in four to six years.

Many social interactions are guided by the presence of these head-borne weapons. Horns are pointed and used in aggressive encounters, and females of most species have smaller versions of the males' horns. Antlers, in contrast, are large, awkward weapons found generally only on males. These magnificent structures are used more for showing off in front of females and rival males and less in actual sparring, although fights do take place, and injury and even death may occur. Because energy stress and nutrient deficiency can reduce the size of a male's antlers, antler size is correlated with health and strength. Larger-antlered males mate more often and leave more offspring than less well-endowed males; thus, the genes of the healthiest and most dominant males become more frequent in subsequent generations. Alaskan moose grow the largest antlers of any living animal (see 5.3), and only in caribou do females have antlers (a few lack them), which are retained throughout the winter to defend the feeding craters they dig through the snow. An unfortunate side effect of the hunting of trophy animals, the males with the largest antlers and horns, is the removal of the fittest and most dominant males from breeding populations. Most antlers are then dropped after the mating season to aid exhausted males in escaping predators.

REFERENCES: MODELL 1969; GEIST & BROMLEY 1978; CHAPMAN & FELDHAMER 1982; BARRETTE & VANDAL 1986; SCRIBNER ET AL. 1989; REIMERS 1993; STRICKLAND & DEMARAIS 2000; BLOB & LABARBERA 2001; DITCHKOFF ET AL. 2001; SCHAEFER & MAHONEY 2001; KRUUK ET AL. 2002

5.17   Misleading Displays

If an animal can't fight a threatening predator or bluff it into withdrawing, it might try to act its way out of danger with diverting behaviors known as distraction displays. An injured bird might seem easy pickings to a predator, but some ground-nesting birds, including shorebirds and waterfowl, call loudly and feign injury by spreading and dragging a wing (a broken wing display) to draw the predator away from their nests (Fig. 5.17a). They flutter and expose colorful feathers to make themselves conspicuous to the invader. Of course, an "injured" bird keeps a safe distance from the enemy it's luring away, but what really makes distractions by the parent birds necessary is that the nests are immovable and their concealment can't be improved. Distraction displays are behaviorally interesting because, rather than trying to avoid a predator, the animal performing the act draws the predator's attention. The displays are most common when the young are most vulnerable.

Playing dead is another misleading behavior, a response so closely associated with opossums that it is known as "playing possum." When unable to escape a predator, opossums often fall over in a catatonic state (Fig. 5.17b). They lie still and openmouthed while drooling saliva, defecating, and secreting repellent odors from their anal glands, a scene that's usually enough to repel a predator. The opossums remain fully alert with their eyes open during these episodes, evaluating the immediacy of the threat before returning to normal. Curiously, their heart rates don't change even at the height of the danger. Hognose snakes also bluff predators they can't scare away by feigning death as they lie twisting on their backs (Fig. 5.17c).

It's another surprise of nature that animals other than humans are capable of such deception.

REFERENCES: HARVEY & GREENWOOD 1978; CHAPMAN & FELDHAMER 1982; EHRLICH ET AL. 1988

Fig. 5.17. Misleading displays: (a) the broken-wing display of a killdeer, *Charadrius vociferus*; (b) an opossum, *Didelphis marsupialis*, playing dead; (c) a (nonvenomous) eastern hognose snake, *Heterodon platyrhinos*, playing dead.

a

b

c

5.18   Tail Flagging

Several ideas have been offered to explain why, when disturbed, white-tailed deer run with their white tails up and rump patches exposed. Most likely, tail flagging during flight serves as a general alarm signal to other deer that, by promoting cohesion, reduces the likelihood of harm. Mobile fawns have the most to gain from staying with others, and they are the most likely to flag. Flagging may also serve as a signal to alert the predator that it has been seen, so a chase isn't worthwhile. In addition, dropping the tail after running may make the deer inconspicuous if the predator keeps searching for a white tail. Anecdotal evidence suggests that a doe may tail-flag to draw a predator's attention away from a bedded young fawn.

An alternative behavior when a predator approaches is simply to freeze and blend in with the background. This response takes less energy and is more likely, logically enough, when a deer is alone or in deep cover or when the predator is far away. Although white-tailed deer flee when a predator approaches, mule deer are more likely to group together and defend their ground, without giving tail signals. This behavioral difference likely derives from their

Fig. 5.18.   The tail flagging of a white-tailed deer, *Odocoileus virginianus.*

different environments, with the western mule deer occupying habitat that is more open with fewer refuges. It is in the aptly named white-tailed deer that we see tail-flagging.

REFERENCES: BILDSTEIN 1983; SMITH 1991; CARO ET AL. 1995; LINGLE & WILSON 2001; ATWOOD & WEEKS 2002; LINGLE 2002

5.19   Wall Walkers

Defying gravity, animals such as flies, ants, and gecko lizards can hang on to surfaces of any orientation, a clear advantage for small creatures that travel in the three-dimensional world of terrestrial plants. These animals use a tight matching of surfaces to generate the intermolecular attraction that holds them up. The attachment can be strong; one study showed that a beetle could hold fifty times its body weight on a smooth surface.

The feet of flies match the contour of the surface exactly through footpads that resemble soft-bristled toothbrushes, with thousands of fine hairs, each of which is branched with flattened ends to give many points of attachment. Flies leave tracks when crossing a glass window (Fig. 5.19a), showing that they secrete a thin film of an oily liquid to increase attachment. The wet, thin-layer adherence of flies is the chemical attraction of a sandwich of

Fig. 5.19. Wall and window walking: (a) house fly, *Musca domestica;* (b) tokay gecko, *Gekko gecko.*

two close surfaces with a thin fluid between. For something similar, think of trying to separate two nested wet glasses.

Geckos, which are lizards known especially for their wall climbing (Fig. 5.19b), have foot pads covered with hundreds of thousands of hairs, each with hundreds of flattened split ends that touch the surface. Just as with flies, the branched, flattened ends create a large surface area for contact, but for geckos, weak intermolecular attraction creates dry adhesion without oil or adhesives. The intermolecular attractive forces are known as van der Waals forces and result from two molecules being less than one nanometer (10^{-9} meter) apart and having both positive and negative ends. Geckos can race over vertical surfaces because they peel their toes back as they lift their feet, and the change in angle between the ends of the hairs and the underlying surface cancels the molecular attraction.

Ants and bees, on the other hand, extend soft foot pads forward hydraulically. Just like suction cups, their foot pads mold to the walls and ceilings they contact and provide electrostatic attraction, like that of plastic food wrap on a clean dish, through a tight matching of touching surfaces. Despite Hollywood stories of Spider-Man, only small, light animals such as these can walk on walls.

REFERENCES: STORK 1980; PAIN 2000; PENNISI 2000; FEDERLE ET AL. 2001; AUTUMN ET AL. 2000, 2002

6. Birds

Because of birds' colorful beauty, song, abundance, and flight, millions of people enjoy the hobby of bird watching (birding). Usually, one first notices the size, color, and shape of a bird, so this chapter begins with visible patterns in their bills, wings, and tails. But people are most curious about bird behavior—vocalizations, flight patterns, nesting activities, and feeding behavior—so behavior is the focus of most of these descriptions, including the dawn chorus, timing of migration, and concealment of seeds for later feeding. Understanding these behaviors increases the enjoyment of bird observation, whether the behavior applies to all birds or only special cases.

Related descriptions include:

6.1 Bills and Beaks

Any task is easier with the right tool for the job. Birds use their bills (beaks) to grasp, shred, crush, and transport a wide range of foods, and the shape of each bill enables the catching and consuming of specific kinds of foods. Shape and function are strongly correlated, so bill shape lets you easily infer a bird's diet.

Fig. 6.1. Some of the diverse bill shapes of birds: (a) flesh-tearing bill of a kestrel, *Falco sparverius*; (b) seed-cracking bill of an evening grosbeak, *Coccothraustes vespertinus*; (c) fish-holding bill of a brown pelican, *Pelecanus occidentalis*; (d) sand-probing bill of a willet, *Catoptrophorus semipalmatus*; (e) straining bill of a mallard duck, *Anas platyrhynchos*.

As flesh-eating predators, hawks and owls have a sharp hook on the end of a strong bill (Fig. 6.1a). The hook is used to rip flesh from prey held by the feet or, as with shrikes, to kill small prey. Carrion-feeding vultures have the same hooked bills as other meat eaters, although they lack feathers around the head, which lessens the messiness that comes with poking one's head in a rotting carcass.

Seed eaters such as finches and grosbeaks have conical bills to crack seeds open (Fig. 6.1b); the deeper and heavier the bill, the larger the seed the birds may eat. Fruit eaters that simply swallow the seeds with the fruit don't have bills that are as heavy because they don't need the same crushing force.

Birds such as warblers, which glean insects from leaves and buds, have sharp, thin, pointed bills that are very maneuverable tools. Creepers, which search on tree trunks, have longer, downward-curved bills for ease in picking insects from bark. Birds such as flycatchers, which capture insects in flight, have very wide bills that when opened form a basket for scooping up prey. These flying insect nets are enhanced by having bristles at the side of their broad bills to expand the area for catching prey; the larger the insect prey, the heavier the bills.

The bone-jarring drilling of woodpeckers is achieved with a strong neck, reinforced skull, and straight, stout bill that is strongly calcified for chiseling away wood in the search for insect larvae. Flower feeders, typified by hummingbirds, have long, narrow, often downcurved bills for probing flowers for nectar.

Fish-eating birds such as herons typically have heavy, pointed bills for spearing or grabbing their prey. Those that take large fish may also have a small hook at the end or small serrations along the edge to help in holding on to and manipulating their slippery food. Of course, pelicans (Fig. 6.1c) also have an expanded throat pouch to carry fish ("A wonderful bird is the pelican; his bill can hold more than his belly can," wrote D. L. Merritt). Sandpipers use elongated, sensitive, flexible bills to probe the mud or sand for aquatic invertebrates (Fig. 6.1d). Ducks and spoonbills use their flattened bills to strain food from the water (Fig. 6.1e).

REFERENCES: EHRLICH ET AL. 1988; FAABORG 1988; ENGLEN 2000

6.2 Wing Shape

A bird's flight abilities can be recognized by the match of its wings to one of four categories of wing shape. (1) The wings of fast-flying birds such as ducks, falcons, and terns are pointed, swept back, and flapped actively in flight (Fig. 6.2a). Swallows, another example, are a delight to watch because of their powerful, turning flight. (2) The wings of hawks, vultures, and other soaring birds, in contrast, are quite broad compared to their length, with large feathers protruding separately from rounded outer margins. These slotted tips, appearing as fingers, reduce drag by spreading out the vortices that develop as air flows over the wings. More wing area for a given body weight permits more-efficient soaring (Fig. 6.2b). (3) The wings of most birds, including all smaller species, are elliptical in shape and intermediate in breadth and other traits; they give high maneuverability. (4) The wings of some seabirds are very long, narrow, and pointed, a shape that enables continuous gliding through the turbulent winds that sweep over open oceans.

Size and speed records of birds are related to wing shape. The fastest birds (category 1 wing shape) are peregrine falcons in a steep dive (reported to be from 160 to 200 mph) or ducks and swifts in level flight (up to 70 mph). The longest wings are those of the wandering albatross, which locks its wings in place to become a living glider over the ocean surface (nearly 12-foot wingspan; category 4), while the wings with the largest area belong to the Andean condor (category 2, with a span of about 10 feet and very wide).

REFERENCES: WOOD 1982; EHRLICH ET AL. 1988; FAABORG 1988; TUCKER 1993; SIBLEY 2002

a   b

Fig. 6.2.   Different wing shapes: (a) for maneuverability in a common tern, *Sterna hirundo;* (b) for soaring in a red-tailed hawk, *Buteo jamaicensis.*

6.3   Tail Shape

Varying significantly in form, birds' tails reveal nearly as much about their flight patterns as do the outlines of their wings. The best aerodynamic shape for a tail when fully spread is triangular, the same shape used in hang gliders. But birds are neither gliders nor airplanes; they can reshape their tails as needed by folding or spreading them. A triangular tail takes on a forked shape when folded because the inner feathers are shorter than the outer ones. In contrast, tails with longer central feathers are wedge-shaped when folded.

Size of the tail affects flight ability. Larger tails make it possible to turn more quickly, so birds that require high maneuverability, such as swallows, which chase flying insects, have broad tails that can be used as a rudder (Fig. 6.3a). For lift and stability, birds that fly slowly must be able to spread their tails and point them down. Tails add aerodynamic drag, however, so birds such as swifts, which fly at high speed, have small tails that they can fold tightly. Deeply forked tails give greater turning ability but less stability, so birds with forked tails must move them actively. Aerial feeders and forest birds, both of which need maneuverability and resistance to damage, have larger tails (Fig. 6.3b) than do terrestrial feeders and those of open habitats.

Contributions to flight aren't the only factor in tail design, however. For barn swallows and many other species, longer tail feathers help males attract mates, so some of the elaboration in tail shape has developed for reasons other than their influence on flight. Exaggerated tails, such as those of magpies and scissor-tailed flycatchers, are best explained as features for sexual attraction.

REFERENCES: THOMAS 1997; HEDENSTROM 2002; SIBLEY 2002

a

b

Fig. 6.3. Different tail shapes: (a) for acrobatic agility in a barn swallow, *Hirundo rustica*; (b) for woodland flight in a blue jay, *Cyanocitta cristata*.

6.4 Brighter Males

In most species of birds, males are more brightly colored than females and have higher-contrast visual patterns, differences that originate in the separate reproductive roles of the two sexes. Standing out against the green and brown of most backgrounds, gaudy plumages serve two visual purposes: they help males compete against other males to establish and maintain territories, and they attract females. Birds that are monogamous and remain paired throughout the year have similar appearances of the two sexes, but those that establish territories for just the breeding season often develop different plumages (sexual dimorphism; Fig. 6.4a). Usually, older males are brighter than younger ones, and brighter males are socially dominant. In some species, the brightness of a male's color is evidence of his resistance to parasites, and a bright male advertises his good health to the females he courts. In house finches, reddish-orange colors come from carotenoid pigments in the food they eat, and the reddest feathers, from the best nutrition, are found on the healthiest males. In blackbirds,

b

a

c

Fig. 6.4. Examples of bright male coloration: (a) red male and pale female northern cardinals, *Cardinalis cardinalis*; (b) male wood duck, *Aix sponsa*; (c) male painted bunting, *Passerina ciris*.

carotenoids are in short supply and are withdrawn from their orange bills when needed to ward off immunological challenges. In contrast, drab coloration helps conceal females from predators, especially during incubation. Bright colors are costly for both energetic reasons and conspicuousness to predators; species with strong dimorphism are more apt to suffer local extirpation. Thus, males revert to a less showy, more femalelike appearance after the breeding season. A few species such as phalaropes have reversed sex roles in which females choose the breeding territories and males incubate the eggs, and in these species, appearances are also switched, with females more brightly colored. For visual animals such as birds and mammals, color is a vital cue for communication.

REFERENCES: EHRLICH ET AL. 1988; FAABORG 1988; DUNN ET AL. 2001; HORAK ET AL. 2001; HILL ET AL. 2002; BLOUNT ET AL. 2003; DOHERTY ET AL. 2003; FAIRRE ET AL. 2003

6.5   Nest Design

Despite great diversity in shape among the nests built by birds, there is a best design for each species's lifestyle. Nests serve three purposes: structural support for incubation, insulation against temperature extremes, and, above all, protection of the eggs against predators, since a nest of eggs is certainly an appealing meal to a hungry predator. One form of protection is to make the nests hard to reach; they may be (1) suspended from the farthest tips of thin branches,

b

Fig. 6.5.   Different nest designs: (a) pendant nest of a Baltimore oriole, *Icterus galbula*; (b) mud nests of cliff swallows, *Petrochelidon pyrrhonota*; (c) stick nest of a northern mockingbird, *Mimus polyglottos;* (d) alpine ground nest of an American pipit, *Anthus rubescens.*

a

c

d

as are the pendulous basket nests of orioles (Fig. 6.5a); (2) placed within cactus spines, such as with those of the cactus wren; (3) hidden in cavities in trees, as with those of most woodpeckers; (4) attached to cliff faces, such as with the mud nests of cliff swallows (Fig. 6.5b), or (5) made unreachable at the tops of trees, as are the large stick nests of eagles and osprey (theirs are the largest nests, often 3 feet deep and 7 feet across). Cavity nests provide protection from weather as well as from hunters, and, for added warmth, the cavities may open on the side of the tree that faces the sun. Some nests are positioned so they can be defended, for example, when grouped together in colonies or placed near bee and wasp nests. Nests in colonies tend to be simple in order to retard the buildup of parasites. Most nests are hidden; especially for small birds, which constitute the majority of species, nests are open at the top, camouflaged, and concealed among leafy branches (Fig. 6.5c). Birds whose young are precocial (see 6.6) often save time and energy in nest construction by scraping the ground to form minimal nests; the young of these ground nesters are able to run and feed themselves soon after hatching, so the nests are needed for shorter times and can offer less protection to the young. Ground nests are often raised a little to withstand the threats of heavy rain and mud, and ground nesting is necessary for those that breed in arctic and alpine zones (Fig. 6.5d). The shape of each nest reflects the size and lifestyle of the bird that built it.

REFERENCES: EHRLICH ET AL. 1988; FAABORG 1988; CARPENTER 2002

6.6 Precocial Young

Baby birds display a wide range in mobility right after hatching. Robins are typical of most small birds, whose young are little more than helpless blobs of pink flesh that need time to develop feathers and open their eyes (Fig. 6.6a). Requiring parental protection and feeding to survive, they are described as altricial, from the Latin word for "nourishing." Baby chickens, ducks, and others, in contrast, are able to run around and feed themselves within hours after hatching (Fig. 6.6b). They are described as precocial, from the Latin for "early maturing," and these are the kinds of young birds that people take home as pets. Different bird species represent the full range of developmental ability at hatching, from completely helpless to entirely independent.

These developmental patterns have evolved as alternative solutions to the challenges of gathering food and defending against predators. Birds with precocial young must better provision their eggs so that the young can develop to independence at about hatching time, whereas altricial young require more parent-provided food and care after hatching. The difference is illustrated in their eggs; those of altricial birds are typically only about 20 percent yolk, whereas those of precocial birds may be up to 50 percent or even more yolk, with double the energy content. Species of altricial birds must also protect against predators by nest concealment or active parental defense, and they must feed their young well enough for the hatchlings to grow rapidly. Because each baby bird requires more time and energy, parents of altricial young typically have smaller clutch sizes (e.g., blackbirds, with two to six eggs) compared to those with precocial young (e.g., ducks, which produce seven to twelve eggs).

REFERENCES: EHRLICH ET AL. 1988; FAABORG 1988

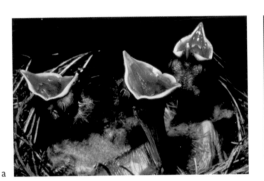

a

b

Fig. 6.6. Newly hatched birds: (a) altricial (dependent) young of American robin, *Turdus migratorius*; (b) precocial young of piping plover, *Charadrius melodus*.

6.7 Dawn Chorus

Of all the sounds made by birds, songs, which are partly learned, are the most complex. Starting early in the morning each day of the breeding season, male birds offer a wake-up concert by singing back and forth from perch to perch, producing the species-specific songs that are the sounds of spring. The intensity of singing peaks near dawn and dusk, mostly because the dim light restricts foraging success but not social interactions. The dawn chorus begins with species that have larger eyes and can see better in the first, dim light; thus, robins sing before house sparrows. The primary function of bird song is to communicate with females: to attract them, to stimulate them to mate and build nests, and to synchronize reproductive readiness. Songs serve secondarily to communicate with other males: to defend territories or to maintain individual status in dominance hierarchies. Females may sing in reply to males, too. Other bird vocalizations are known as calls; they have specific functions and are innate, less complex, and vocalized by either sex throughout the year. They may warn of the approach of a predator or simply signal the position of a bird.

Fig. 6.7. Singing eastern meadowlark, *Sturnella magna*.

Songs vary from male to male within a species, permitting individual recognition. The rate at which a male sings may be energetically constrained, resulting in the strongest birds singing for longer times and potentially attracting the most females. Because each male learns parts of the songs he sings, older birds in some species have a larger song repertoire, including songs for different purposes, and the greater vocabulary can be more attractive to females. Songs may vary regionally, too, producing different bird dialects; in both birds and people, an accent can be a clue about where an individual came from. Singing then diminishes after the breeding season.

REFERENCES: KACELNIK 1979; EHRLICH ET AL. 1988; FAABORG 1988; KROODSMA 1989; KROODSMA & BYERS 1991; HUTCHINSON 2002; THOMAS ET AL. 2002

6.8   Geese Honking

Why geese should honk so noticeably as they fly is unclear because vocalizations of such volume use up energy that could otherwise be used for flight. There are two hypotheses for

why geese honk loudly. The first is that these sounds help keep the flock together and well oriented with respect to each other. Geese live in family groups with monogamous pairings and are very protective of their young, and they are known to recognize individuals by their calls. Honking might be communication among individuals that helps prevent offspring from becoming lost, for example. The second possibility is based on the

Fig. 6.8.   Canada goose, *Branta canadensis*, honking in flight.

energetic demands of maintaining the lead position in flight. Because of wind resistance, it is tiring to be the leader. Honking may help the geese assess their flight condition and determine when another individual should take the lead. Although it is difficult to establish clear reasons for what geese are communicating, the popular notion that they honk to encourage their leader is human wishful thinking.

REFERENCES: SCHMITT 1991; AAAS 1999

6.9   Woodpecker Drumming

The living jackhammers known as woodpeckers hammer rapidly on trees not only to excavate holes and forage for edible insects but also to communicate with other woodpeckers. Drumming serves the same functions as song—to attract mates and to claim territories—but

Fig. 6.9.   Pileated woodpecker,
Dryocopus pileatus, drumming on a pine.

it carries farther away and so reaches individuals that are more widely spaced. The use of drumming as a signal is especially apparent to us when a male drums repeatedly against a drainpipe, metal gutter, or aluminum siding to produce a loud and annoying racket. These surfaces resonate with louder sounds than hollow trees, and the drumming can even leave dents or small holes. Drumming for communication ceases after the breeding season. The birds may also excavate nest cavities or forage in wooden siding, but these activities use lighter, less regular tapping.

Different species of woodpecker often differ in the cadence of their drumming, especially between those with similar appearances, such as hairy and downy woodpeckers. Others such as red-bellied woodpeckers use tapping, which is slower and more regular than drumming, for within-pair communication. The reinforced skulls and strong necks and bills of woodpeckers protect them while hammering. One of the most unusual features of woodpecker behavior is their use of structures outside their bodies to create audible communication.

REFERENCES: EHRLICH ET AL. 1988; FAABORG 1988; EBERHARDT 1997; STARK ET AL. 1998; WILKINS & RITCHISON 1999; CORNELL LABORATORY OF ORNITHOLOGY 2002

6.10   Mobbing

Occasionally, several smaller birds dive-bomb a hawk soaring overhead or make a noisy ruckus near an owl perched in a tree. This behavior, known as mobbing, is active harassment of an animal perceived to be a threat in order to chase it away. The subject of the

Fig. 6.10. Red-tailed hawk, *Buteo jamaicensis*, being mobbed by common crows, *Corvus brachyrhynchos*.

attack is usually stationary or slow-moving, and the attackers can be a mix of several different species. The sounds generated by the birds are annoying and confusing to the predator, and they warn other potential prey of the predator's presence, thus eliminating the element of surprise. With impaired hunting efficiency, predators usually leave the area after being mobbed. Because mobbing protects their young, both by driving the threat away and by distracting it from their nests, birds engage in mobbing behavior more during the breeding season. A second advantage is that young birds recruited to the mobbing may learn better to recognize the predator threats around them. The targets of mobbing—hawks and owls especially, but also opportunistic nest predators such as crows—are dangerous, but smaller birds are usually maneuverable enough to escape. Still, mobbing is risky because of the chance of retaliation; the target is a predator, after all, so birds mob less when the predator is very dangerous or when protective cover is far away.

Cawing loudly, crows commonly mob hawks (Fig. 6.10), and owls and blackbirds mob crows. Mobbing may also be directed toward terrestrial predators such as snakes and weasels. One of the best ways of seeing an owl during daylight hours is to chance upon loud cawing in a tree, an obvious signal that something interesting and worth investigating is taking place.

REFERENCES: HARVEY & GREENWOOD 1978; SHEDD 1982; BROWN & HOOGLAND 1986; CHANDLER & ROSE 1988; EHRLICH ET AL. 1988; PETTIFOR 1990; PAVEY & SMYTH 1998; DESROCHERS ET AL. 2002

6.11 Soaring and Kettling

Given the high energetic costs of active flight, many birds take advantage of rising air currents wherever they can. Air rises where winds are deflected upward over ridges and where uneven heating of the earth's surface creates pockets of lighter, warmer air. Soaring birds spiral upward in updrafts and thermals and glide from one updraft to the next. Sometimes hawks concentrate in large numbers to soar and spiral in a column of rising heated air, forming what is known as a kettle from the effect of many birds spinning slowly as a group. Red-tailed hawks, broad-winged hawks, and turkey vultures form extensive aggregations like this within large thermals.

Soaring flight occurs when the sink rate due to gravity is offset by the climb rate due to rising air. Soaring birds have evolved a shape that reduces the sink rate; their wings are broad (see 6.2), and the birds have reduced wing loading (ratio of body weight to wing area). The climb rate for migrating hawks in thermals has been measured at up to 3 meters per second, which is countered by a sink rate of less than 2 meters per second. Birds with greater wing loading have a slower climb but a faster glide. All large birds use soaring and gliding flight

 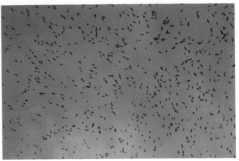

a   b

Fig. 6.11. Soaring: (a) a red-tailed hawk, *Buteo jamaicensis*; (b) a large aggregation of broad-winged hawks, *Buteo platypterus*, rising on thermals.

when flying long distances because the increase in wing loading with greater size makes flapping flight ever more costly. It is not surprising that energy efficiency is important for bats and large butterflies such as monarchs, too, which also use soaring flight patterns in rising air currents. For all these creatures, soaring flight is ultimately solar-powered.

Wing area is proportional to the square of body length, whereas weight is proportional to the cube of body length; thus, for the same body shape, wing loading (weight/wing area) is higher with a bigger bird. Weighing over 30 pounds, mute and trumpeter swans are the heaviest flying birds in North America. The lowest wing loading and slowest sink rate for any bird in the world belong not to the smallest bird, however, but to the tropical magnificent frigate bird, which has adapted a body shape for continuous soaring in trade-wind zones over oceanic waters. Because of the difference in wing loading, these birds display enormously different flight behavior, from labored fast flight to leisurely gliding.

REFERENCES: GIBO & PALLETT 1979; KERLINGER ET AL. 1985; EHRLICH ET AL. 1988; FAABORG 1988; LESHEM & YOM 1996; SPAAR 1997; WEIMERSKIRCH ET AL. 2003

6.12 V-Formations

Ducks, geese, and pelicans are often seen flying in an angled line or V-formation. Two hypotheses have been proposed for this behavior. The simpler one is that a V-formation allows

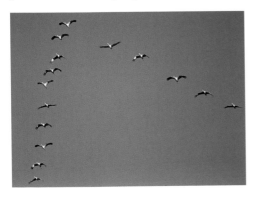

a group of large, heavy birds to communicate with each other and maintain visual contact while minimizing the chance of a collision whenever they change directions. The second hypothesis is a more interesting one, however; it claims that an energetic advantage accrues to linear flight patterns by improving aerodynamic efficiency. In flight, air rushes over a bird's curved wings, creat-

Fig. 6.12. V-formation flight in a skein of Canada geese, *Branta canadensis*.

ing lift due to higher pressure below the wings and lower pressure above. Air at the wing tips then flows upward into pockets of lower pressure, creating vortices that could provide lift to a trailing bird. The distance that we see between birds in V-formations is not one that would maximize the increase in lift, probably due to the difficulty of tracking the vortices precisely. But there is evidence of an energetic advantage because birds that follow the leader flap their wings at a lower frequency, and pelicans flying in formation have a significantly lower heart rate (a measure of energy expenditure) and glide more often compared to when they fly alone. The savings in energy increase the distance that large, heavy birds can fly.

REFERENCES: LISSAMAN & SCHOLLENBERGER 1970; BADGEROW & HAINSWORTH 1981; O'MALLEY & EVANS 1982; HAINSWORTH 1987, 1989; EHRLICH ET AL. 1988; WEIMERSKIRCH ET AL. 2001

6.13   Raptor Attacks

Hawks, eagles, and falcons have the highest visual acuity when visual images focus through the lenses of their eyes onto a part of the retina known as the deep fovea, a small region dense with receptor cells. This region is not in the middle of the retina, and with eyes that rotate little in their sockets, the birds have to turn their heads approximately 40° to the side to have images focus on the fovea and thus get the best vision. When watching a distant object, therefore, raptors tilt their heads from side to side.

But flying after prey with its head tilted to the side would cause a bird to lose aerodynamic shape and be slowed by increased drag. Their solution? Peregrine falcons pursue prey in a curved path (a closing, logarithmic spiral) so that their speed remains maximal at the same time that they use the angled vision that gives the highest acuity. And then seconds before contact, they straighten out in flight, abandon use of the fovea, and use binocular vision to home in on their target.

Fig. 6.13. Peregrine falcon, *Falco peregrinus*, in flight.

REFERENCES: FAABORG 1988; TUCKER 2000A, 2000B; TUCKER ET AL. 2000

6.14   Migration Weather

Many birds migrate southward in the fall and back northward in the spring to avoid harsh winters but still take advantage of the flush of growth, both plant and animal, that unfolds each spring in northern climes. Most waterfowl follow traditionally recognized migration corridors through the Mississippi valley and western plains and along the Atlantic and Pacific coasts, but there is great diversity in the routes followed by migrating birds. Flying long distances is energetically expensive, so birds use tailwinds to lessen the costs of flight. By knowing weather patterns, an observer can anticipate when waves of migrants will pass overhead wherever one happens to be.

Fig. 6.14. Migrating flock of snow geese, *Chen caerulescens.*

Air masses move about 600 miles each day from west to east across North America. Because the wind flows clockwise around a high-pressure (cold) cell, winds blowing toward the south are found near the leading edge of a high-pressure system; thus, in autumn, waves of birds migrate southward when cold, clear weather comes in with a weather high. Most migrants wait a day after a cold front passes, though, to avoid turbulence associated with the front itself. The reverse process takes place in the spring. Winds blowing northward occur near the leading edge of counterclockwise-spinning low-pressure systems, so, as long as heavy clouds and rain don't curtail flight, waves of migrants are found with spring warm fronts. Just as one would expect of an energy-efficient traveler, monarch butterflies migrate using the same tailwinds and weather patterns as birds.

REFERENCES: GIBO & PALLETT 1979; LINCOLN & PETERSON 1979; EHRLICH ET AL. 1988; FAABORG 1988

6.15   Migrant Returns

The news media regularly report that swallows (Fig. 6.15a) return to Capistrano, California, and buzzards (Fig. 6.15b) to Hinckley, Ohio, on a precise day each year. Redwing blackbirds (Fig. 6.15c) reappear in northern marshes in mid-March, and other birds also arrive in northern areas on or about the same yearly date. How do birds know when the calendar says they should return? Day length increases in the spring and decreases in the fall in a highly regular pattern, so the most reliable cue, the one that determines when most birds migrate, is photoperiod (day length). Birds become restless when the photoperiod reaches a critical length, and this restlessness predisposes them to begin migration at the arrival of good flying weather. Short-distance migrants may rely more on weather cues than on day length, but a long-distance migrant could not possibly be affected by the weather at its destination. Thus, photoperiod is the primary cue.

Of course, the timing of spring migration is set ultimately to achieve the best average time to begin the breeding season, and that time happens to be about March 19 for cliff swallows to return from Argentina to start rebuilding their mud nests in southern California and about March 15 for turkey vultures (buzzards) to return from southern states to nest among the rocky ledges and fields of northeastern Ohio.

REFERENCES: EHRLICH ET AL. 1988; FAABORG 1988

a

b

Fig. 6.15. Birds known for their regular spring return schedules: (a) cliff swallows, *Petrochelidon pyrrhonta*, to Capistrano; (b) turkey vultures, *Cathartes aura*, to Hinckley; (c) red-winged blackbird, *Agelaius phoeniceus*, to northern marshes.

c

6.16 Winter Irruptions

During some winters, large incursions of northern birds move from Canada down into the northern tier of states in irregular but dramatic explosions of bird numbers. Most noticeable are crossbills, evening grosbeaks, pine siskins, and redpolls (Fig. 6.16a). Irruptions of these birds are triggered by the extensive failure of seed crops in northern coniferous forests, leading the birds to move southward in search of food. Seed shortage is magnified when bird populations are high, as they may be following a year with high seed production. Because low-seed years typically follow high-seed years, the shortage is then exacerbated.

a

b

Fig. 6.16. Birds that sometimes appear during the winter in northern states: (a) common redpoll, *Carduelis flammea*; (b) snowy owl, *Nyctea scandiaca*.

Different from the irregular irruptions of seed-feeding birds is the more cyclical invasion of predatory birds such as rough-legged hawks, northern goshawks, and snowy owls (Fig. 6.16b). A three-to-five-year cycle in numbers of small rodents in Canada produces the three-to-five-year cycle in appearance of snowy owls and a few other rodent predators in northern states; the predators range more widely when their prey in the north are scarce. A nine-to-ten-year cycle in northern snowshoe hares leads to a cycle of equivalent length in the appearance of goshawks. The factors causing prey cycles are not fully understood but include differences in food availability, changes in features of the prey themselves at high and low density, and interactions with predators. Snowy owls were seen frequently during the winter of 2001–2 in New England, for example, and many were in poor condition from being stressed by a shortage of food. The birds we see at feeders and in fields each winter may be influenced strongly by what's going on in the forests and tundra of Canada.

REFERENCES: EHRLICH ET AL. 1988; SMITH & SMITH 2001

6.17   Flock Feeding

Many birds spend much of their time together in flocks (as the saying goes, "birds of a feather flock together"). There are two main advantages to remaining part of a group: feeding efficiency and predator avoidance. When food is spread out widely or in unpredictable locations, a flock can search an area more effectively than isolated individuals can. As a result, feeding in a group increases the likelihood of each bird's finding food regularly and experiencing fewer hungry days. Furthermore, young birds learn how to forage by watching older birds. Decoys in open water attract ducks, showing that some birds use the presence of others to indicate where to feed. In contrast, when food is dispersed uniformly throughout an area, birds can find the food efficiently on their own.

The second factor in favor of flock feeding is predator avoidance. With multiple sentinels, a flock is better able to detect the approach of a predator such as a falcon; being part of a group reduces the likelihood of each individual's being attacked, while warning calls from sentinels reduce the predator's probability of success. Groups may even make it hazardous for the predator to attack.

Different species that feed on similar foods, such as chickadees and tufted titmouse, sometimes feed together in mixed flocks in wintertime. Other mixed flocks occur where food is abundant, as in marshes (Fig. 6.17), and share the advantages of both foraging effectiveness and predator avoidance.

REFERENCES: FAABORG 1988; WALTHER & GOSLER 2001

Fig. 6.17.   A mixed flock of ducks and wading birds: great blue heron, *Ardea herodias*; snowy egret, *Egretta thula*; black-necked stilt, *Himantopus mexicanus*; and others.

6.18 Diet of Worms

A red-breasted American robin will stand on a freshly cut lawn in an upright, alert posture, run a few steps, stop abruptly, cock its head to one side, and then reach down to grab a worm. Constituting 20 percent of a robin's diet during the summer, earthworms are active

near the ground surface early and late each day, especially following a rain (see 10.8). At these times it seems as though the robins are heeding an imperial call to gather for feeding (many plays on words have alluded to the German assembly of 1521 that is known as the Diet of Worms). The behavior of robins when foraging suggests that they find worms from the sounds the worms make, but it's not entirely clear how they localize their prey. In addition to improving hearing, head tilting can also sharpen visual perception by focusing images on the fovea of the eye's retina, a region of closely packed light receptors that provides sharper vision (see 6.13). Early studies of robin feeding concluded that they use visual cues to find food, but subsequent research has shown that the birds can localize prey using sound alone. It benefits any forager to have a backup means of finding food, and robins can use either sensory ability; vision takes precedence, but when prey are underground, the birds are able to listen for sounds of worms moving—as surprising as that may seem—and localize their snacks that way.

Fig. 6.18. An American robin, *Turdus migratorius*, finding a worm by both sight and hearing.

REFERENCES: HEPPNER 1965; EHRLICH ET AL. 1988; MONTGOMERIE & WEATHERHEAD 1997

6.19 Caching Seeds

Nutritious and long-lasting, seeds and nuts are collected when they're abundant each fall by a number of birds to cache for eating when food is scarce during the winter and early spring. Blue jays can collect more than half the acorn crop from a stand of oaks and cache them up to a mile away; they prefer smaller acorns, which they cache singly under leaf litter (Fig. 6.19a). Each western Clark's nutcracker, a relative of the eastern blue jay, may cache 30,000 pine seeds each autumn at a distance of up to 10 miles from their source. Using their bills, nutcrackers scoop out trenches in the ground and deposit the seeds one to several at a time, covering them with soil and debris. Depending on where they've been cached, a few seeds may be forgotten and grow into new trees far from the parent plant (see 1.10), but the birds' long-term memory for recovering their caches is remarkable. Nutcrackers can remember the locations of seeds for many months at a time. Proof of their memory has been demonstrated experimentally: birds that bury seeds find their caches six times faster than other birds that are simply looking for hidden seeds.

Recovering caches is not an issue for acorn woodpeckers of western North America (Fig. 6.19b). A cooperatively breeding group of these birds stores large numbers of acorns in holes

a

b

Fig. 6.19.   Acorn-caching birds: (a) blue jay, *Cyanocitta cristata*; (b) acorn woodpecker, *Melanerpes formicivorus*.

drilled in the bark of their granary trees, often oaks and sycamores, which they defend against other birds. They can store up to 50,000 acorns in a single dead tree. The amount and quality of storage sites for their acorns determine where the birds live, and their cached acorns provide them with food during the winter months.

REFERENCES: DARLEY-HILL & JOHNSON 1981; KOENIG 1981; VANDER WALL 1982; SHETTLEWORTH 1983; MUMME & DE QUEIROZ 1985; EHRLICH ET AL. 1988; TOMBACK & LINHART 1990; BALDA & KAMIL 1992; BEDNEKOFF ET AL. 1997; KOENIG & HAYDOCK 1999

6.20   Owl Pellets

A feeding owl engulfs its prey whole and then regurgitates undigested material in compact pellets. Each pellet usually represents the leftovers from a single meal. Owls commonly eat rodents such as field mice, so most pellets contain fur and small bones, but feathers indicate bird prey, while exoskeletons indicate insects. The size of the pellet correlates with the size of the owl, and a pellet from a large bird such as a snowy owl may contain the bones of eight or nine different victims: a multicourse meal. Owl pellets accumulate underneath where the owls roost, and in dry climates the pellets can last for months. Gulls, herons, and some other birds occasionally regurgitate pellets, too, but owls do so regularly.

If an owl pellet is taken apart, either dry or softened in warm water, one may see the remains of that meal's victim; the teeth, especially, and other bones can be used to identify

Fig. 6.20.   Pellet collection: (upper four) eastern screech owl, *Otus asio*; (leftmost) great horned owl, *Bubo virginianus*; (lower two) long-eared owl, *Asio otus*; (large one on the right containing turtle eggshells) great blue heron, *Ardea herodias*. The heron pellet shows that birds other than owls can also produce pellets.

the species of prey. About half of the prey's bones can be recovered from a pellet, usually including the jaws and femurs but rarely the skull, which is usually crushed. By their size and shape, the pellets also indicate which species of owls were feeding nearby.

REFERENCES: DODSON & WEXLAR 1979; EHRLICH ET AL. 1988

6.21　Active Feeders

Finding small invertebrate prey in the mud of shallow waters is not easy, but some birds have found ways to improve the odds, even when it makes them perform strange-looking behaviors. Phalaropes are small shorebirds that use thin bills to feed on tiny food items in the water. They swim quickly in tight circles to concentrate food that they stir up from the bottom (Fig. 6.21a). They are the spinning tops of the bird world; their characteristic spinning motion reminds one of a dog chasing its tail.

Snowy egrets appear to wear stylish slippers, having bright yellow feet that contrast strongly with their black legs (Fig. 6.21b). They are among the most active herons, shuffling their gaudy feet over the soft sediments to surprise their prey and cause movement. Phalaropes and snowy egrets associate with several other bird species that stir up prey, including other wading birds such as glossy ibis and American avocets, as well as cormorants and some ducks. Glossy ibis feed by probing, not looking, for prey, which makes them good partners for the visually feeding snowy egrets. Active feeders benefit from the disturbances created within mixed-species groups.

REFERENCES: ERWIN 1983; EHRLICH ET AL. 1988; FAABORG 1988

Fig. 6.21. Active feeders: (a) red-necked phalarope, *Phalaropus lobatus*, spinning in the water; (b) snowy egret, *Egretta thula*, shuffling its yellow feet while feeding.

6.22   Cold Feet

Birds can lose much of their body heat to the environment around them from the warm blood that flows through their thin legs. Legs must be well vascularized so that food and oxygen can be supplied to the leg muscles, but all legs must remain flexible and mobile; they cannot be encumbered with overly thick insulation. The solution for cold-climate-dwelling ptarmigans is to have thick feathers on their legs and feet. Not only are feathered feet insulated, but they also serve as built-in snowshoes for travel across northern landscapes.

The challenge of retaining body heat is even greater in wading birds, which often stand in icy water. One way for them to conserve heat when at rest is to stand on one leg and hold the other against the warm body. Another is to constrict surface veins so that blood is shunted toward the inside. But an unseen mechanism is equally important. Heat loss is reduced when the major artery and vein of the leg are adjacent to each other; then the returning cold venous blood is warmed by the outflowing arterial blood, and the arterial blood is cooler when it reaches the feet. The result is a thermal gradient down the leg. With cooler blood at the extremities, the temperature difference between the feet and the outside environment is reduced, so less heat is lost. Wading birds such as herons also have an interlaced network of arteries and veins in the thigh, called a rete, that increases the amount of heat exchanged between warm arterial blood and cool venous blood. This mechanism of countercurrent heat exchange is found not just in the legs of wading birds but also in the legs of numerous mammals and even the tails of beavers and flippers of whales.

REFERENCES: EHRLICH ET AL. 1988; FAABORG 1988; RANDALL ET AL. 1997; SMITH & SMITH 2001

b

Fig. 6.22.   Cold feet: (a) willow ptarmigan, *Lagopus lagopus*; (b) a long-billed curlew, *Numenius americanus*, standing in the water on one foot.

a

7. INSECTS

The tremendous diversity of insects makes possible so many observable patterns that it would take multiple lifetimes to learn them all. This chapter describes a few general features of insects, mating and molting in particular, along with a sample of observations of specific groups. Butterflies and moths are better represented than other insects on these pages because of their attractiveness, ease of observation, and popularity; like most people, I'm attracted to butterflies. The discussions of these insects illustrate what could be described with many of the other insect groups, too, including a little anatomy, physiology, behavior, and ecology.

For additional observations having to do with insects, refer to:

7.1 Insect Mating

Reproduction is the primary function of the adult stage in insects, with growth allocated to juveniles. As a result, adult-stage insects are often seen during the spring and summer engaged in mating activities. Males use scents, elaborate visual displays, and sometimes even sounds (as with crickets) to court females, but what we see most often are the couplings that result from such courtship. While mating, a pair may fly away to escape the attention of competing males, and their flight makes them visible to us. Tandem flights of damselflies are common near streams; male wasps carry females to less conspicuous locations; paired butterflies often flutter from one plant to another when disturbed, with an active flier carrying a quiescent mate (males fly in some species and females in others); and coupled midges zip away to escape the frenzy of swarming males. Sometimes pairs remain coupled for days; the insect record for remaining mated is seventy-nine days for a walking stick insect, which is far longer than needed for the transfer of sperm.

Females of many species are able to mate multiple times and store sperm, so after mating, males may act in one or more ways to ensure their paternity. Some male flies and beetles hold on to or perch over their mates to repel other males, sometimes by physically wrestling with the intruders. Male water striders ride on the backs of their mates to provide protection, and male damselflies guard females that lay their eggs within the males' territories. In certain species of butterflies, males leave mating plugs over the females' genitalia as chastity belts to prevent remating by the females. Much of the activity of adult insects has to do with reproduction in one form or another, and, as a result, males and females are often seen closely associated.

REFERENCES: THORNHILL & ALCOCK 1983; RIDLEY 1989; ROMOSER & STOFFOLANO 1994

a   b

Fig. 7.1. Mating insects: (a) greenish blue butterflies, *Plebejus saepiolus*; (b) forktail damselflies, *Ischnura ramburii*.

7.2 Insect Swarms

During summer days near wetlands, millions of midges, gnats, and mosquitoes emerge from their aquatic juvenile stages and rise to form vibrant, hovering clouds. These swarms serve

Fig. 7.2. An evening swarm of midges (family Chironomidae) (California).

an important purpose: to allow males and females to find each other. Because many of these insects live for only a day or two, mating activity may be frenzied. Swarms of newly emerged adult insects reappear consistently at the same places and same times of day, and in these swarms it's an insect orgy. Individuals in a swarm are not stationary; they seem to dance up and down and side to side. Most members of a swarm are males, and even though not all will find a mate, their success rate is higher in an aggregation than elsewhere alone. A female finds a partner as soon as she enters a swarm, and the pair then departs to mate elsewhere.

People often are annoyed by these clouds, but swarms are commonly of nonbiting midges and provide more entertainment than hazard. Often the swarms are oriented with respect to environmental markers such as trees or sunlit patches of ground, where they hover unless blown by breezes. Emergence of swarming insects can be highly synchronized; using environmental cues of warmth, day length, and light level, as well as their own aggregation scents, members of the same species appear almost simultaneously, often in clouds 2 to 20 feet above the ground at sunrise or sunset. Even heavy feeding by birds, bats, and dragonflies barely dents their numbers. Insects aggregate for other reasons, too, but mating swarms of small insects, particularly fly relatives, are a conspicuous summertime sight.

REFERENCES: CHAPMAN 1982; STOKES 1983; TAYLOR 1991; ROMOSER & STOFFOLANO 1994

7.3   Mate Finding

The highest priority for a male butterfly is to find a receptive mate, and to do so, males search for females using either of two strategies. When resources are concentrated—host plants for egg laying or floral nectar for adult feeding—males defend locations near where females are likely to travel. Males perch in their territories for hours at a time, flying up to inspect any insect that passes nearby. They select resting sites with unobstructed views and often return to preferred perches. Because insect eyesight does not resolve detail at much distance, males will even fly at and investigate a passing human. It's a surprising feeling to walk along a forested trail and find oneself being checked out by a lonely butterfly! Species

a   b

Fig. 7.3. Two strategies of male butterflies for mate finding: (a) perched Empress Leilia butterfly, *Asterocampa leila*; (b) patrolling eastern tiger swallowtail, *Papilio glaucus*.

vary in how long individual males remain on their perches and how strongly they defend these encounter sites.

The alternative strategy for males is to patrol paths or edges where females travel. Tiger swallowtails (Fig. 7.3b) illustrate this behavior as they fly along residential streets, often repeating the same route. If host plants and nectar sources don't occur in localized concentrations, or if there are no other places where females are likely to be found, then patrolling is the dominant strategy. The private lives of insects around us are every bit as interesting and complex as our own.

REFERENCES: SCOTT 1975; BREWER & WINTER 1986; DENNIS & SHREEVE 1988; RUTOWSKI 1991; VAN DYCK ET AL. 1997

7.4   Hilltopping

With insects for whom it's not easy to find an individual of the opposite sex, hilltops sometimes serve as singles bars, excellent places to look for and pick up a mate. Because of the limits of vision in insect compound eyes—which are excellent for detecting movement but cannot focus farther than a few feet away—male and female insects simply may not see each

other in the usual places they fly. As a result, individuals of widely dispersed species and those whose host plants are small and occur at low density improve their chances of finding a mate if everyone flies uphill to local high points, an instinctive behavior that increases their density on hilltops.

Fig. 7.4. Hilltopping male pipevine swallowtail, *Battus philenor* (Arizona).

Especially in open areas of southern and western North America, hilltopping is part of the mating strategy of many wasps, bees, flies, beetles, and butterflies, including anise and pipevine swallowtails (Fig. 7.4), checkered and western whites, white admirals and red-spotted purples, and great purple hairstreaks. The insects that congregate on hilltops are mostly males; they patrol the summits or wait on selected perches, chasing intruders of all kinds, especially other males of their own species. The earliest arrivals choose the highest, most preferred sites on the hilltops, which they defend. Unmated females fly up a hill and then depart after mating; consequently, males remain longer and in higher numbers on hill-tops than do females. The behavior of males on hilltops can shift from territorial perching to active patrolling as the number of competing males increases.

Different species are active on hilltops at different times of day, although it is not known why they spread themselves out this way. It may be simply to avoid the distractions of having too many other flying insects to chase and investigate. On sunny spring or summer days, you can catch glimpses of the social lives of a number of these insects by looking for rendezvous points on hills where they gather.

REFERENCES: SHIELDS 1967; BREWER & WINTER 1986; ALCOCK 1987; RUTOWSKI ET AL 1989; RUTOWSKI & KEMP 2002

7.5   Ascending Flight

Occasionally two or more butterflies flutter around each other in ascending spiral flight, a behavior that derives from mate seeking. In the yellow butterflies known as sulphurs, which are often visible flying over agricultural fields, upward flight takes place when a male pursues a female who rejects him. When the butterflies first encounter each other, an unwilling female signals a lack of readiness to mate by her posture on the ground or by short avoidance flights. But if a male persists in courting her, she flies upward; the more persistent the male and the more unreceptive the female, the higher they spiral. Eventually, a rejected male flies straight back down to the vegetation while the female returns more slowly to her time-consuming search for places to lay her eggs.

Fig. 7.5.   The ascending flight of interacting clouded sulphur butterflies, *Colias philodice*.

Ascending flight also occurs among pairs of males, typically among numerous species of territorial butterflies that chase intruders in their territories. The upward chases may become actual competition for the territory, too, with the winner—most often the resident—being the male that flies the longest. Sometimes the pair may rise so high that they are hardly visible. Whichever individuals are involved, ascending spiral flights in butterflies reveal intense mating activity.

REFERENCES: RUTOWSKI 1978; STUTT & WILLMER 1998; SCHAPPERT 2000

7.6 Puddle Clubs

Some butterflies will astonish you by where they feed. People usually associate butterflies with flowers, and most do sip regularly on flower nectar, a high-energy drink that fuels their active flight. Other butterflies rarely if ever visit flowers and prefer to feed instead on tree sap and rotting fruit. In addition to these sources, many also land on moist sand or mud to imbibe water with whatever is dissolved in it, a behavior known as puddling. Especially when the day is hot and sunny but moisture is available near streams or in puddles remaining from previous rain, clusters of butterflies—puddle clubs—gather at the wet spots, uncoil their proboscises (mouth parts), and feed (Fig. 7.6a). Wet soil isn't their only source; they'll

Fig. 7.6. Puddle clubs of butterflies: (a) Palamedes swallowtails, *Papilio palamedes*, on mud (South Carolina); (b) white admiral butterflies, *Limenitis arthemis arthemis*, on a roadkill toad (New York); (c) Colorado alpines, *Erebia callias*, on coyote scat (Wyoming); (d) arctic blue butterflies, *Agriades glandon*, on moist wood (Wyoming).

c

d

also sip from carrion (Fig. 7.6b), animal excrement (Fig. 7.6c), sweat-soaked clothing, campfires, and urinals. Puddling is more than drinking, though; when puddling, butterflies release surplus fluid from the anus.

Experimenters have shown that sodium is the primary benefit to puddling butterflies and moths, although amino acids and other compounds may also be consumed. All animals require sodium for normal physiological functions, but plants are richer in potassium than in sodium, so sodium is often in short supply for herbivores (see 5.11). Puddle clubs are conspicuous displays of animals foraging for sodium. Evaporation at the surface concentrates sodium ions from these different sources, making them prime feeding spots. But another part of the story is that the individuals doing most of the puddling are males. It has been shown in one moth species that the sodium accumulated from puddling is passed on, along with sperm, to a female at mating in a nuptial gift, and she uses the male-provided sodium to provision her eggs. She focuses on laying her eggs; he helps by providing nutrients. It's possible that on the rare occasions when females puddle, they're obtaining nitrogen as much as they are sodium to further their egg production. But puddle clubs are generally stag parties, through which males help provide for their own offspring.

REFERENCES: ARMS ET AL. 1974; SMEDLEY & EISNER 1995, 1996; SCHAPPERT 2002; SCRIBER 2002

7.7 Monarch Migration

Monarch butterflies are unique in their life history and migratory patterns. Having originated in the tropics, monarchs cannot tolerate freezing winters; consequently, the low temperatures (below 60°F) and shortened day lengths of fall spur them to avoid the oncoming northern winter by migrating southward. Using the same tailwinds and soaring flight as migrating birds (see 6.11), millions of monarchs fly southward at a rate of about 50 miles per day to pass the winter in cool but above-freezing temperatures. Monarchs throughout eastern North America and the Great Plains fly to fir forests in the mountains of central Mexico, whereas those west of the Rocky Mountains fly to eucalyptus and pine groves in a series of stops along the California coast (e.g., around Monterey). In all overwintering sites, they gather in impressively dense aggregations. While migrating a distance of several thousand miles, most of the butterflies build their fat reserves for the coming winter by taking in nectar en route. Along the way, particularly during cold and windy weather, they cluster for the night in roost trees. Some populations of monarchs remain year round in southern Florida and California, and despite the separation created by the Rocky Mountains, a little mixing does occur between the eastern and western butterflies.

Monarchs move northward each spring to take advantage of the spring emergence of milkweeds, their food plants, throughout North America. In February and March, masses of monarchs become active, mate, and fly northward to reoccupy their summer habitats. East of the Rockies the initial migrants reproduce in the southern tier of states, and their offspring continue the migration

Fig. 7.7. Overwintering aggregation of monarch butterflies, *Danaus plexippus* (California).

by moving farther northward. One of the most remarkable features of monarch migration is that, unlike the migratory patterns of birds, a subsequent generation returns to northern states the following year; northern returners are several generations later than those that had flown south.

Monarchs are exceptional butterflies. They live as adults for two to five weeks during the summer and, with hormonal control delaying reproduction and aging, for six months or more during the cold of winter. Then they migrate thousands of miles, with the full migration route completed by different generations. Monarch migration is a fantastic phenomenon not yet fully understood but threatened by loss of overwintering habitat in Mexico.

REFERENCES: STOKES 1983; ACKERY & VANE-WRIGHT 1984; STOKES ET AL. 1991; GIBO & MCCURDY 1993; BROWER 1995; PYLE 1999; HERMAN & TATAR 2001

7.8   First Butterflies

Butterflies disappear in northern regions when winter settles in, so the first butterflies that emerge each spring are distinct signals of a change in seasons. The first ones we see appear worn because they've endured the long winter while hidden in protected bark crevices, woodpiles, and outbuildings. Mourning cloaks (Fig. 7.8a), commas, and tortoiseshells pass the winter as adults. The first sunny spring days above 50° or 60°F call them forth, and on such days, you may see them basking on sunlit low branches or on the ground. Few flowers are open that early, but these large butterflies aren't nectar feeders even during the height of summer; they feed mostly on sap that flows from broken tree branches. The wings of early-appearing butterflies are pale because of loss of scales and the fading of pigments through the fall and winter months; the wings are usually tattered as well from long use. Cold spring days return them to a torpid state. Because they endure through winter and summer, mourning cloaks may live as long as ten months as adults, making them among North America's longest-lived butterflies, rivaled only by monarchs. For butterflies with a single generation per year, the full life span from egg to egg is usually a year, but with a few exceptions, the adult stage lasts only a week or two (the full life span is much less for those with multiple generations per year).

a

b

Fig. 7.8.   The first butterflies to appear each spring in northern latitudes. (a) mourning cloak, *Nymphalis antiopa*, which overwinters as an adult; (b) spring azure, *Celastrina ladon*.

As temperatures rise with the arrival of spring, the first fresh, newly emergent butterflies begin to appear, including small blue spring azures (Fig. 7.8b) and black-dotted cabbage whites. These species, smaller and unable to withstand the harsh conditions of winter as adults, overwinter as pupae and are ready to emerge and fly when the days have warmed sufficiently. Warmth calls forth flowers, too, and later-appearing butterflies feed more on nectar. Large, worn butterflies and smaller, glistening new ones each signal a stage in the gradual unfolding of spring.

REFERENCE: OPLER & KRIZEK 1984

7.9   Nymphs and Larvae

Caterpillars don't look anything like what they eventually turn into, but newly hatched grasshoppers are easily recognizable as the grasshoppers they are, just smaller. As insects develop from the egg to the adult stage, they undergo a process of metamorphosis, which is literally a change in form. Although young insects range widely in how closely they resemble the adult form, insect species are generally grouped according to two developmental patterns. In those with simple metamorphosis, such as grasshoppers (Fig. 7.9a), the immatures lack fully developed wings and reproductive structures but resemble the adult form, and each time they shed their exoskeleton, their developing wings become larger and more apparent. Young of this type are usually called nymphs. In contrast, insects with complete metamorphosis, such as flies, bees, and butterflies, go through a stage of dramatic change in shape that requires two molts: one to a resting stage, the pupa, in which a dramatic internal transformation takes place, with wings developing inside the pupal case; and a second molt to produce the emerging adult. An immature of a species that undergoes complete metamorphosis (Fig. 7.9b) is called a larva.

Nymphs live and eat very much like their adult forms, but complete metamorphosis allows different stages of the same species to live very different lives; just think of caterpillars as opposed to butterflies and maggots as opposed to adult flies. Dragonflies, mayflies, and stoneflies are intermediate between the two extremes: they undergo simple metamorphosis, but their young are aquatic, while the adults are aerial and terrestrial. Adaptation to different environments has left the young of these insects less similar to their adults than is usual in most cases of simple metamorphosis.

REFERENCE: ROMOSER & STOFFOLANO 1994

a   b

Fig. 7.9.   Juvenile insects: (a) the nymph of a grasshopper (unidentified species); (b) the larva (caterpillar) of a black swallowtail, *Papilio polyxenes*.

7.10   Inchworms

The twiglike caterpillars known as inchworms are distinctive because of their looping gait. Most caterpillars have two distinct sets of legs: three pairs of true legs near the front (on the thorax) of their cylindrical bodies and five pairs of prolegs in the middle and on the end. The prolegs are fleshy, missing the full skeletal structure of the true legs, and disappear in the adult stage. Missing the middle three pairs of prolegs from their elongate bodies, inchworms move by clasping a twig with their thoracic legs at the front end, releasing the two pairs of prolegs (all they have) and bringing the rear end forward to grasp the twig again, and then releasing the thoracic legs and extending the body forward. This behavior creates an upwardly directed loop in their elongate bodies alternating with a straightened shape as they move. When looped, they resemble the uppercase Greek letter omega, Ω (Fig. 7.10a). They can move surprisingly quickly this way.

These caterpillars metamorphose into small to medium-sized adult moths that, like butterflies, have slender bodies and broad wings. Inchworms are also known as geometers (from the Greek for "distance-measurer"), and the distance they cover in a single loop depends on the size of the caterpillar. Some inchworms escape predators by mimicking twigs, which they do by grasping the stem with their rear prolegs and straightening their bodies upward at an angle (Fig. 7.10b). With their narrow cylindrical shape, inchworms are preadapted to escape predators by looking like twigs, needles, and catkins (which are hanging strands of flowers like those in birches and willows). One inchworm in Hawaii is the only known caterpillar predator; from a twig-mimic pose, it can twist rapidly to grasp a nearby fly.

REFERENCES: BREWER & WINTER 1986; WAGNER ET AL. 1997

a

b

Fig. 7.10.   Inchworms (moth family Geometridae):
(a) large maple spanworm, *Prochoerodes transversata*;
(b) an unidentified inchworm.

7.11   Cocoons and Chrysalids

Many people think that moths emerge from cocoons and butterflies emerge from chrysalids. Actually, all caterpillars of butterflies and moths pass through a resting stage, a pupa, in the process of metamorphosing into adults, and the pupal case forms after the final caterpillar skin is shed. Pupae are vulnerable, so camouflage and a hard covering increase their survival.

Most moth caterpillars use modified salivary glands to spin a silken cocoon, and some add larval hairs, excrement, plant material, or other environmental debris to the silk. Others make tents by tying leaf edges together, while sphinx moth caterpillars burrow into the soil to form chambers hidden from view. Whatever the form of the cocoon, a pupa rests inside it. The largest cocoons in North America, produced by cecropia moths, have an insulative layer between inner and outer walls (Fig. 7.11a). In contrast, butterflies produce naked pupae, also known as chrysalids, that are attached to plant stems and hang in some species (Fig. 7.11b) and are held upright by a silken girdle in others (Fig. 7.11c). A few butterflies spin a loose silken cocoon in an underground chamber.

Pupae appear quiescent, but astonishing transformations take place inside as old tissues break down and new tissues develop. Masses of embryonic cells, known as imaginal discs,

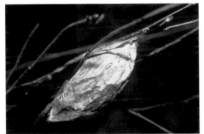

a

b

c

Fig. 7.11.   (a) The cocoon of a cecropia moth, *Hyalophora cecropia*; (b) the pendant pupa of Gillett's checkerspot, *Euphydryas gillettii*; (c) the upright pupa of black swallowtail, *Papilio polyxenes*. The pupae of butterflies are also known as chrysalids.

inside a caterpillar grow and differentiate into adult structures during the pupal stage. You can see the wing pads, antennas, mouthparts, and legs through the outer shell of well-developed pupae. Aided at the right time by muscular contraction, uptake of air at the time of emergence, and enzymatic softening, the new adult insect induces a split in the pupal case and crawls out. The timing of emergence may depend on climatic conditions rather than occur automatically after a set time; the longest delay known for a moth before emergence from its pupa is thirty years. After the resting stage, the seeming magic of metamorphosis produces another winged adult.

REFERENCES: COVELL 1984; DOUGLAS 1986; ROMOSER & STOFFOLANO 1994; POWELL 2001

7.12   Shed Skins

It can be eerie to find dead, hollow insects perched on plant stems, but these are just shed skins. The skin is a hardened external skeleton (exoskeleton) that provides protection, water repellency, and a site of attachment for leg and wing muscles used for movement. This body design may seem restrictive, but a strong, flexible exoskeleton is excellent for small animals such as insects. The main limitation is that to increase in size, an insect must shed its old skin and grow a new, larger one. And that's just what they do.

With the time of molting under hormonal control, juvenile insects shed their skins a standard number of times (the stages between molts are known as instars), leaving the old exoskeletons (also known as exuviae) behind in a set of different sizes, just like a nested set of Russian dolls. The process begins with some digestion of the old covering and splitting along lines of weakness. The rest of the old skin then splits off, sometimes in pieces, leaving a wrinkled new skin underneath that stretches to a larger size before it dries. The outer skin or cuticle is made of the polysaccharide chitin along with some proteins and waxes, and it hardens when cross-linkages form between protein molecules—exactly what takes place when leather is tanned. The largest and most noticeable old skins are those from the final molt, left behind when the insect turns into a fully formed adult. These ghostly reminders—seen often during cicada appearances or after dragonfly and mayfly emergences from water—are waste products that mark the transition of an insect to the next stage of its life.

REFERENCES: BORROR ET AL. 1989; ROMOSER & STOFFOLANO 1994

b

Fig. 7.12.   Shed insect exoskeletons: (a) cicada (unidentified species), showing both the shed skin and the newly emerged adult; (b) a stonefly (unidentified species).

a

7.13   Caterpillar Webs

Conspicuous silken webs spun by tent caterpillars are noticeable on North American trees and shrubs each spring. Like many other animals, tent caterpillars grow best when warmth accelerates their development. They can bask in the sun to warm up or move under a leaf when too hot, but at night and under overcast conditions, they cluster on silken carpets within their webs, where heat produced by their activity raises the temperature several degrees over that of external air. Without the tents, their development couldn't begin as early in spring and would take longer to complete; the quality of their food supply, which is more nutritious early in the spring, would decline; and they would be exposed for a longer time to natural enemies such as parasitic wasps and predatory bugs. Caterpillars that forage away from their tents leave scent marks as trails to follow back to safety. Western tent caterpillars show another thermal response: eggs and tents are found predominantly on south-facing, sun-exposed branches.

The caterpillars of some butterflies and other moths live in communal webs, too. For most, group living provides protection from parasitic wasps that lay their eggs on or inside the caterpillars, an action with fatal consequences. When groups are too small, the newly

a

b

c

Fig. 7.13.   Caterpillar webs: (a) fall webworm, *Hyphantria cunea*, on pin cherry, *Prunus pensylvanica*; (b) brown-tail moth, *Euproctis chrysorrhoea*, on shadbush, *Amelanchier* sp.; (c) Baltimore checkerspot, *Euphydryas phaeton*, on turtlehead, *Chelone glabra*. The last web also shows a wasp parasitoid, *Benjaminia* sp., attacking the caterpillars.

hatched caterpillars are unable to weave a large enough web to be protected. Large groups, on the other hand, conspicuously attract wasps, so an intermediate group size is just right for protection.

REFERENCES: STAMP 1981; CASEY ET AL. 1988; JOOS ET AL. 1988; FITZGERALD 1995; GREEN ET AL. 1998; RUF & FIEDLER 2000

7.14   Banded Woolly Bears

Among the best-known caterpillars because of their autumnal movement in search of over-wintering sites, banded woolly bears (woolly worms) are covered with bristly hairs that are

hardly wool-like but display an orange-brown band between black ends. They are the caterpillars of the Isabella tiger moth, a fairly plain yellowish moth 2 to 2.5 inches across. Woolly bears star in a common myth: the narrower the brown band, the harsher the upcoming winter. Some people also think that when the black band is wider at the head end than at the tail, the beginning of winter will be harsher than winter's end. Despite variation in the bands—some caterpillars are entirely brown, while others are entirely black—the color bands have no correlation to the harshness of the coming winter. They may, however, correlate to the conditions of caterpillar growth, crowding and food abundance in particular, and thus provide some link to recent summer weather. The youngest and smallest caterpillars are dark and add brown hairs as they grow, so the width of the brown band depends in part on their overall size. Some specialists think that a wide brown band results from development in dry conditions. Environmental influence is to be expected; caterpillars of most species change in appearance with each molt, and their color is influenced by local conditions. For example, both monarch and swallowtail caterpillars are darker when reared in a colder environment, and some hawkmoth caterpillars change color depending on their food plants. Alas, despite limited effects of past weather on their color pattern, woolly bears are no better than their human observers in predicting future weather.

Fig. 7.14.   A fall woolly bear, caterpillar of the Isabella tiger moth, *Pyrrharctia isabella.*

REFERENCES: BERENBAUM 1989; FINK 1995; *OLD FARMER'S ALMANAC* 1998; BARNES 1999; HAZEL 2002; SOLENSKY & LARKIN 2003

7.15   Moths and Lights

Moths at night are attracted to lights, a behavior that is only partially understood. All animals orient to features of their environment, so it is not surprising that most moths respond to lights because moonlight is a primary guide for movement at night.

Fig. 7.15. Polyphemus moths, *Antheraea polyphemus*, attracted to a light.

Some moths appear to spiral in toward light sources. One hypothesis for this behavior is that they fly at a constant angle to the light of the moon, and when that "moon" turns out to be a nearby lightbulb, flight at a constant angle leads them to spiral in toward the source. Other moths appear to fly straight toward lights, and a few may be attracted as much to the hum of the light source as to the light itself. Whatever the pattern of their flight, when moths reach the light, it is bright enough to become more of a "sun" from their perspective than a "moon," so they are apt to settle down in the brightness, just as they would during the daytime. Moths near bright lights may also suffer sensory overload and become trapped. Some workers have suggested that the increase in outdoor lighting in urban areas might be affecting this relationship, with moths evolving less responsiveness to lights.

The strength of the attraction depends on the color of the light. All moths have visual pigments that provide perception of short, ultraviolet wavelengths—especially attractive to them and beyond what humans can see—but they see less well at the long-wavelength, red end of the spectrum. You might be able to watch a moth without disturbing it if you use a red light.

REFERENCES: FRANK 1988; ADAMS 1997; HIMMELMAN 2002; BRISCOE ET AL. 2003

7.16   Firefly Flashes

Appearing near dusk on summer evenings, fireflies produce a series of regular flashes as they float over lawns and meadows. The flashes we see are mostly those of amorous males advertising their presence and availability to females. Occasionally, females perched on the vegetation flash back in reply, and after signaling back and forth in a species-specific pattern, a pair finds each other, turns off the lights, and stays together for much of the night. So that they can recognize the right mates, each species of firefly produces nerve-controlled flashes that are specific in color, duration of pulse, and pulse frequency (the flash rates of all fireflies slow a little at lower air temperatures). The flight patterns of the insects (they are actually beetles) and the times during the evening they fly are also distinctive, so different flash patterns in the same area indicate the presence of more than one species. It is one of the unexpected twists of nature that females of one firefly (genus *Photuris*) mimic the flash patterns of other species (genus *Photinus*) to attract males and eat them (see 4.17). These femmes

Fig. 7.16. Fireflies: (a) time-lapse image of fireflies flashing over a field in the evening; (b) a flashing individual (unidentified species).

a

b

fatales gain not only food but also their prey's protective chemicals, which in turn make the predatory fireflies distasteful to their own bird and spider predators.

Found in specialized photocyte cells within luminescent lantern organs in their abdomens, molecules of the protein luciferin become energized when acted upon by the enzyme luciferase in the presence of oxygen and chemical energy from molecules of ATP, the cell's energy currency. The energized luciferin then emits light of surprising intensity for a cold, chemical process. Larvae of fireflies and their relatives, known as glowworms, luminesce for protection from toads and birds, which find them distasteful, an entirely different function from the mate-attracting luminescence of adults (see 4.4). Firefly activity is greatest on warm, moonless summer nights in moist areas of the eastern, southern, and midwestern United States, but fireflies are declining in environments with greater photopollution and loss of fields.

REFERENCES: LLOYD 1966, 1969; STOKES 1983; TWEIT 1999; DECOCK & MATTHYSEN 2001; LEWIS 2001; LEWIS & LLOYD 2003

7.17 Aphid Feeding

Aphids use their sharp, sucking mouthparts (stylets) to penetrate a plant, puncture the phloem, and feed from the sugary solution within. Because phloem sap is under pressure, it flows readily into and through the aphids, resulting in droplets of sugary "honeydew" secretions formed at their rear ends. Aphids sometimes have less effect on the plants than do leaf-chewing and xylem-feeding insects, but an infestation of aphids can reduce plant growth by removing sap, altering its amino

Fig. 7.17. Heavy aphid (unidentified species) feeding on fireweed, *Epilobium angustifolium*, showing reduced vigor of the attacked flower buds, with ants patrolling the aphid aggregation.

acid composition, clogging the phloem, adding water stress, and introducing pathogenic viruses. Sometimes aphids alter growth of the plant so much as to form a gall (see 3.5) in which the aphids live and reproduce, but more often the result of a high density of aphids is just a recognizably smaller plant part. For protection, some aphids conceal themselves under masses of a white "wool" that they secrete.

Other insects take advantage of aphid clusters. Aphids are easy prey for the larvae of ladybird beetles (ladybugs), which are sold to gardeners for aphid control. Sometimes ants have a mutually beneficial interaction with these little plant feeders; patrolling aphid-infested plants, ants deter potential aphid predators while feeding on aphid honeydew secretions. Aphid clusters on a plant indicate the likelihood of ant presence and reduced plant growth.

REFERENCES: MEYER 1993; ROMOSER & STOFFOLANO 1994; RIEDELL & KIECKHEFER 1995; RAVEN ET AL. 1999

7.18 Anthills

Ants live nearly everywhere, so they and the mounds of soil they pile up from digging their underground nests are familiar to everyone. Anthills range from volcano-shaped craters to formless mounds along sidewalks and in lawns, fields, and deserts. Some of the hills in these antscapes may last for a hundred years or more. As highly social insects that live mostly below the ground, where temperature and humidity are moderated, ants dig out tunnels and chambers for their nests and transport the excavated soil to the surface. If you look closely, you'll see that the material brought upward is granular; anthills are made up of coarser, sandier material than the surrounding soil. These particles give anthills a soft quality because their soil is looser and lighter than the substrate. In digging their nests, ants transport soil particles to the surface either in their mouths or held loosely under their chins. Complex

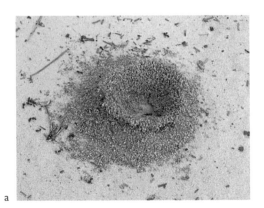

a

b

c

Fig. 7.18. Ant hills (unidentified species): (a) small crater; (b) large mound of a prairie ant; (c) ant trails.

underground chambers are used for wastes, nurseries, and simply resting. Radiating away from the nests are major trunk trails, kept clear to serve heavy ant traffic.

Some species of ants are distinguished by the kinds of hills they build. Harvester ants scatter plant debris away from a cleared zone around the nest entrance. Fire ants build loose mounds penetrated by numerous holes. Pavement ants pile up soil along cracks in sidewalks, and other ants create volcano-shaped cones with a single entrance in the middle. Some ants decorate the surfaces with small rocks, pieces of charcoal, and plant material to absorb solar energy and warm the nest; in fact, occasional garnets or pieces of fossils in the decoration zones of western anthills tell you that more of these items may be found under the surface. There can be treasures in anthills.

REFERENCES: HOLLDOBLER & WILSON 1990; LEWIS ET AL. 1991; HULUGALLE 1995; ARCHBOLD BIOLOGICAL STATION 2000

7.19   Velvet Ants

In drier regions of North America, you'll sometimes encounter what looks like a brightly colored, densely hairy ant scurrying across the sandy soil. The bold black and red or yellow

patterns on the velvety exterior give a strong warning not to touch, for it is actually not an ant but a solitary wasp that possesses a long, powerful stinger, which it can use repeatedly. Females lack wings and are active during the day, which is why they are seen running around on the ground. They resemble ants by their form and coloration and spend much of their time looking for the underground larvae and pupae of other insects on which to lay their eggs. The sting is reported to be so painful that one large species of velvet ant is known as the cow killer, surely something to avoid. With wings but without stingers, males appear to be a completely different kind of insect. Ranging up to an inch in length, velvet ants feed mostly on nectar as adults and are not aggressive unless harassed. But even their powerful sting doesn't keep all potential predators at bay: horned lizards are able to eat velvet ants.

Fig. 7.19.   Red velvet ant, the cowkiller *Dasymutilla occidentalis.*

REFERENCES: MANLEY & SHERBROOKE 2001; *DESERT USA* 2002

7.20   Wasp Nests

Few things repel people as quickly as a nest swarming actively with wasps. Although many wasps nest primarily underground, some species form visibly conspicuous nests. The most impressive by far are the gray, football-shaped, paper-encased nests made by hornets (which are kinds of wasps) and suspended at heights from 3 to 30 feet on trees or buildings (Fig. 7.20a).

With a single opening to defend, these nests grow gradually larger, housing thousands of hornets with several tiers of combs, all surrounded by several layers of flaky, pastry-like paper. Made of long wood fibers, the paper is tough, waterproof, and light in weight, and dead air between the paper layers insulates the nest against temperature extremes. The smaller, exposed, honeycomb nests of paper wasps (genus *Polistes*), which support dozens rather than hundreds of wasps, are found suspended from thin stalks along the eaves of buildings (Fig. 7.20b). Their nests are formed with cells that are visibly six-sided, a mathematical pattern that gives the most efficient packing in limited space, and they are quite similar to hornet nests without the paper casing. To make nests, the wasps chew strands of weathered wood and bark that they mix with saliva to form a paperlike substance (Fig. 7.20c).

Another kind of nest that is often encountered is made from mud; these wasps are solitary rather than colonial and are less threatening. Mud daubers, which gather mud by rolling it into tiny balls, form irregular, mud-walled, several-celled structures that they provision with spiders for their young to feed on (Fig. 7.20d). Potter wasps, in contrast, construct single mud nests that resemble dainty pots or jugs with flared entrances that they provision with caterpillars. Females of solitary species build nests and provision them but don't defend them; they are much less threatening than social wasps.

a

b

d

c

Fig. 7.20. Different kinds of wasp and hornet nests: (a) enclosed paper nest of the bald-faced hornet, *Vespula maculata*; (b) open paper comb of paper wasp, *Polistes* sp.; (c) a wasp, *Vespula* sp., making paper; (d) nest of mud dauber, *Chalybion* sp.

Although mud nests are inhabited during the winter months, paper nests are abandoned in the fall and may be torn into by skunks or birds searching for larvae.

REFERENCES: MORSE 1963; HANSELL 1989; BUDRYS 2001; UNIVERSITY OF VERMONT EXTENSION 2002

7.21   Insect Singers

It may be a stretch to think of insects "singing," but cicadas, crickets, and grasshoppers can certainly produce quite a racket. Cicadas are the loudest, using muscular contractions to vibrate parts of their cuticles called tymbals to produce a metallic buzzing sound. It's just like pushing the sides of a soda can rapidly in and out. In contrast, grasshoppers and crickets make a chirping sound by rubbing two parts of their exoskeleton together, usually two wings or a leg and a wing, in a process called stridulation. One part has a file with regularly spaced ridges, while the other has a hard projection, the scraper, which is rubbed over the file. In crickets, each closure of the wings produces a pulse of sound at about 5,000 hertz that lasts for 1/400th of a second. These are the most conspicuous mechanisms used by insects for producing sounds, but others include the whirring of wings, the tapping of heads against the substrate, the gnashing of mandibles, and the hissing of air released from the spiracles (openings in the exoskeleton that allow for gas exchange).

Fig. 7.21.   Insect singer: a stridulating cricket (unidentified species).

For these insects, song can serve to bring males and females together for reproduction. Within the din made by thousands of cicadas singing all at once, a female can use a song's specific frequency to pick out the one made by a male of her own species. Cricket song speeds up in warmer temperatures, but males of each species sing their own innate, species-specific song to entice females. Even the whine of a female mosquito, so annoying to most people, excites male mosquitoes that happen to be nearby.

REFERENCES: BENTLEY & HOY 1074; ROMOSER & STOFFOLANO 1994; MARCHAND 2002

7.22   Insect Stingers

Many people fear insects because small creatures can hide in cracks and crevices and because many can bite or sting. Getting stung is the biggest worry, and it's true that stings of wasps can be very painful. The stingers are too small to see without a hand lens, and when you find a large, daunting stinger on an insect (Fig. 7.22a), it isn't something to fear: large needlelike structures can't be used to sting. Stingers are modified from ovipositors, structures on females for inserting their eggs in specific locations. Evolutionarily, ovipositors originated as extensions from terminal abdominal segments that fit together to form a tube. They were

a   b

Fig. 7.22.   Female insects: (a) Mormon cricket, *Anabrus simplex*, with a large ovipositor; (b) an Old World paper wasp, *Polistes dominulus*, with a small stinger.

used initially for sawing into plant tissues and subsequently developed for penetrating other organisms. For those using the ovipositor as a sting, eggs are released at the base of the sting.

Sensory hairs on an ovipositor can help the insect evaluate the quality of an oviposition site. Because large grasshoppers lay their eggs in the ground, their ovipositor is modified for digging. Some wasps lay their eggs on other insects deep within the wood of a tree, and to reach distant sites, their ovipositors may be several times longer than the body of the wasps themselves. Enormous ovipositors look dangerous, but what they really tell you is that the insect is a female.

REFERENCE: CHAPMAN 1982

8. Mountains

The vegetation changes as you go up a mountainside. This chapter describes the responses of trees to elevational gradients and the characteristics of plants (and an animal) that must cope with cold climates on the tops of mountains. The higher the mountain, the stronger the environmental differences across the elevational gradient, and the more severe the challenges of life on top. These descriptions focus particularly on what one can see in the mountains of northeastern and western North America.

Additional observations related to mountains include:

8.1   Elevational Zonation

The forest of a mountainside changes in the conditions for growth over an elevational gradient. Cooler temperatures, shorter growing seasons, thinner soils, and water that is frozen and unavailable for part of the year are all factors that affect tree growth all the way up to the highest elevations, where forests stop and alpine tundra begins. The composition of the forest shifts from one elevation to another as different tree species become abundant. From the bottom of a mountain in northeastern North America to the top, the forest changes from mostly hardwoods (maple, beech, oaks) to entirely conifers (spruce, fir), and the number of tree species in the forest declines. Furthermore, the trees at higher elevations are not as tall because of less fertile soils and a shorter growing season. Along a similar gradient in the central Rocky Mountains, the replacement is from ponderosa pine and Douglas-fir in the foothills to lodgepole pine in the middle zone and to fir and spruce at higher elevations. The specific elevational sequence of any one mountainside depends on longitude, moisture, fire frequency, and the trees that grow in that region, but elevational zonation is conspicuous wherever there are mountains simply because forests reflect changing conditions for growth.

REFERENCES: PEET 1978; VANKAT 1990; SMITH & SMITH 2001

a   b

Fig. 8.1.   Forests change with elevation, often from (a) taller, mostly deciduous forests at low elevations to (b) shorter, mostly evergreen forests at higher elevations (Adirondack Mountains, New York, at elevations of 1,850 and 4,000 feet).

8.2   Color Zonation

The colors of autumn reveal conspicuous patterns on the landscape, particularly where hardwood forests of northeastern lowlands give way to conifers at higher elevations. The composition of the forest shifts as some tree species replace others along an elevational gradient, and each species has its own pattern of seasonal activity and senescence. Spectacular reds develop at the lowest elevations, for this is where sugar maples and red maples stand out in a forest of yellow birch, hemlock, ash, and beech. With leaves that take on autumnal golden yellows as their leaves senesce, paper birch is conspicuous at middle elevations, amid red spruce and a sprinkling of mountain ash. Mountaintops always appear dark green because of

Fig. 8.2. Autumn color zonation by elevation on Whiteface Mountain (New York), from red sugar maples, *Acer saccharum,* at low elevations to yellow paper birch, *Betula papyrifera,* at middle elevations (and in the disturbed zone along the highway) to green balsam fir, *Abies balsamea,* at higher elevations.

their coniferous forests, dominated by balsam fir. In the central Appalachians, ridges with reddish brown oaks add another hue to a similar colorful pattern. A sunny late September day from near the top of an Adirondack mountain provides a dramatic view: reds cloak the landscape down low, yellows fill in middle elevations, and dark greens encircle the peaks. It is as if a cartographer used color coding to show the topography of the landscape.

REFERENCES: HOLWAY & SCOTT 1969; MARCHANT 1987

8.3   Streamside Spruce

Water availability is the most important determinant of where different plant species grow. A conspicuous example of water's effect is seen in the ribbons of dark green spruce that run

down through the pale green lodgepole pine forests of western mountain slopes. Because their stomates don't close as tightly in dry conditions, spruce have lower efficiency in using water than do

Fig. 8.3.   Dark green spruce, *Picea* sp., in the midst of lighter green lodgepole pine, *Pinus contorta,* forests indicate the presence of streams (Alberta).

pines (stomates are the pores in a leaf's surface that are necessary for photosynthesis; when open, they allow the inflow of carbon dioxide from the surrounding air but also the outflow of water vapor from spaces within the leaf). As a result, spruce grow where the land is wetter and cooler, such as at higher elevations and alongside streams. With their deeper color, spruce stand out as dark green stripes along stream beds, leaving the landscape color-coded for observers.

REFERENCE: KNIGHT 1994

8.4   High Treelines

There's a limit to how far up high mountain trees can grow. The limit is easily seen as the timberline or treeline, although the "line" is actually a transition zone from montane forest below to alpine tundra above. Declining conditions for tree growth are responsible. Every gain of 1,000 feet in elevation produces approximately a 3.5°F decrease in average temperature, a relationship known as the lapse rate. Trees generally aren't found where the average temperature of the warmest month is less than 50°F because when the weather is this cold, growth is too slow and the frost-free time too little. Treelines are higher on south-facing slopes, where solar warming is greater, than on north-facing slopes.

Fig. 8.4.   High treeline in the Rocky Mountains (Wyoming).

The climatic challenges of growth high on a mountain are numerous. Not only do colder temperatures slow growth, but high winds and blowing ice crystals dry the foliage and harm leaf cuticles. As a result, leaves don't last as long. Furthermore, high light intensities can lead to a loss of chlorophyll needed for photosynthesis (a loss known as chlorosis), accumulations of ice can break needles and branches, freeze-thaw cycles damage water transport tissues, and seed production is infrequent. Trees stop where winter-caused damage cannot be made up in summer growth.

REFERENCES: ARNO & HAMMERLY 1984; MARCHAND 1987; GRACE 1989; KNIGHT 1994

8.5   Low Treelines

Lower limits to tree growth (reverse treelines) are visible on mountains of the arid West, where montane forest gives way to sagebrush, junipers, and grasses at lower elevations. These

a b

Fig. 8.5. Low treelines: (a) the usual limit to tree growth at the prairie's edge on western mountains; (b) trees on the moister northern slope but missing from the drier southern slope (Montana).

drought-induced treelines develop because of insufficient moisture in arid lowlands for the growth of trees. Because granitic soils resist drought and support tree growth better than limestone soils, the composition of the substrate can shift the location of lower treelines. The shallow and unstable soils of talus and scree slopes also limit tree growth. Exposure matters, too; prevailing winds from the south and west remove snow from windward slopes and deposit it on leeward slopes; consequently, with more moisture, dry treelines are lower on north-facing slopes. Where the actions of blowing winds and different soils intersect, trees grow only along the crests of dry ridges. Forests cease where rainfall is less than 15 inches per year, while low-elevation open woodlands and chaparral cease where rainfall is less than 10 inches per year. With less precipitation than that, grasslands and deserts characterize the landscape.

REFERENCES: ARNO & HAMMERLY 1984; WHITNEY 1985

8.6 Crooked Wood

Environmental conditions that exclude trees from the high alpine region on a mountaintop also force them to grow short and shrublike just below the treeline. Here the trees, mostly different species of firs, are battered by strong, cold, drying winds. During the harsh winter, though, snow forms an insulating blanket over the landscape; it shields low plant growth from winds that blow above the snow surface, while temperatures within the snow cover remain only a few degrees below freezing. As a result, snow-covered branches are protected and meet the oncoming spring in good health, but stems that protrude above the snow retain only a few surviving buds, mostly on the leeward side. Continued growth produces a flaglike appearance (a flag tree; Fig. 8.6a, b). Swirling, abrasive ice crystals at the snow surface produce the greatest damage, so if a stem protrudes 2 or 3 feet above the snow cover, then more buds survive at the top and form a broomlike appearance. Snow blast erodes protective wax secretions from the tree's needles, hastening their death. Near the treeline,

Fig. 8.6. Crooked wood at upper treeline: (a) dwarfed form with a flagged stem (balsam fir, *Abies balsamea*, Mt. Washington, New Hampshire); (b) flag tree (balsam fir, Whiteface Mountain, New York); (c) krummholz cluster sculpted by the wind (subalpine fir, *Abies lasiocarpa*, Beartooth Mountains, Wyoming).

trees appear dwarfed and sculpted by cold winds and are known as krummholz, which is German for "crooked wood." The thickness of the shrublike layer is a biological indicator of how deep the snow is at midwinter; just by looking at the branches, one can visualize where winter winds blow.

REFERENCES: ARNO & HAMMERLY 1984; MARCHAND 1987; HADLEY & SMITH 1989

8.7 Fir Waves

Waves of dead and dying trees undulate across high ridges in the dense fir forests of northeastern mountains. Young firs grow well on these slopes; despite the cold, windy weather and thin, rocky soil, they reach high densities of similar-sized trees. As the trees grow taller, however, severe environmental conditions make survival more and more difficult: (1) in the winter, moisture from blowing winds freezes on fir branches, producing accumulations of rime ice that break the newest twigs; (2) a high density of trees formed by abundant seed germination leads to dieback of lower, shaded branches; and (3) high winds physically stress shallow roots, causing breakage and allowing fungal infections to invade. These stresses intensify as trees age, and they eventually reduce the rate of photosynthetic gain below that needed for survival. The trees gradually die. Eventually, dead trees in the dieback zone fall, opening the forest floor for new seedlings to begin growing. Firs die in waves through this process, with the crests of the waves being several hundred feet apart and moving at a rate of several feet per year in a direction toward the prevailing winds. The full cycle at one site takes about sixty years. The resulting waves of wind-induced mortality sweep through high-elevation fir forests in a repeated pattern of growth and death.

REFERENCES: SPRUGEL & BORMANN 1981; MARCHAND 1987, 1995; FOSTER 1988

a   b

Fig. 8.7. Fir waves of balsam fir, *Abies balsamea*, (a) and (b) on Whiteface Mountain (New York).

8.8 Subalpine Invasion

Forest trees are currently invading subalpine meadows in mountainous regions, gradually closing some of these formerly open habitats. Three processes can cause such a change. The first is succession: following fire or other disturbance, late-succession plants replace coloniz-

ers in a sequence that returns the meadow back to a self-replacing forest. The second factor is decreased grazing: tree seedlings that are browsed or trampled do not survive heavy grazing, and when grazing ceases, trees may invade. The third factor is global climate change. A warmer climate means that soils dry out sooner, the snow-free period lasts longer, and trees can more easily colonize high-elevation areas that had excluded them previously. A warm period began in the late 1800s, and we are now seeing the results of that change through the invasion of Douglas-

Fig. 8.8. Invasion of a subalpine meadow in the Rocky Mountains by young trees (Wyoming).

fir and lodgepole pine into dry montane and subalpine meadows of western mountains. The invasion is discontinuous, however, because seed crops are episodic. Invading trees alter the patterns of wind and snow accumulation in the meadows, leading to further changes. This expansion of woody vegetation, most noticeable in the West, reflects a dynamic shift in the conditions for growth.

REFERENCES: BUTLER 1986; JAKUBOS & ROMME 1993; KLASNER & FAGIE 2002

8.9   Soil Tubes

After the snow melts in western mountain meadows and rangelands, wormlike ropes of soil about 4 inches in diameter appear draped across the surface. Produced by pocket gophers, which push soil upward as they burrow along under the surface, soil tubes are most apparent where the soil is rocky. These subterranean rodents feed on taproots and herbaceous shoots, consuming foods with high protein and storing those with low protein for later feeding. Much of the soil they excavate backfills old tunnels, but some is pushed upward over the surface. Wintertime tunnels within the snow give an easy means of travel and allow the pocket gophers to cross inhospitable habitat; they also provide protected access to aboveground shrubs for winter feeding. The soil they backfill into their snow tunnels is left behind following snowmelt as sinuous, fallen tubes of excavated soil that endure into the summer.

A pair of these small mammals can keep a meadow in conspicuous upheaval. Their extensive burrowing changes the soil structure, mixes the vertical layers, accelerates erosion, and allows air and water to filter in. The effects are similar to those made by earthworms at lower elevations, though more extensive. Estimates are that an average pocket gopher moves about 23 cubic yards of soil each year. The large, newly created soil mounds of pocket gophers become colonized by small flowering plants to create distinct gopher gardens that alter plant composition of the meadow and increase local plant diversity. One almost never sees these engineering animals, but their impact on the mountain meadows, prairie grasslands, and even volcanic landscapes where they live is extensive. Just like beavers, they strongly alter their habitat.

REFERENCES: BURT & GROSSENHEIDER 1964; ZWINGER 1972; VLECK 1981; CHAPMAN & FELDHAMER 1982; ANDERSEN & MACMAHON 1985; STUEBE 1985; ANDERSEN 1987, 1990; COX 1989; ROGERS ET AL. 2001; REICHMAN & SEABLOOM 2002

a   b

Fig. 8.9.   Soil tubes, (a) and (b), of northern pocket gopher, *Thomomys talpoides* (Wyoming).

8.10   Floral Diversity

The shortness of the growing season at high elevation forces plants in mountain meadows to flower in a rushed sequence to be pollinated and produce seeds before the return of winter cold. With many plant species flowering at the same time, competition for pollinators is strong, and it is advantageous, therefore, for each species to be distinctive; an insect attracted to one floral shape and color that provides nectar rewards is more likely to remain faithful to that one plant species as it transfers pollen among individuals. Diversification in shape and color is promoted by the response of different kinds of pollinators to different floral cues (see 1.1). The diverse signals by which plants attract pollinators lead to the exuberant diversity of floral color and shape in mountain meadows. It is a spectacular appearance.

REFERENCES: HOLWAY & WARD 1965; MOSQUIN 1971; KUDO 1992; MOLAU 1993; HORRIDGE 1998

a   b

Fig. 8.10.   Floral diversity of a midsummer mountain meadow, dominated by (red) Indian paintbrush *Castilleja* sp., (pink) sticky geranium *Geranium viscosissimum*, and (yellow) little sunflower *Helianthella* sp. (Wyoming); (b) white-lined sphinx moth, *Hyles lineata,* feeding from tall delphinium, *Delphinium occidentale.*

8.11   White and Yellow Meadows

In contrast to the diversity of floral color and shape seen in midsummer, white and yellow saucer-shaped flowers dominate alpine meadows soon after snowmelt. Because flowers function to attract pollinators, the open shapes and absence of blues and pinks in early spring suggest that the earliest pollinators are small and attracted to the most reflective flowers. Open shapes lacking distinct colors are generally associated with fluctuating numbers of unspecialized insect pollinators. Sure enough, flies are the most abundant early pollinators in the alpine zone, and they lack color vision. The pattern of white and yellow flowers is repeated throughout the summer in the alpine region of New Zealand, where, because of

a

b

c

Fig. 8.11. Early spring white and yellow montane meadow (Wyoming): (a) soon after the snow has melted, with two of the abundant early flowers, (b) marsh marigold, *Caltha leptosepala*, and (c) subalpine buttercup, *Ranunculus eschscholtzii*.

this island country's isolation, the vegetation has evolved in the absence of color-seeing butterflies, hawkmoths, and long-tongued bees. The vegetation of the arctic also has a preponderance of white and yellow flowers for the same reason: most arctic pollinators are flies. As the diversity of pollinators increases mid-summer in alpine meadows, especially with the emergence of native bees, so does the diversity of floral color and shape (see 8.10).

REFERENCES: BILLINGS & MOONEY 1968; KEVAN 1972; BILLINGS 1974; LLOYD 1985; KEARNS & INOUYE 1993; SWENSON & BREMER 1997; LEE ET AL. 2001

8.12   Cushions, Rosettes, and Mats

Above the treeline, plants must tolerate cold temperatures, nearly constant wind, and the unavailability of water, which is so often frozen. Furthermore, the shortness of the growing season restricts the vegetation mostly to perennials that grow only a little each year (the few alpine annuals are tiny). To escape drying winds, the leaves of many alpine plants stay low in a boundary layer of air close to the ground where winds are slowed. To sense the difference, a person can lie on the alpine turf and as a result feel warmer and less windblown than when standing.

Three common plant forms take advantage of the boundary layer in the alpine zone. (1) Streamlined cushion plants grow close to the ground in tight clusters of small leaves with short flowering stems, all from highly branched, anchoring taproots (Fig. 8.12a, b). They

Fig. 8.12.   The forms of alpine plants: (a) the cushion plant moss campion, *Silene acaulis*; (b) the cushion plant alpine forget-me-not, *Eritrichium nanum*, (c) the basal leaf rosette of diamond-leaved saxifrage, *Saxifraga rhomboidea*; (d) the prostrate mat of net-vein willow, *Salix reticulata*.

grow slowly, taking decades to reach dinner-plate size, with the elongation of stems suppressed hormonally by cold-stressed roots. Slow growth in these conditions is illustrated by the discovery of a 350-year-old cushion of moss campion a couple of feet across. (2) Rosette plants produce a circle of leaves flat against the ground around a taller flowering stem (Fig. 8.12c). (3) Other alpine plants grow as mats, prostrate and spreading close to the ground (Fig. 8.12d). Despite their short stature, all three forms attract pollinating insects with exuberant displays of clustered small flowers or tall floral stems poking upward from the ground.

REFERENCES: ZWINGER & WILLARD 1972; HAGEN & SPOMER 1989; MCCARTHY 1992; SLACK & BELL 1995

8.13 Leaf Fuzz

Alpine plants suffer water loss from cold winds whenever their stomates (leaf pores for gas exchange) are open for photosynthesis. To slow that loss, many plants are covered with long hairs that trap a layer of air next to the leaf surface. Without this protection, a steeper gradient would exist between water-saturated air within the leaf and dry air blowing by the

Fig. 8.13.   Thick hairs on alpine leaves: (a) *Senecio fuscatus*; (b) Labrador tea, *Ledum groenlandicum*; (c) woolly pussytoes, *Antennaria lanata*.

surface, and water vapor would diffuse outward more rapidly. The steeper the gradient in humidity, the faster the loss of water. When stomates are found on only one side of a leaf, only that surface may be velvety.

The above is the long-accepted explanation for fuzzy leaves on alpine plants, but some leaf surfaces without stomates are also hairy. Another explanation is that thick hairs reflect some visible light that, when too intense, can slow photosynthesis. Hairs can also trap invisible wavelengths of solar energy, making buds with dark hairs warmer than the surrounding air and thus accelerating flowering and seed development. The earliest-flowering plants usually have buds like this. Although green photosynthetic surfaces lie beneath the pubescence, alpine plants characteristically have a soft and fuzzy texture, perhaps to regulate light interception as well as to slow airflow across the leaf surfaces.

REFERENCES: BLISS 1962; ZWINGER & WILLARD 1972

8.14   Old Lichens

Exposed rocks form an inhospitable habitat for most living things, but lichens are nature's pioneers and can survive well on barren rock surfaces. Lichens are blended structures of fungi and photosynthetic algae or cyanobacteria in which both parts benefit. The fungus provides a latticelike structure, attachment to the rock, and retention of moisture, while the algae or cyanobacteria contribute photosynthetic gain.

Lichen growth produces blotches of yellow, orange, green, tan, and black colors on forbidding substrates, developed from the fungal filaments of the lichen constructing a flattened body with entrapped photosynthetic cells. One of the best-known is yellow map lichen (Fig. 8.14a), which is particularly common on acidic rocks at high elevations in North America. It appears in maplike patterns with a yellow-green thallus, the platelike form of a lichen, with black borders of pure, unlichenized fungus (Fig 8.14b). For map lichen, *Rhizocarpon geographicum* is the scientific name of both the fungus and the lichen; the photosynthetic partner (photobiont) is the alga *Trebouxia* spp. Weathering of the rock surface increases in the presence of lichens because they release organic acids that make minerals available for growth. You can't peel a lichen off a rock without taking some of the rock surface, so in a very real sense, lichens eat rocks.

a   b

Fig. 8.14.   Slow-growing crustose map lichen, *Rhizocarpon geographicum*: (a) on an undisturbed alpine boulder; (b) close-up showing black fungal areas without symbiotic algae.

Crust-forming lichens form very slowly, taking from less than a year to several decades (depending on light and temperature) to expand 1/16 inch, so the diameter of a lichen on a rock can indicate approximately how long the rock surface has been exposed and undisturbed. One measurement in northern Alaska, in particular, gave growth at 1/8 inch per century. Colonization of a rock surface is through windblown propagules that settle in small crevices or rough areas. Initially, young thalli fuse together and expand outward, but the lichen's initial rapid growth slows after it reaches about half an inch in diameter. The slowdown in growth is due to a loss of photosynthetic efficiency and the limitations of lateral transport from the central photosynthetic area to the dark marginal region. Some lichens on rocky substrates near glaciers are several thousand years old and have been used to measure the ebb and flow of glacial ice. Taking life at a slow pace can lead to a great age.

REFERENCES: HALE 1967; BESCHEL 1973; CALKIN & ELLIS 1980; ARMSTRONG 1983; INNES 1985; ARMSTRONG & SMITH 1987; VITT ET AL. 1988; EVERSMAN 1995; SLACK & BELL 1995; ARMSTRONG & BRADWELL 2001; BRODO ET AL. 2001; SANDERS 2001

8.15   Pink Snow

Circumstances that appear alienating may not be as severe as they seem; living things can and do adapt to the challenging conditions of freezing temperatures, limited nutrients, and intense solar radiation. Summer snowbanks at high elevations sometimes display a pink tint, forming what is known commonly as watermelon snow. When disturbed, pink snow may even smell faintly like overripe watermelon. The reddish cast comes from large resting cells of the widely distributed single-celled alga *Chlamydomonas nivalis*, which is associated with the water that surrounds ice crystals. Although a mucilaginous coat gives some adherence to snow crystals, cells in the highest snow layer may wash away, leaving a higher intensity of pink just under the surface and down about 5 inches into the snow. The red color derives from carotenoid pigments (especially one known as astaxanthin) that protect chlorophyll from the intense sunlight and damaging ultraviolet radiation of high elevations. UV light exposure also spurs production of other chemicals, phenolic antioxidants, for additional protection. When the temperature drops below freezing, photosynthesis ceases. Moving water from melted snow concentrates the algae in patches on the snow surface, where rates

a   b

Fig. 8.15.   Snow tinged pink by growth of *Chlamydomonas nivalis*: (a) edge of a snowbank; (b) a late-season snowbank (Wyoming).

of photosynthesis can be as high, surprisingly, as 10 percent of that of green plants. Another alga, *Chlamydomonas brevispina*, produces a greenish tint just below the snow surface in northern forests, while other algae produce variants of these colors. But don't eat colored snow; with pigmented algae, nature makes snow cones that are enticing but give intestinal distress.

REFERENCES: MOSSER ET AL. 1977; MARCHANT 1982; GRINDE 1983; WEISS 1983; HAEDER & HAEDER 1989; DUVAL ET AL. 1999; RAVEN ET AL. 1999; WILLIAMS ET AL. 2003

8.16 Patterned Ground

Rock polygons characterize the frosty ground of alpine ridges, and plant growth reflects these patterns. Repeated freeze-thaw cycles in saturated soils produce frost heaves that sort the surface material into regular polygonal networks of mixed soils bounded by narrow rock-filled trenches. Convection cells develop in the soil because newly thawed water becomes denser and heavier as it warms up at the surface (water is densest at 39°F, whereas colder meltwater is actually lighter; it is an unusual property of water that the coldest liquid is not the heaviest). Two mechanisms are involved in forming patterned ground: the expansion of frozen soil, which separates soil from rocks, and the redistribution of accumulated rocks by gravity. The width of the polygons is determined by the convection cells of water flowing up and down in the soil; daily freezing affects the soil about 5 inches down, while seasonal freezing has deeper effects. The polygons appear most conspicuously where the water table fluctuates between just above and just below the surface, and they elongate on downslopes, appearing more as stripes than polygons because gravity stretches out the rock concentrations.

Instability of the soil affects plant growth in the alpine zone, producing gradients in the vegetation from rock zones outward. Near the middle of the polygons, soil upwells, mixes, and weathers more, producing higher nutrient concentration and pH, but the greater instability slows successional changes. Heath vegetation is thicker and plants and seedlings survive better near the edges, where rocks ameliorate temperature and drought. Because change occurs slowly in cold climates, these vegetational patterns persist for centuries. Fossil patterned ground may still be apparent in regions where the ground no longer freezes regularly but where glacial ice passed thousands of years ago.

REFERENCES: JONASSON & SKOLD 1983; RISSING & THORN 1985; GLEASON ET AL. 1986; KRANTZ ET AL. 1988; PIELOU 1991; ANDERSON & BLISS 1998; KESSLER & WERNER 2003

a
b

Fig. 8.16.   Patterned ground from freeze-thaw processes on an alpine ridge: (a) polygons in flat areas; (b) stripes on slopes (Wyoming).

8.17   Frost Hummocks

Alpine soil is saturated along streams, near ponds, and in low swales, and in these wet areas, mounds of soil a foot or two in diameter and cloaked in vegetation appear in an orderly grid. The importance of water in their development is apparent because the hummocks are highest where it is wettest, and they diminish in height where drier. With a solid substrate of rock or frozen ground underneath and the water table near the surface, cycles of freezing and thawing produce a small initial rise in the ground level at one spot. Mosses and sedges then colonize that higher site, and organic material collects among the sedge roots. The hummock grows in height as peat accumulates underneath. Small willows subsist in the surrounding trenches, which are wetter and more protected from the wind. In winter large hummocks are exposed to blowing ice crystals, which kill some of the capping vegetation. As the plants die back and expose the accumulated soil, abrading winds erode the hummock, eventually leaving behind a flattened frost scar. Soil rebuilds in the scars, while continued freeze-thaw activity raises new frost boils, and the cycle begins slowly again to repeat the growth and breakdown of hummocks.

Fig. 8.17.   Frost hummocks of wet soil near alpine ponds (Wyoming).

REFERENCES: BILLINGS & MOONEY 1959; ZWINGER 1972

9. FORESTS

Commanding our attention, forests are more than just groups of trees; many other organisms live there as well. In a forest one can see the scrape marks of deer and bear, the thick growth of mistletoes and shelf fungi, and the damage of bark beetles and sapsuckers. The trees themselves are the first objects of our interest, though, including how large they are and when they leaf out and senesce. This chapter begins with different kinds of forests and then considers signs left by residents of the forest.

In addition to all of Chapter 2, "Trees," more observations about forests may be found in:

9.1 West Coast Conifers

Giant trees live in the coastal ranges of western North America, including conifers that reach impressive heights and girths (Table 9.1). Here, the evergreen habit is advantageous. Photosynthesis in these trees continues for much of the winter because of moderate temperatures and fog-provided moisture, and their conical shape is better than that of most deciduous trees at intercepting the angled light that comes from low winter sun. Growth in the summer is restricted by a lack of available water, but the smaller, needle-shaped leaves of conifers remain closer to ambient temperatures in warm summer months and experience less heat stress and subsequent water loss than do broad leaves.

These trees reach large sizes through sustained growth over many centuries. Their thick bark protects them from fire, while their large size produces a buffer against low availability of water or nutrients. The enormous volume of sapwood in a large conifer provides a water reservoir for dry times, and conifers replenish their water reservoir faster than deciduous trees because their vessels refill rapidly when water is available. Among these trees is the largest living organism on earth (by total weight), the General Sherman giant sequoia, which has a height of 275 feet, a trunk diameter of 28 feet, an estimated weight of 2.7 million pounds, and a volume equal to that of eleven blue whales.

REFERENCES: WARING & FRANKLIN 1979; AMERICAN FORESTRY ASSOCIATION 1988, 1994

Fig. 9.1.   The grandeur of West Coast conifers: (a) giant sequoia, *Sequoiadendron giganteum* (notice the person with outstretched arms at the base of the tree); (b) coastal redwoods, *Sequoia sempervirens*; (c) sugar pine, *Pinus lambertiana* (California).

Table 9.1. West Coast conifers. Size data are given for the largest living specimens known in 2004 (American Forests 2004), along with approximate ages (Brockman 1979; Waring & Franklin 1979).

Species	Max. age (yr.)	Max. diam. (in.)	Max. height (ft.)
Alaska-cedar	3500	452	129
Coast Douglas-fir	1200	600	301
Coast redwood	2200	950	321*
Giant sequoia	3000	1020	274
Ponderosa pine	726	294	227
Sitka spruce	750	668	204
Sugar pine	600	435	209
Western redcedar	1200	761	159

* In 1988, the tallest living redwood was 362 feet high.

9.2   Pine Plains

Well represented in New Jersey, New York, and Wisconsin, pine plains (pine barrens) are fire-adapted pine-and-oak communities that occur on well-drained, nutrient-poor sandy soils. Fire maintains these communities; without regular disturbance, the pines and oaks would be replaced by trees less tolerant of burning. Pine plains have trees adapted genetically to frequent fires by having thick bark, rapidly regenerating shoots, and closed cones (see 2.21).

At the center of the New Jersey pine barrens is a forest of dwarf pitch pine and oaks with a canopy height only 4 feet above the ground. As in all pine barrens, wildfire kills aboveground growth, but, taking in the nutrients that are released by fire, the trees resprout quickly to reform a sprawling, dense, shrubby forest. Huckleberry and blueberry shrubs add to the thickness of the vegetation and increase its flammability. The pine plains are swept regularly by fire because the extensive, high, dry, infertile sands have few rivers or swamps to serve as firebreaks. It is this high frequency of fire in an arid environment—perhaps only ten years between outbreaks—that makes the forest of the pine plains so stunted; even pitch pine and oaks can't reach a larger size between their episodic burning. It makes one feel like Gulliver among the Lilliputians to walk through this pygmy forest.

Fig. 9.2.   Pine plains, where the canopy of pitch pine, *Pinus rigida*, is 4 feet high (New Jersey).

REFERENCES: ROBICHAUD & BUELL 1973; BOERNER 1981; GIVNISH 1981; BUCHHOLZ & GOOD 1982; BUCHHOLZ 1983

9.3 Aspen Clones

Found in all Canadian provinces, thirty-three states, and even parts of Mexico, quaking aspen, *Populus tremuloides,* is the most widely distributed species of tree in North America. These trees grow in discrete clusters, and all the trees in a cluster have a similar appearance. Although germination and growth of an aspen seed is rare, growth from root suckers of the same aspen root system is quite common, so genetically identical clones develop wherever a seedling germinates. Connected trees share water, nutrients, and sugars, and each clone produces predominantly male or female flowers. Being genetically the same, all the trees in a clone usually senesce at the same time in autumn and are attacked equivalently by insect pests and fungal and bacterial pathogens. Actually, slight variation can be found within a clone because rare mutations take place in the developing stems as the trees grow. Different clones on a mountainside start turning yellow at different times because of their genetic differences. Although seed crops are periodically large, few seedlings become established because seeds remain viable for only a short period of time and require specific conditions to survive. Germination is enhanced when the soil surface has been cleared by fire; recent forest fires in western North America, such as the Yellowstone National Park fires of 1988, have promoted abundant new growth of aspen.

Aspen clones can reach astonishing sizes and ages. The largest yet reported is a clone in Utah that covers 106 acres, contains 47,000 trunks, and is estimated to weigh over 6,000 tons. Considering the weight of genetically distinct individuals, this makes the Utah clone the largest individual on earth. The age of a clone can't be measured directly, but even though the oldest individual tree within them may be only seventy-five years old, the largest clones probably date back ten thousand years to the end of the last ice age.

REFERENCES: KEMPERMAN & BARNES 1976; BURNS & HONKALA 1990; BARTOS ET AL. 1991; GRANT 1993; MITTON & GRANT 1996; TUSKANM ET AL. 1996; ROMME ET AL. 1997; USDA 2003

Fig. 9.3. Quaking aspen, *Populus tremuloides*, clones: (a) from the inside; (b) on a mountain slope in autumn golden colors (Wyoming).

9.4 Greening Wave

A spring wave of greening and flowering takes place from the ground up in eastern deciduous forests. With the increasing warmth of early spring, forest-floor herbs, shrubs, and even seedlings of canopy species benefit from unfolding their new leaves quickly so they can harvest early-spring sunlight before the trees above them leaf out and block the light. As a result, the vegetation turns green from the forest floor upward.

Fig. 9.4. The unfolding of new leaves and flowers from the ground floor up in the eastern deciduous forest (New York).

Many forest-floor herbs also flower in the favorable light and moisture conditions before the canopy fills in. Most herbaceous plants are insect-pollinated, and their flowers are more visible in the openness of early spring, while air movement is greater for wind-pollinated plants before tree leaves fill in. With warming soil, sunlight, and plentiful nutrients, a profusion of wildflowers carpets undisturbed forest floors in March and April. The blooming period is brief, waning as the canopy closes, so forest-floor herbs share pollination from available early-season flies and bees. To reproduce successfully, each flower attracts diverse pollinators and remains receptive for an extended duration, until spring blends into summer (see 1.6).

REFERENCES: MOTTEN 1986; GARLAND 1997

9.5 Bud Break

As spring arrives each year, red maple, quaking aspen, and birch are always among the first trees to leaf out, while walnut, hickory, elm, oak, and ash are among the last. Sugar maple and beech are intermediate. Latecomers could photosynthesize more if they produced leaves earlier, but they don't because they would then be at higher risk for internal damage from freezing. With each species on its own schedule, buds rest on branches, biding their time in the wait for days that are long and warm enough.

The difference in timing is correlated with the kind of water-conducting tissues (xylem) found in each species. Trees with larger-diameter vessels (ring-porous) are more likely to experience early spring rupture of the continuous water columns in their tissues, so they cannot leaf out until the cambial layer

Fig. 9.5. Different time for leafing out in the spring in sugar maple, *Acer saccharum*, (leaves opening) and black walnut, *Juglans nigra* (bare limbs) (New York).

inside the bark, which produces new tissues, begins to grow new xylem vessels. Trees with smaller-diameter vessels (diffuse-porous) leaf out earlier. Furthermore, trees that have a single growth flush of new leaves delay leafing out to minimize the likelihood of being subject to a late frost, whereas those that produce new leaves over a longer time (indeterminate shoot growth) can begin leafing out earlier because they risk losing fewer leaves. Why these trees have different developmental patterns relates to their origin in temperate or tropical habitats in their evolutionary past. The changing ranges of different tree species as glaciation has ebbed and flowed have produced the mixed deciduous forests we see today, and bud break may not match the best time for an individual tree to leaf out where it grows now.

REFERENCES: LECHOWICZ 1984; WANG ET AL. 1992; HACKE & SAUTER 1996; KOZLOWSKI & PALLARDY 1997; HEINRICH 2002

9.6 Fall Colors

An artist's palette of warm colors characterizes autumn. While conifers retain their ever-green needles in the fall, deciduous trees withdraw sugars, proteins, and minerals from the

a

b

c

d

Fig. 9.6. Fall colors: (a) northeastern forest edge; (b) collection of sugar maple leaves, *Acer saccharum*; (c) red maple, *Acer rubrum*; (d) white oak, *Quercus alba* (New York).

leaves that are soon to drop and grow a separation layer (an abscission layer) at the base of the leaf stems to block the delivery of water and nutrients from the branch into the leaves. With the nutrient supply halted, the green chlorophylls of photosynthesis degrade without being replaced, as they are during the summer, and accessory pigments that break down more slowly become unmasked, especially yellows, oranges, and reds from decay-resistant carotenoids and anthocyanins. During the growing season, these pigments absorb part of the sun's energy not captured by green pigments and pass it along to chlorophyll for photosynthesis. They may also block damaging ultraviolet light (UV-B). As green chlorophyll disappears, additional colors arise from the conversion of colorless compounds (flavonoids and leftover sugars) into additional light-reflecting anthocyanins. The more acidic the leaf sap, the more brilliant the reds produced; alkaline sap creates purple shades.

Gleaming red-leafed maples typify the October forests of the Northeast and draw many leaf-peeping visitors each autumn. Maples are among the few forest trees that produce red colors, so early American landscape paintings that portrayed scarlet trees were assumed to be fanciful exaggerations by those unfamiliar with the forests of North America. Leaf senescence in the temperate zone is spurred by shorter days and frost. Fall colors develop first in the cooler weather of higher latitudes and higher elevations; then as temperatures decline during the autumn months, a wave of peak color sweeps down mountainsides and from north to south (see 8.2). Bright colors develop best with sunny fall days and cold, frost-free nights because more sugars are produced under these conditions. Trees develop color in a predictable sequence, from red maples to aspens to sugar maples to oaks. Drought, air pollution, disease, and other stresses can lead to early leaf senescence and color development. All compounds eventually degrade, however, and the brilliant fall colors slowly fade to brown.

The bright colors may be simply by-products of leaf senescence, but recently proposed ideas indicate functions for these pigments. One suggestion is that brilliant reds may advertise the trees' chemical protection to color-seeing, damaging insects. It is more likely, however, that red anthocyanin pigments serve to protect senescing leaves from excess light and damaging free-radical molecules while nutrients are being withdrawn back into the trunk. An observation that supports this latter idea is that reddish anthocyanins are more noticeable in plants in times of stress and in the parts of leaves that have been damaged by frost.

REFERENCES: LANNER 1990; PEEK 1995; MCGUIRE 1998; MARCHAND 1999; HAMILTON & BROWN 2001; HOLOPAINEN & PELTONEN 2002; LEE & GOULD 2002; PAIN 2002; WILKINSON ET AL. 2002

9.7 Blowdowns

Wind is a primary agent of disturbance in a forest. The causes of tree blowdowns, also known as windthrow, can range from explosive volcanoes (e.g., Mount St. Helens, in Washington), to tornadoes, hurricanes, and simply strong gusts. Catastrophic blowdowns leave large gaps in the forest canopy and occur especially in exposed landscapes and where the soil is shallow, saturated, or frozen. In some blowdowns, most of the trees have been uprooted, leaving a bizarre scene of wreckage. Even in protected areas, loss of a few trees can open the canopy enough to allow wind to damage trees around the periphery, producing an elongate and expanding gap in the canopy. The effect of incoming winds is reduced where trees grow at high density and receive support from interlocking root systems. Blowdowns affect predominantly

a

b

Fig. 9.7. Blowdowns: (a) damage from an ice storm; (b) root base of a fallen tree; (c) pit and mound topography of the forest floor of an old-growth forest (New York).

c

larger-diameter trees. Direct damage to some trees can produce indirect damage to others, as when one tree falls into a neighbor or exposes surrounding trees to higher wind speeds (see 8.7). Typically, more trees are uprooted than are broken.

Blowdown produces unevenness of the ground beneath the fallen trunks as root masses are yanked from the soil and left as upturned root plates. The sizes of root pits correlate with the sizes of the trees that fell. Pit-and-mound topography is characteristic of northern old-growth forests, giving evidence that blowdowns, even when infrequent, leave lasting effects on the structure of the forest. After each disturbance, succession begins again with reseeding and regrowth, leaving a mosaic of forest patches at different successional stages.

REFERENCES: BORMANN & LIKENS 1979; FOSTER & REINERS 1986; SMITH ET AL. 1987; LIECHTY ET AL. 1997; GREENBERG & MCNAB 1998; ZHANG ET AL. 1999; BARBOUR & BILLINGS 2000; CLINTON & BAKER 2000; LARSON & WALDRON 2000; PETERSON 2000; RUEL 2000; ULANOVA 2000; LINDEMANN & BAKER 2001

9.8   Fire Regrowth

Most people respond to forest fires with horror because of the gripping visuals presented by the media and the threats to human habitations, but in many plant communities, fire is a common and natural form of disturbance. In the absence of humans, fire is simply one of several factors that periodically alter the biological community, and it does so in a cycle that takes a forest from a dense state with mature and senescent trees to an open woodland that allows new trees to begin to grow.

Fire requires fuel—accumulated dead and dying vegetative debris—as well as an ignition source, usually lightning. The spread and intensity of the fire then depends on the large-scale factor of regional climate and the small-scale factors of slope, firebreaks (e.g., streams), and vegetative structure and flammability. Fires produce dramatic changes to the forest by reducing overcrowding; allowing more sunlight to reach the forest floor; returning nutrients from dead material back into the soil to spur new plant growth; increasing the availability of groundwater by reducing transpirational losses; cleaning out insect pests, parasitic plants, leaf litter, and downed timber; and promoting biological diversity by suppressing the growth of otherwise dominant competitors and by creating a mosaic of forest patches at different successional stages. In regions where fire is suppressed, the fuel load may reach such a high level that when a fire gets started, it is larger and more intense than if fires had been more frequent. Fires differ in size and intensity, too, ranging from surface fires that don't kill canopy trees to crown fires that do.

Frequent-fire habitats support vegetation adapted to withstand and recover rapidly from fire's periodic occurrence. Some trees such as pitch pine resist damage by having thick bark that peels off in flakes when burning, carrying the fire with it. Many fire-adapted conifers produce closed cones that release enormous quantities of seed after being popped open by the heat of the flames (see 2.21). After fire has swept through, herbaceous plants intolerant of shade invade the sunlit areas, producing a profusion of wildflowers, as took place in Yellowstone National Park after the extensive fires of 1988 (see 14.2). Then new generations of plants begin to grow and start the cycle all over again.

REFERENCES: KIRKMAN ET AL. 2001; HEYERDAHL ET AL. 2001; SMITH & SMITH 2001

a   b

Fig. 9.8.   Regrowth, (a) and (b), after a forest fire, showing wildflowers and lodgepole pine, *Pinus contorta*, seedlings (Wyoming).

9.9   Browse Lines

Animals can feed only where they can reach palatable food. In the winter, the preferred succulent food of deer and other large herbivores is no longer available, so these large mammals browse on tender but fibrous tree twigs. Feeding by deer is recognizable because, lacking upper incisors, they leave ragged edges on the stems they strip. Hungry deer in dense populations eat everything in their reach, leaving a threshold height, called the browse line,

a   b

Fig. 9.9. Browse lines: (a) northern white-cedar, *Thuja occidentalis*, around the edge of an Adirondack lake (New York); (b) apple, *Malus pumila*, orchard (Montana).

above which the unreachable foliage is thick and below which it is thin. Browse lines are five to six feet high and are most apparent in coniferous forests with abundant deer. Northern white-cedar has nutrient-rich, soft foliage and is especially apt to show browse lines in the northern United States. When deer are abundant in Texas, oaks develop a wintertime browse line. And everywhere, seedlings and saplings survive better where deer are fenced out.

Browse lines reveal an upper limit to herbivory, but a lower limit may be produced by snow cover. Rabbits feed on the bark of saplings while standing atop the winter's usual accumulation of snow, and the height of their gnaw marks indicates the depth of midwinter snow.

REFERENCES: STOKES & STOKES 1986; *ADIRONDACK DAILY ENTERPRISE* 2001; RUSSELL ET AL. 2001

9.10 Masting

Mast seeding is the synchronized production of large seed crops by trees that grow in the same area. Acorn production in red oaks may be a hundred times higher in a mast year, for example, than in an off year. Thin rings in mast years give evidence of the drain on the tree's resources and point to a trade-off in allocation of the tree's energy between growth and reproduction. As a result, trees are unlikely to have two mast years in a row, and mast years occur irregularly.

More than one factor can make masting advantageous. When many seeds are produced at once, seed predators become satiated before consuming all the available seeds, so many survive, are dispersed, and germinate (predator satiation hypothesis). Masting may attract additional seed predators, but what counts is the number of seeds that survive; in beech, for example, fertile seeds in a mast year are only half as likely to be consumed by seed predators. The second advantage of masting comes from synchronized heavy flowering, which can enhance pollination, especially in wind-

Fig. 9.10. Heavy seed production (masting) of a northern red oak, *Quercus rubra*.

pollinated plants (pollination efficiency hypothesis). Synchronous seed production, then, is a by-product of synchronous flowering. A third possible advantage is that a tree may leave more offspring in a mast year if, when there are more seeds, predators disperse and cache seeds at greater distances.

Masting occurs in long-lived, large-seeded trees, particularly those that are wind-pollinated and those at high latitudes and high altitudes. Climate triggers a mast year; for sugar maple and yellow birch, mast years correlate with warm, dry springs (when buds first develop) and wet summers a year later (when seeds mature). But the variability in seed production is too great to be explained solely by climate; masting is an adaptive reproductive strategy for trees to enhance seed survival. The high variability in seed crops produces effects that cascade through the food web from seed-eating mice and voles through their weasel and owl predators.

REFERENCES: SILVERTOWN 1980; SORK 1983; NILSSON & WASTLJUNG 1987; WALLER 1993; KELLY 1994; HERRERA ET AL. 1998; SHIBATA ET AL. 1998; HEALY ET AL. 1999; KOENIG 2000; OSTFELD & KEESING 2000; KELLY ET AL. 2001; KELLY & SORK 2002; VANDER WALL 2002; KOENIG & ASHLEY 2003

9.11 Bark Galleries

Tunnels in the wood just under the bark of trees are the work of bark beetles. Adult beetles bore through the outer bark, especially on trees under stress, to the cambial layer of the inner bark, where they excavate channels for laying their eggs. After hatching and beginning to feed, the larvae dig additional channels in which they leave the frass (droppings) and dust from their feeding. Some beetles etch their galleries in the wood beneath the cambium, giving them the name engraver beetles. Different species of beetles produce different patterns in their tunnel galleries, from S-shaped to Y- or H-shaped; different species are also found in different parts of the tree, from high on the trunk to low, and additional species bore into the wood. Mites and fungi may subsequently invade the tunnels. Pines and other conifers are common hosts of bark beetles, but elms, chestnuts, hickories, and other trees are affected, too.

The tunneling activity can harm the trees. In an infestation of bark beetles, galleries may girdle the tree, cutting off the movement of sugars to the roots and killing the tree. The beetles may also introduce a fungus that reduces the movement of water. Reddish dust on the bark or beneath the tree indicates the presence of the beetles, but the beetle galleries become most apparent after a tree dies and the bark peels off. The beetles emit aggregation scents that, along with tree odors, draw in other beetles for a group attack on a tree. Trees fight the attack by oozing resin where the beetles bore in. Not all of the effects are negative; the beetles may thin the forests and create habitat for additional plants and animals, at the same time forming galleries that display their own artistic designs.

REFERENCES: ROSE & LINDQUIST 1973; WHITE 1983; KLEPZIG ET AL. 2001; UNIVERSITY OF ARIZONA COOPERATIVE EXTENSION 2002

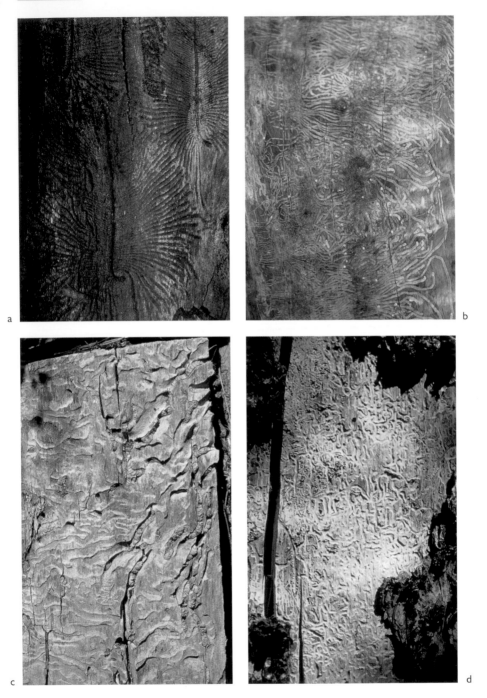

Fig. 9.11. Bark beetle galleries on (a) slippery elm, *Ulmus rubra*; (b) apple, *Malus pumila*; (c) cottonwood, *Populus* sp.; (d) lodgepole pine, *Pinus contorta*. Different species of bark beetles leave galleries of different designs.

9.12 Buck Rubs

Deer sometimes rub their heads and antlers against trees and branches, bruising or shredding the bark and breaking saplings. They do this for two reasons, both related to mating. Rubs in August or September remove the drying velvet (old skin) from around the males' newly developed antlers, occasionally leaving tattered bits of velvet on a broken branch. Most rubs, however, are made a little later in the fall; they communicate a buck's presence during the rut (mating period) and serve to attract females and deter subordinate males. Young, strong, dominant bucks make the most rubs. Rubs start a foot or two above the ground level and then extend upward for another foot or so. The bucks anoint the rubs with secretions from glands near the base of their antlers, leaving scent marks that are enduring signposts for other deer. Bucks with a strong reproductive drive will rub most anything, but they prefer smooth-barked trees such as aspen, or in the southeastern United States, trees with aromatic bark such as cedar and sassafras. They often rub a tree as they first approach it along a trail, so a fresh buck rub can reveal the direction a male is traveling. To communicate the same signals, bucks also tear at the ground with their hooves to make scrapes in which they urinate. Rubs and scrapes are visual and olfactory signs of intense activity of hot-blooded young bucks.

REFERENCES: MURIE 1975; STOKES & STOKES 1986; OZOGA 1999; SMARTNET 2000

a

b

Fig. 9.12.   Buck rubs of white-tailed deer, *Odocoileus virginianus*, on (a) alder, *Alnus* sp., and (b) striped maple, *Acer pensylvanicum*.

Fig. 9.13.   Marked trees: (a) browsing of willow, *Salix* sp., by white-tailed deer, *Odocoileus virginianus*; (b) gnawing of quaking aspen, *Populus tremuloides*, by a beaver, *Castor canadensis*; (c) grizzly bear, *Ursus arctos*, claw marks on Engelman spruce, *Picea engelmannii*; (d) bison, *Bison bison*, horn scratches on spruce.

9.13   Marked Trees

When bark has been bitten or scratched away from a tree trunk or branch, a story is there to figure out. Small branches with cut ends and chewed bark indicate the feeding of deer (ragged cuts; Fig. 9.13a) or rabbits (sharp cuts), while bark stripped away from tree trunks can indicate feeding by various animals, large and small. The size of the tooth marks indicates which animal is responsible, from the tiny teeth of mice to the large ones of moose, which can strip away large sections of bark. Trees gnawed by beavers are easily recognizable (Fig. 9.13b).

More noticeable is when bark scraping has been used for communication, particularly by deer (see 9.12) or bears. Bears mark trees to signal their presence as well as just for a good rub. Choosing a tree near a main trail, they rear to bite or claw the trunk 5 or 6 feet above the ground, often ripping away patches of bark and rubbing their heads and backs against the tree. They leave scents on the exposed wood and a little fur in the oozing sap. Most impressive are the claw marks of a grizzly (Fig. 9.13c), which advertise the size and power of their producer. These marks are made mostly during the summer breeding season.

REFERENCES: MURIE 1975; CHAPMAN & FELDHAMER 1982; STOKES & STOKES 1986

9.14   Sapsucker Holes

Neat rows of small, round, bullet-sized holes in tree trunks are made by sapsuckers, a group of woodpeckers. By drilling into the living tissues of a tree, these birds cause the sap to ooze outward through the holes, providing a liquid food that the sapsuckers return to feed on (Fig. 9.14a). But that's not all; the sap attracts insects as well, particularly ants, and sapsuckers feed on these sap-coated insect snacks, too. The birds prefer aspens, birches, maples, and

a   b   c

Fig. 9.14.   Sapsucker holes: (a) yellow-bellied sapsucker, *Sphyrapicus varius*, with recently made holes; (b) apple, *Malus pumila*; (c) American mountain-ash, *Sorbus americana*, with older holes stretched to an oval shape by the increase in trunk diameter as the tree grew.

apples for their drilling, often choosing less healthy trees. Because the holes are clustered, sap accumulates in that part of the tree, and when the birds drill new holes, typically just above previous holes, the sap flows easily because it is already concentrated on that side. There is no damage to the tree unless fungal infections gain access to the living tissues inside.

Other animals benefit from sapsucker holes, too. Admiral butterflies, honeybees, flies, wasps, and even chipmunks feed at the holes, and hummingbirds that migrate back to northern latitudes before flower nectar is available feed principally at sapsucker holes. Later on, these sap sources become important food within hummingbird-defended territories.

REFERENCES: SUTHERLAND ET AL. 1982; MILLER & NERO 1983; OTVOS & STARK 1985; WILLIAMS 1990; EBERHARDT 2000

9.15   Leaf Nests

After leaves drop from deciduous trees in the autumn, large clumps of dead leaves and twigs 1 to 2 feet in diameter sometimes remain throughout the winter at least 20 feet above the ground or wedged in the fork of two branches. Whenever you see a ragged clump like this, you have found a squirrel nest. Nest building occurs primarily in late summer and autumn, and the nests are most visible when silhouetted against the sky after the tree has shed its leaves. Known in Europe as dreys, the nests are made by red, gray, and fox squirrels from twigs and leaves and are lined by bark stripped from nearby trees. No entrance is visible. Other materials such as moss and grass may be added, and these increase the insulative properties of the nest. Squirrels may den in tree cavities instead, but it is the leaf nests that are so visible to us. Several squirrels sometimes share a nest, although a pregnant or nursing female will not tolerate the presence of others. She may also form a well-lined baby chamber in the nest. Old nests disintegrate over time but remain in trees awaiting renovation and renewal by a new generation of squirrels.

REFERENCES: BURT & GROSSENHEIDER 1964; BARKALOW & SHORTEN 1973; SPRAGINS 2002

a   b

Fig. 9.15.   Leaf nests, (a) and (b), of eastern gray squirrels, *Sciurus carolinensis.*

9.16 Witches'-Brooms and Mistletoes

Bacterialike pathogenic cells, fungal rusts, and mistletoes cause the formation of dense clusters of stunted, abnormal stems on the branches of shrubs and trees. Given their brushlike form, these growths are descriptively known as witches'-brooms, and in eastern North America, the most frequently seen witches'-brooms are produced on hackberry trees by the concerted action of a fungus and a mite.

Among the most distinctive witches'-brooms, however, are those made by parasitic dwarf mistletoes on coniferous trees in western North America. These witches'-brooms include compact branching of the host tree as well as growth of the infecting mistletoe. Like other parasitic plants, mistletoes develop absorptive organs that extract water and nutrients from their hosts. In mistletoes, the connection takes place from the attachment structure, the haustorium, through outgrowths called sinkers that invade the host cambium and transport tissues.

Mistletoes are spread by sticky seeds that adhere to the feet and feathers of birds; in the American Southwest, for example, phainopepla birds are well-known dispersers of desert mistletoe. Once dispersed, a germinating seed begins a mistletoe infection at a needle bundle or in a crevice of a host tree's bark, where a flattened root for attachment can develop. Growing tissues then penetrate the bark through buds or lenticels (see 3.8), and the infection spreads slowly, building a witches'-broom in ten to twenty years. The weight of a large witches'-broom may be enough to cause limbs to break. Mistletoes take sugars, water, and nutrients from their host trees, diminishing the vigor of the tree; they also photosynthesize with their own chlorophyll, but at a slower rate than their hosts. The high rates of transpiration of mistletoes increase their damage to the hosts, particularly during times of water

a

b

c

Fig. 9.16. Witches'-broom of dwarf mistletoe, *Arceuthobium campylopodum*: (a) and (b) on Engelman spruce, *Picea engelmannii*; (c) close-up showing the needle-shaped leaves of the dwarf mistletoe (compare to the spruce needles below).

shortage. Though harmful to the trees, mistletoe witches'-brooms may be useful to birds and mammals such as red squirrels and owls, which use them for nesting and foraging.

The leaves of many parasitic mistletoes resemble the leaves of their host plants. A cryptic appearance occurs most frequently when nitrogen accumulates in the mistletoe, suggesting that this mimicry helps to conceal the nutritious mistletoe leaves from herbivores. Mistletoes whose leaves have less nitrogen than those of the host usually don't resemble the host.

REFERENCES: EHLERINGER ET AL. 1986; RAVEN ET AL. 1999; SELLERS 1999; WALKER 1999; MARCHAND 2001; WATSON 2001; AUKEMA 2003

9.17 Spanish Moss

Trees draped with hanging masses of grayish green Spanish moss are a sure indicator of the southeastern United States. Termed an epiphyte or air plant because of its growth on other plants, this filamentous plant with scalelike leaves on long stems is neither Spanish (it was said to resemble the beards of early Spaniards) nor a moss (it is a bromeliad flowering plant, *Tillandsia usneoides*, related to pineapple and many tropical epiphytes). Nor is Spanish moss harmful to its supporting trees, since it is not parasitic, although great masses may block sunlight to the tree's leaves, and it can absorb so much rain that branches crack under the added weight. Seeds of Spanish moss are blown to other trees, especially live oaks, where they lodge and germinate in cracks in the bark. Short, irregular scales on the plant's stem help trap water, and the plant takes in nutrients from dust and decaying organic matter on the tree. To photosynthesize rapidly, Spanish moss requires high nighttime relative humidity, though it can grow well under a range of light levels. Low temperatures restrict it from growing farther north.

REFERENCES: UHLIG 1956; RICKETT 1967; MARTIN & SIEDOW 1981; MARTIN ET AL. 1981, 1985; WALKER 1999; BEAUFORT COUNTY PUBLIC LIBRARY 2001

a   b   c

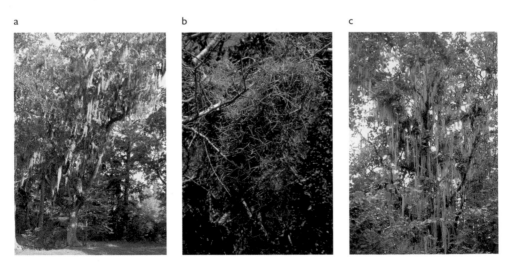

Fig. 9.17. Spanish moss, *Tillandsia usneoides*, (a) draped on live oak, *Quercus virginiana*, and (b) a close-up; (c) lichen, *Usnea* sp., that resembles Spanish moss (a and b, North Carolina; c, Oregon).

9.18   Club Mosses

Diminutive ground pines, ground cedars, and princess pines—all club mosses—appear to be miniature versions of the conifers above them, ignored amid the greenery of summer but conspicuous on the mottled brown forest floor of fall or in the snow of winter. They are evergreen but not trees. Waxy leaves seal these small plants during the water shortages of winter, while internal chemical antifreezes protect them from damage by ice. Other plant chemicals known as alkaloids (a wide-ranging group that includes cocaine, caffeine, and nicotine) confer bad taste and repel herbivores. With these different forms of protection, ground pines, ground cedars, and their club moss relatives have endured for hundreds of millions of years in the same basic form. Club mosses grew abundantly in ancient forests where, after dying, they changed over time into the coal found underground today. As relatives of ferns rather than pines, they don't produce true cones, although some develop conelike clusters of modified, spore-producing leaves. These plants grow in concentrated patches through clonal reproduction, with adjacent individuals connected by underground rhizomes. An entire patch may be a single genetic unit. Just think of a patch of club mosses as a Lilliputian model representing forests that grew 300 million years ago.

REFERENCES: COBB 1963; VITT ET AL. 1988; STAGER 1998; RAVEN ET AL. 1999

Fig. 9.18.   Club mosses: (a) ground pine, *Lycopodium obscurum* (also known as princess pine or tree clubmoss); (b) running cedar, *L. complanatum*; (c) bristly clubmoss, *L. annotinum*. Brown reproductive structures are visible in (a) and (c).

9.19   Forest Fungi

Conspicuous on the trunks of dead and dying trees, shelf fungi are generally woody or leathery in texture, often form overlapping clusters, and may have orange or purple tinges to their typical gray-to-brown shades. They are visible signs of extensive living activity in the wood; the invisible fungus inside is an interwoven mat, known as a mycelium, which consists of miles of threadlike fungal filaments, called hyphae, that are thinner than a human hair and, like the exoskeletons of insects, are strengthened with chitin. These filaments infiltrate dead organic remains; fungi are decomposers, secreting enzymes that digest dead material and absorbing the digestion products through the very large surface area of their hyphae. The greedy hyphae of some fungi "forage" by growing toward concentrations of food. While high in carbon, dead wood is low in the nitrogen needed to make proteins, so some fungi also trap and consume tiny animals by lassoing roundworms in the soil and digesting and absorbing the worms' outer layers.

The enduring shelf fungi seen in forests on standing and fallen dead trees are constant reminders of the presence of these decomposing fungal mats. Shelf fungi, mushrooms, and other fungi, noticeable especially during late summer and fall, are simply reproductive structures. Through gills or pores on the underside of these exposed fruiting bodies, millions of spores are released to grow new filament mats (shelf fungi are known as polypores for the many small pores on their undersides). If you measure size by the total area over which it grows, a fungal mat of the honey mushroom, *Armillaria ostoyae*, is the largest living organism in the world; a single one in Washington state extends for 1,500 acres, and another in Oregon covers 2,200 acres.

REFERENCES: MILLER 1979; BARRON 1992; MARCHAND 2000

Fig. 9.19.   Shelf fungi (polypores): (a) on yellow birch, *Betula alleghaniensis*; (b) on northern red oak, *Quercus rubra*; (c) on a rotting tree trunk.

10. FIELDS AND MEADOWS

The openness of fields and meadows lets one see small mammals, non-native plants, spiders, insects such as spittlebugs and antlions, and many other kinds of plants and animals. But openness is often temporary; most fields and meadows change from year to year, as colonizing plant species replace others in a successional sequence. One consequence is that many of the inhabitants of fields and meadows are able to disperse readily to wherever conditions are suitable. In open fields, many features of nature are visible, but changes in the habitat are inevitable.

Other descriptions that pertain to fields and meadows are:

10.1 Old Field Succession

When no longer plowed, the exposed soil of an abandoned field becomes colonized first by herbaceous plants and then in subsequent years by shrubs and trees. This is the process of succession. Even though windblown seeds are rarely carried farther than 200 yards, small, wind-dispersed seeds of weedy annuals such as mustards and fleabanes reach the field the first year, with short-lived perennials appearing the second year. The arrival of a few golden-rod seeds in an open field leads to the growth and expansion of goldenrod clones until little space remains. Bird-dispersed seeds usually follow wind-dispersed seeds, often producing clumps of plants because the feces of single birds are likely to contain multiple seeds; furthermore, birds often perch (and defecate) in the same places. Mammal-dispersed seeds arrive more slowly, taking a decade or longer, making hickories among the last trees to arrive in the field. Woody shrubs and trees first invade the perimeter of abandoned fields and fill in slowly toward the middle.

The vegetation changes because of a mix of factors: variation in size of seeds and dispersal mechanisms leads to different rates of arrival, and the first plants to reach the field may alter growing conditions for later-arriving plants. Some early arrivals facilitate the colonization of later successional species by providing some shade from intense sunlight, for example, whereas other colonists inhibit the arrival of new species by taking over open spaces. Even herbivores have an effect: high densities of meadow voles slow field succession measurably by their eating the tips of tasty seedlings. Although the rates of colonization vary, different plant species arrive over time and, within decades, a field becomes a forest.

REFERENCES: HARTNETT & BAZZAZ 1985; MCCAUGHEY & SCHMIDT 1987; MYSTER 1993; BAZZAZ 1996; KREBS 2001; MANSON ET AL. 2001; SMITH & SMITH 2001

Fig. 10.1. Succession taking place as an abandoned field gradually returns to a forested state; young trees appear in this field that were not there ten years before.

10.2   Invasive Aliens

Invasive alien plants transform the landscape when they outcompete and displace native species. Primary features that make a plant invasive are a high seed dispersal rate and an ability to grow in diverse conditions; additional features include vegetative growth, rapid development to reproductive age, reduced energetic costs of new leaves, frequent and large seed crops, and small seed size. Small seed size increases seed abundance, dispersal, and rates of germination. Vigor of alien plants is enhanced by growth in stands that are dense enough to exclude other species, by escaping harmful pathogens found in the soil of their native lands, and by having to repel fewer natural enemies in their new land than do native plants (the enemy-release hypothesis). Broad evidence indicates that invasives encounter fewer fungal and viral pathogens where they've been introduced. Competitors for growing space are less effective in slowing the growth of invasives than are predators and pathogens.

With seeds brought in by human transport, some intentionally and some unnoticed, non-native plants colonize in areas where disturbances—roads, trails, construction, logging,

Fig. 10.2.   Invasive alien plants: (a) purple loosestrife, *Lythrum salicaria*; (b) butter-and-eggs, *Linaria vulgaris*; (c) spotted knapweed, *Centaurea maculosa*; (d) leafy spurge, *Euphorbia esula*.

and agriculture—have disrupted the native plant communities. Roads serve as conduits for the spread of seeds into new areas. There is evidence, too, that global increases in nitrogen availability have shifted the competitive balance toward some invasive aliens over natives. Sometimes plants in new locations have diverged genetically from those in their source populations, and they become larger and grow faster. Alien plants can alter habitat suitability, take over native pollinators, be less palatable to native herbivores, and reduce plant diversity; they constitute a silent invasion that forms a major threat to native plant communities. Examples of alien plants are Canada and bull thistles, common mullein, hawkweed, red clover, birdsfoot trefoil, English plantain, purple loosestrife (Fig. 10.2a), wild parsnip, butter-and-eggs (Fig. 10.2b), spotted knapweed (Fig. 10.2c), leafy spurge (Fig. 10.2d), common buckthorn, and Japanese honeysuckle.

REFERENCES: REJMANEK & RICHARDSON 1996; WILLIAMSSON & FITTER 1996; WILLIAMS 1997; AUSTIN 1998; WHITE & SCHWARTZ 1998; WILLIS ET AL. 1999; KOLAR & LODGE 2001; NAGEL & GRIFFIN 2001; SAKAI ET AL. 2001; LEE 2002; VAN DER PUTTEN 2002; DAVIS 2003; GELBARD & BELNAP 2003; MITCHELL & POWER 2003

10.3   Grass Runways

In grassy fields during the summer, field mice and voles, mouse relatives, scurry along the ground on established trails through the vegetation, creating a network of worn runways that are small (1–2 inches wide) but distinct. These trails are most visible right after the melting of winter snow, with small paths and tunnels penetrating through the dead leaves and stems that settle on the muddy surface. Runways are clear signs of activity. Small rodents are mostly nocturnal to avoid hawks and other predators, but they move some in the daytime, too, because their high metabolic rate requires a lot of food energy. Easily attacked by predators, these small mammals cannot travel long distances safely, so they spend only a few minutes at a time out of their burrows traversing their trails. They eat one-third their weight in food each day, which requires a lot of foraging. Flattened vegetation shows where their activity is concentrated, while clipped stems reveal their menu choices.

Fig. 10.3.   Runways for field mice and voles in (a) winter and (b) summer.

a

b

Trails connect to their underground or under snow burrows and nests. Field mice and voles are small animals that lose body heat rapidly, but their burrows insulate them from cold winter air; when the air temperature is below -10°F, deer mice are restricted to their warmer tunnels. But when above ground, whether during the winter or in daytime, they travel rapidly on the highways they construct through the meadow.

REFERENCES: BURT & GROSSENHEIDER 1964; CHAPMAN & FELDHAMER 1982; CONLEY & PORTER 1986

10.4   Bubble Masses

The stems of meadow plants are occasionally draped with salivalike globs of white, wet froth less than an inch long. These bubble masses are the protective coverings of spittlebugs,

soft-bodied insect nymphs with sucking mouthparts (belonging to the traditional insect group Homoptera, which includes aphids, hoppers, and cicadas) that rest head down on plant stems and, hidden from view, feed on watery plant sap that flows in large volumes into and through their bodies. Spittlebugs can reduce plant growth even more than leaf chewers. As fluids exit the ends of their digestive tracts, the spittlebugs blend in mucus from glands and inject air into the mix. This bubbly froth flows by gravity back down over the bugs, providing protective concealment from predators such as ants and a constantly humid environment in which to feed and grow. Using fingers to rub the froth away, one can find a nymph or two inside each spittle mass. Common on goldenrods, spittlebugs are also found on many other plant species, and their spittle masses are typically seen somewhere in the middle of the plant's stems. Most people won't touch the bubbles, which illustrates their repellency.

Once spittlebugs molt into adults, they are known as froghoppers because of a vague resemblance to tiny frogs, and they fly from plant to plant, no longer using froth for protection. Froghoppers hold the record as nature's champion high jumpers. Less than ¼ inch long, they can generate four hundred times the force of gravity when they leap, and reach more than 2 feet into the air.

REFERENCES: MILNE & MILNE 1980; BERENBAUM 1989; MEYER 1993; MEYER & WHITLOW 1992; BURROWS 2003

Fig. 10.4.   Bubble masses: (a) on a goldenrod; (b) the spittlebug itself, a froghopper nymph (unidentified sp.), revealed after the "spittle" has been rubbed away.

a

b

10.5 Web Decorations

To catch flying insects, orb-weaving spiders weave nearly transparent webs of complex design from thin strands of silk they secrete, but some spiders that stay on their webs during the daytime make the web easier to see by adding a conspicuous white cross- or disc-shaped silk structure, the stabilimentum, in the middle. It's a zigzag of heavy stitching, sometimes resembling a zipper, that was given the name *stabilimentum* because it was originally thought to add stability to the web. The form of the stabilimentum may change from disclike for a juvenile to crosslike for an adult.

One hypothesis for the existence of this structure is that it warns birds of the presence of the web so that they won't fly through and damage it, but there are other ideas as well. When a spider is small and sits in the middle of a silken pad, the stabilimentum may hide the spider from its predators by blurring its own outline. Or it may reflect sunlight and so keep the spider cooler on a hot day. An intriguing hypothesis, originating from the fact that the stabilimentum reflects ultraviolet light more than does the rest of the web, suggests that because insects are attracted to the ultraviolet reflectance patterns of flowers, they may actually be drawn to the reflectance pattern of the spider's web. Although the stabilimentum of garden spiders has been shown to attract some kinds of insects, it does not attract all. A problem for the spider is that any conspicuous signal may also attract the spider's own predators, and web decorations do have conflicting effects. Silver argiope spiders, *Argiope argentata*, produce stabilimenta to attract stingless bees as prey, but those that decorate their webs don't survive as

a

b

Fig. 10.5. Web decorations (stabilimenta): (a) orange garden spider, *Argiope aurantia*; (b) silver garden spider, *Argiope argentata*.

long. Evidence supports both the prey attraction and predator protection hypotheses for stabilimenta; they are multipurpose tools that can serve different functions.

REFERENCES: SCHOENER & SPILLER 1992; KERR 1993; PRESTON-MAFHAM & PRESTON-MAFHAM 1996; BLACKLEDGE 1998; TSO 1998A, B; BLACKLEDGE & WENZEL 1999, 2000; HERBERSTEIN ET AL. 2000; CRAIG ET AL. 2001; SEAH & LI 2001; BOWER 2002; HAUBER 2002

10.6 Crab Spiders

An unwary insect that lands on a meadow flower to imbibe nectar may be in for a fatal surprise. Crab spiders lie in wait among flowers to ambush their insect prey because flowers are a predictable place to find insects attracted by nectar and pollen rewards. Not many spiders choose this mode of hunting because of the dangers of being visible in such an open site, but crab spiders tend to match their chosen substrate in color, and at least one species is known to shift from yellow to white and back again over several days. By blending in with the flowers they sit on, they are hidden from both the birds that might eat them and their insect prey. The best way to find a camouflaged crab spider is to look for a bee, fly, or butterfly that is immobile and perched awkwardly on a flower such as goldenrod or daisy; the odd posture is an excellent clue that the insect has become a meal, and mealtime is under way. Crab spiders feed devotedly on one insect at a time and do not store prey; thus, a feeding spider is no threat to other pollinators that land on the same flower. Predictably enough, their success rate is higher when sitting in large, dense patches of flowers because such aggregations attract more insect pollinators. Small bees, which are more likely to be captured, learn to avoid flower patches with crab spiders.

With their front legs spread wide to attack, crab spiders select larger-than-average insects as their prey, which they subdue by injecting a fast-acting poison with digestive enzymes. It

Fig. 10.6. Crab spiders (unidentified species) (a) on a white flower and (b) feeding on captured prey on yellow flowers.

is characteristic of spiders that hunt without prey-restraining silken webs to produce fast-acting poisons. The preferred place to bite is just behind the head of the prey because poison spreads quickly from there, but if the victim struggles from a bite in another place, the spider simply hangs on to both its prey and its perch until the struggle ceases. The spider then sits in place drinking a nutrient broth from its victim.

REFERENCES: PRESTON-MAFHAM & PRESTON-MAFHAM 1996; SCHMALHOFER 2001; DUKAS & MORSE 2003

10.7   Antlion Pits

Conical pits in sheltered, sandy soils conceal tiny but fierce predators. An antlion—the larva of an insect that looks like a damselfly but is related to lacewings—lies within the sand at the bottom of each pit, with its jaws ready to capture an ant or other insect that ventures too close. The antlion first senses vibrations from approaching prey and opens its mandibles. When an insect enters the pit and scrambles to escape, the steep sandy walls give way, helped along by the antlion tossing sand grains upward to keep the prey sliding down. At the bottom, the antlion pierces the unfortunate insect with sharp, curved mandibles; forward-pointing bristles on its body then keep the antlion in place against the pull of the prey as it struggles frantically. Finally, the predator sucks the fluids from its food. Antlions have an exceptionally low metabolic rate, which is advantageous for a sit-and-wait predator, so they can endure long periods without feeding. Starvation reduces their size, but they maintain their pits longer when hungry.

In excavating their pits, antlions back around in a spiral, expelling the larger sand grains because large particles are tossed away more efficiently than small ones. At high densities, antlions interfere with each other by tossing sand into other antlions' pits and taking prey from each other (shadow competition). If an antlion frequently experiences sand thrown into its pit, it relocates farther away, a behavior that leads to a more regular spacing of pits. Antlions are also known as doodlebugs because of the meandering trails they leave in the

a

b

Fig. 10.7.   Antlions: (a) antlion pits, ranging up to two inches across, and (b) an exposed antlion (unidentified species).

sandy surface as they move from one site to another. Antlions are more common in southern and southwestern North America but may be found elsewhere, too. For ants that roam too carelessly, sandy soils conceal great dangers in these pitlike traps.

REFERENCES: LUCAS 1982, 1985, 1989; STOKES 1983; MATSURA & TAKANO 1989; LINTON ET AL. 1991; LOITERTON & MAGRATH 1996; ARNETT & GOTELLI 2001; ANTLION PIT 2001; LOMASCOB & FARJI-BRENER 2001; ARCHBOLD BIOLOGICAL STATION 2002

10.8 Worms and Rain

Rain-soaked roads and driveways become littered with earthworms. Although it looks as though they've surfaced to avoid drowning in their burrows, worms do not drown. The moistness of their skin allows them to absorb oxygen directly, and by keeping their skin

wet, rain may actually give them a chance to become more active above ground. Three ideas have been proposed for the benefits of surfacing: (1) the worms may disperse more readily on the wet surface than they do underground; (2) they may find bits of organic matter, their food, in greater abundance on the surface; and (3) they may encounter mates more quickly on the two-dimensional ground surface than they do in the three-dimensional soil through which they burrow. This last hypothesis is supported by the fact that the

Fig. 10.8. An earthworm at the surface after rain.

worms appearing on the surface are larger than average. Whatever the benefits may be, surfacing produces hazards as well, as many worms are flattened by cars, and others form a rainy buffet that's enjoyed by robins. Of course, worms are more visible on the homogenous substrates of lawns and pavement and more concealed within the vegetation of a field.

REFERENCES: MERTUS 1993; FOX 2001; LOS ANGELES COUNTY DEPARTMENT OF PUBLIC WORKS 2000

10.9 Worm Casts

Burrowing along underground, earthworms ingest soil to extract the nutrients found within. What goes in must come out, however, so they move to the surface regularly to deposit casts, small mounds of processed soil that are rich in bacteria and organic materials. Cast deposition is greatest in the moist months of spring and fall, and the black, rich casts, known as vermicompost, are prized by gardeners. Worm activity is highly beneficial by aerating the soil and improving drainage. Not everyone enjoys the side effects, though, as worm casting is considered a problem on the manicured lawns of golf courses. Less worm activity takes place in poorer soils such as dense clay, abrasive sand, and acidic earth.

Transit time through the gut ranges from a couple of hours to half a day, depending on the grain size and nutrient content of the soil ingested. Casts wash away rapidly during rainfall but may last for days when dry. In one cornfield, soil erosion from worm casts

Fig. 10.9. Earthworm casts on a lawn.

amounted to three pounds per square meter per year. Earthworms also factor significantly in the spread of spores of mycorrhizal fungi, which contribute importantly to plant growth. Castings are rich in nitrogen as well as in nitrifying and denitrifying bacteria. One writer has estimated that vegetated land supports about 900 pounds of worms per acre, which means a whole lot of soil processing is taking place in the ground underneath us. Where the land is disturbed, however, exotic species are replacing native earthworms; a recent listing notes that at least 30 percent of the earthworm species in North America are introduced, including the fisherman's favorite, nightcrawlers. Alien worms are altering the leaf litter and nutrient cycles wherever they're found.

REFERENCES: GANGE 1993; HENDRIX 1995; BINET & LEBAYON 1999; LEBAYON & BINET 1999; PARKIN 1999; MARCHAND 2000; SOUTHERN STATES COOPERATIVE 2001

10.10   Fairy Rings

The ground under a mushroom conceals a mass of filaments that grow by secreting enzymes over dead organic material and absorbing the products of chemical digestion. Mushrooms are the visible reproductive structures of the unseen fungal filaments, collectively called the mycelium, that form the body of the fungus (see 9.19). In the homogeneous habitat of a lawn or field, a soil fungus may grow uniformly outward in all directions, absorbing nutrients as it spreads and, in autumn, sprouting mushrooms near the expanding front. The circles of mushrooms formed this way, known as fairy rings, can spread 1 or 2 feet per year and reach

diameters up to 100 feet, all resulting from the growth of a single fungal mycelium over many years. The vegetation within a fairy circle often grows less well than that outside because dense fungal filaments can impede water drainage through the soil, and absorption by the fungal filaments leaves fewer nutrients—potassium, nitro-

Fig. 10.10.   A fairy ring (unidentified species) in a lawn.

gen, and phosphorus—behind. Chemicals secreted by the fungus may also slow plant growth within the ring. Sometimes a circle of brown grass is a clue to the presence of a fungus, and intensive watering may bring out the mushrooms. Long ago, these circular patterns were thought to be produced by the feet of a ring of dancing fairies, who then sat on the mushrooms to rest, and that is the origin of the common name. Grasses and club mosses occasionally show a similar ringlike appearance resulting from clonal growth outward from a dying center.

REFERENCES: EDWARDS 1984; DJAJAKIRANA & JOERGENSEN 1996; RAVEN ET AL. 1999

10.11 British Soldiers

Little bits of scarlet add brilliance to a sometimes drab field or forest floor. Like the British redcoats of centuries ago, for whom they are named, British soldier lichens draw one's attention by their gaudy, distinctive display. British soldiers, *Cladonia cristatella*, are the best-known lichens in eastern North America because they are so easily recognized and so tolerant of variable growth conditions; a similar species called toy soldiers, *Cladonia bellidiflora*, is found in western North America. British soldier lichen is named for its fungal component (mycobiont), *Cladonia cristatella;* its photosynthetic component (photobiont) is the green alga *Trebouxia erici.* As symbiotic unions of a fungus with photosynthetic algae or cyanobacteria (see 8.14), lichens grow on stable, well-lit, but nutrient-poor substrates. Although the fungal and photosynthetic components can grow separately, they merge into a lichen when starved; the fungus provides structure and water retention, while the algae create organic materials through photosynthesis. The upwardly protruding, red-capped parts of British soldiers are reproductive structures of its fungus, containing tiny sacs, called asci, within which large numbers of spores are produced. The fungus and algae must disperse together to form a new lichen.

This description begs the question of why the reproductive parts should be so brightly colored, a question that remains unanswered. The color may have to do with the complex array of chemicals produced by lichens, some of which deter the growth of neighboring fungi. Alternatively, red may advertise the lichen as inedible or may be just an accidental by-product of the lichen's chemistry. The red is produced by pigments called anthraquinones. Only the top parts are red, and the shadier the habitat, the grayer the rest of the lichen. With the color they provide, it's easy to take a likin' to these brilliant, tiny mushroom relatives.

REFERENCES: HALE 1967; CULBERSON ET AL. 1983; GOLDNER ET AL. 1986; BRODO ET AL. 2001

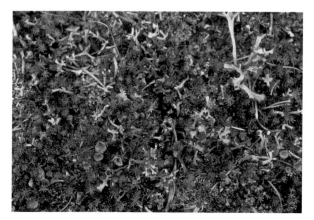

Fig. 10.11. British soldiers, *Cladonia cristatella,* which are conspicuous red lichens in fields and on old wood.

11.   DESERTS AND PRAIRIES

In deserts and prairies, scarcity of water controls the shapes plants take and where they grow. A number of adaptive forms found in deserts, such as gray, hairy leaves, are repeated on mountaintops because of limited moisture there, too, but it's in deserts that xeric adaptations (those that allow growth under dry conditions) are most evident. The biological diversity of deserts is surprisingly rich, and open expanses allow one to observe stark distributional patterns in these habitats, from horizon to horizon.

11.1 Green Ribbons

There's a visible pattern in how water affects the distribution of plants in the arid West of North America. Cottonwoods and willows grow along streams but not in the drier sagebrush prairie; the trees' association with waterways and the dying back of their branches during droughts demonstrate their sensitivity to groundwater depth. From afar, one can trace the meandering path of a stream across the prairie by the ribbon of trees, usually cottonwoods, that marks the stream's presence (Fig. 11.1a). The presence of streamside trees is a common pattern in the West, and these riparian corridors serve as highways for foxes, coyotes, and other animals to traverse the landscape. A similar pattern is seen in southwestern deserts, where spring rains bring a flush of green to the vegetation lining the network of streambeds.

Wherever water flows in western fields, greenery sprouts. Lush crops fill the fields on the downhill side of irrigation canals, while dry sagebrush covers the uphill slopes. Paved roads across the prairie are lined with greener vegetation because of the surface runoff that collects at road edges (Fig. 11.1b); furthermore, evaporation is lessened by pavement, so plants, often non-native species, tap into an increased water supply by sending their roots underneath the road. Wherever precipitation is limited, as in much of western North America, the patterns of vegetative growth are the best indicators of where water can be found.

REFERENCES: PATTEN 1998; ROOD ET AL. 2000; MARCHAND 2002

Fig. 11.1. Green ribbons:
(a) cottonwood trees lining a stream across a western prairie; (b) greener vegetation lining the edges of a paved road.

a

b

11.2 Plant Spacing

Most of the time, plants grow in clumps, but shortages of water in very dry habitats severely limit their growth and yield a very different spatial pattern. Arid-zone plants often spread out evenly as a result of competition for water. The spatial separation of aboveground plant parts is what we see, but the most important interactions take place out of sight, among the roots. Deep taproots that penetrate down 15 feet or more from a shrub and broad lateral roots that reach up to 12 feet away can suck up enough moisture to limit the growth of any nearby plant. An established individual may be so efficient at gathering water that its own seedlings cannot survive near it. A more devious mechanism of competition for space is through toxic secretions (allelopathic chemicals; see 2.22) released from the roots and leaves that restrict the germination and growth of nearby plants. Rain washes over the leaf surfaces of creosote bush in the American Southwest, for example, and leaches out inhibitory chemicals that concentrate in the soil underneath. The uniform plant distributions of arid zones suggest surprisingly powerful inhibitions among the plants that grow there.

REFERENCES: BEALS 1968; SCHULTZ & FLOYD 1999; HYDER ET AL. 2002

a

b

c

Fig. 11.2. The even spacing of shrubs in arid areas: (a) creosote bush, *Larrea tridentata* (California); (b) gray matplant, *Tiquilia nesiotica* (Galapagos); (c) sagebrush, *Artemesia tridentata* (Wyoming).

11.3 Gray Plants

Shades of gray rather than green are the predominant colors of plants in the desert. Under heat and bright sun, light-colored hairs and spines reflect sunlight and so reduce the amount of heat built up in photosynthetic tissues. Heat increases water loss, already a problem in dry environments, so any mechanism that reduces light and heat can help to retain water

a

b

Fig. 11.3. Gray arid-zone plants:
(a) desert holly, *Atriplex hymenelytra*
(California); (b) sagebrush, *Artemesia tridentata* (Wyoming); (c) teddy bear cholla cactus, *Opuntia bigelovii* (New Mexico).

c

and thereby increase the growth of a plant. Leaf hairs are actually hairlike scales called trichomes (see 3.1), which can grow long and thick and reflect sunlight with their pale coloration. Some leaves also have a thick, light-colored cuticle or secrete a gray, waxy substance that protects against ultraviolet radiation. On the top of a cactus such as cholla, dense spines reflect sunlight and provide shade, sometimes so much so that the stem no longer appears green. Of course, the same spines also protect against herbivores that would otherwise feed heavily on the cactus to get at the moisture within. Experimental removal of spines on a cactus leads to higher irradiance of the cactus surface and greater photosynthetic rates but usually at the cost of greater heat load and water loss. The common pale appearance of many desert plants results from several different solutions to excessive light and heat.

REFERENCES: EHLERINGER ET AL. 1976; EHLERINGER & MOONEY 1978; NOBEL 1983; NORMAN & MARTIN 1986; PHILLIPS & COMUS 2000

11.4 Small Leaves

Broad, flat leaves are rarely seen among desert plants because wide surfaces intercept more sunlight and so become hotter and lose more water. Larger size also slows the convective loss of heat to the cooler air that flows over leaf surfaces, so large leaves can literally cook in the heat. The characteristic of having small leaves, known as microphylly, serves to reduce

a   b   c

Fig. 11.4. Small leaves: (a) ocotillo, *Fouquieria splendens*, stems with leaves and flowers; (b) close-up of leaves of ocotillo; (c) leaves of foothill paloverde, *Cercidium microphyllum*.

heat and retain water by lowering transpiration rates (the loss of water through the leaf pores or stomates). The threshold size for desert leaves is about half an inch across, for even in full sun, leaves of this size and smaller can remain below lethal temperatures, roughly 115°F, without the use of water for cooling. Although small leaves reduce the total amount of photosynthetic tissue, light energy is abundant for plant growth. Small leaves may also be shed in a drought and regrown quickly after a rain. As a result, the presence of small leaves and leaflets is common in desertlike environments. Plants that produce larger leaves usually do so only in the rainy season or in shaded habitats.

REFERENCE: PHILLIPS & COMUS 2000

11.5   Green Stems

In one or more ways, desert plants have evolved to cope with water stress. Some have opted for chlorophyll-bearing stems in addition to or in place of leaves because more water can be stored in the stems while photosynthesis can take place near the surfaces of these structures. Some plants, such as cactus, are succulents; with extensive, shallow roots only inches deep, they take up and store large amounts of water after a rain and then minimize the loss of water in dry times with their thick, waxy cuticles, minimal exposed surface area, use of internal organic compounds that hold on strongly to water molecules, and root dieback. Most succulents also use a form of photosynthesis that is very efficient in water usage. Plants with crassulacean acid metabolism (CAM) open their leaf pores (stomates) at night so they can take up carbon dioxide when the air is cooler; that way, they don't lose as much water as they would by opening in the warmer daytime, and they store carbon dioxide in organic acids until the light of day, when photosynthesis can proceed.

Water storage makes the plants attractive to thirsty desert-dwelling animals, however, so succulents gain protection from herbivores by way of bitter taste or the evolutionary modification of leaves into sharp spines (Fig. 11.5a). Spines lack stomatal openings, so they also lessen water loss; furthermore, thick clusters of spines reflect light to reduce overheating. Paloverde (a name meaning "green stick"; Fig. 11.5b) and ocotillo, woody plants of southwestern deserts, make use of two different strategies to cope with water stress: like cactus, the stems of both are green and photosynthetic, and both produce small leaves that can be shed in times of drought. These plants are slow growers, however, because most of the photosynthetic gain of the tree is from its bark, and photosynthesis is less efficient in bark than it is in leaves.

REFERENCES: BOWERS 1993; PHILLIPS & COMUS 2000

Fig. 11.5. Green stems: (a) prickly pear cactus, *Opuntia polyacantha*; (b) foothill paloverde, *Cercidium microphyllum*.

a

b

11.6   Vertical Leaves and Stems

Because intense sunlight increases the heat and water stress on plants in arid environments, a plant response that reduces the heat load is to orient photosynthetic tissue, both leaves and stems, parallel to the sun's rays during the hottest time of early afternoon. Such a vertical arrangement also increases the amount of light striking plant surfaces when the sun is lower during the morning and late afternoon, which is when temperatures are lower and photosynthesis is more water-efficient. Pads (flattened stems) of prickly pear cactus, for example, are noticeably more vertical than horizontal in hot environments (Fig. 11.6a). They're often oriented more north-south than east-west, too, to increase their absorbance of photosynthetically active radiation. Other plants such as grasses, sedges, and yucca cope with brightly lit habitats by having leaves that are erect. Heat isn't the only stress; high light intensities reduce photosynthetic gain by partially reversing the retention of carbon dioxide. Because heat and light are correlated, having green surfaces oriented vertically is a common response of plants to reduce two problems in bright, warm habitats.

REFERENCES: NOBEL 1980; PHILLIPS & COMUS 2000

a
b

Fig. 11.6.   Vertical plant structures: (a) pads (stems) of prickly pear cactus, *Opuntia* sp.; (b) vertical leaves in a hot coastal zone, likely of *Jacquinia berterii* (Virgin Islands).

11.7   Salt Gradients

In many parts of western North America, the water from occasional rain leaches salts from the soil and runs downslope to topographically low areas, where evaporation in warm, dry air leaves concentrated salt accumulations on the soil surface. Over time, a gradient in salinity builds up toward these low areas. High salinity challenges plant growth in two ways. Saline soils have a strong osmotic attraction for water, thus limiting the ability of roots to absorb water; furthermore, an accumulation of salts may be toxic to plant tissues. Salty soils simply accentuate drought conditions, so they are characterized by salt-tolerant plants (halophytes) and thinner vegetation. Extreme sites, such as the Bonneville salt flats of Utah, are entirely devoid of plant growth. Just like people, plants can get too much salt.

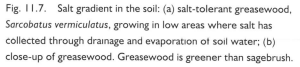

Fig. 11.7. Salt gradient in the soil: (a) salt-tolerant greasewood, *Sarcobatus vermiculatus*, growing in low areas where salt has collected through drainage and evaporation of soil water; (b) close-up of greasewood. Greasewood is greener than sagebrush.

Several mechanisms give plants a greater ability to grow in saline soils. The roots of some maintain high salt levels internally to help draw in water, while increased organic solutes (e.g., sorbitol) in aboveground tissues strengthen their osmotic potential to draw water upward. Succulence and thicker leaves are characteristic, too, as in greasewood, which takes up water to dilute internal salt levels. Saltbush of the arid West prevents the toxic buildup of excessive salts by expelling them through salt glands and leaf hairs, giving a shredded appearance to the leaves. Other plants, especially those that grow in rosette form, may shed outer leaves in which salts have accumulated. The shift to more salt-tolerant species in low areas is visible to us by changes in the overall shade of green of the vegetation.

REFERENCES: GORHAM ET AL. 1981; BOWERS 1993; LARCHER 1995; DONOVAN ET AL. 1996; RAVEN ET AL. 1999; SMITH & SMITH 2001

11.8 Desert Gradients

Conditions for growth vary across all landscapes, including deserts, because soil texture, water-holding capacity, and salinity change gradually across gentle slopes. In southwestern deserts, deep alluvial sediments wash down from mountains to form bajada or piedmont landforms that provide a place for plants with deep taproots. On these slopes lives a vegetation typical of the Sonoran Desert of Arizona, with many species and growth forms: saguaro cactus, ocotillo, and various small trees such as paloverde. The lower elevations of Sonoran Desert landscapes support scattered creosote bush (particularly in calcareous soils), cholla cactus, and bursage (particularly in clay soils), and thus appear more like the Mojave Desert of southern California or the Chihuahuan Desert of southern New Mexico and western Texas. These are tough, drought-tolerant plants. Saltbush dominates in flat areas near streams where salts accumulate. Especially in deserts, the composition of the vegetation is highly sensitive to slight variations in water availability, which is influenced strongly by gradients in elevation and salinity and differences in soil structure. The vegetation shows us the subtle gradients.

Fig. 11.8. Gradients in the Sonoran Desert, from (a) creosote bush in the low desert to (b) a diverse desert flora with giant saguaro cactus on the upper slopes.

a

b

REFERENCES: YEATON & CODY 1979; KEY ET AL. 1984; BOWERS & LOWE 1986; MONTANA 1990; CORNELIUS ET AL. 1991; BARBOUR & BILLINGS 2000; HAMERLYNCK ET AL. 2000; PHILLIPS & COMUS 2000; HAMERLYNCK ET AL. 2002

11.9 Flower Show

When spring arrives in American deserts, bringing with it rain, warmth, and longer days, plants have the chance to flower and set seed before the onset of midsummer heat and dryness. The race to reproduce is on. When winter rains have been frequent, particularly in El Niño years in the American Southwest, the desert becomes carpeted with springtime flowers; splashes of orange, blue, white, pink, and other colors glow against a greenish background, replacing the usual drab browns and grays. After a wet winter, March is showtime in the desert for both annuals and perennials.

Many annuals grow in southwestern deserts, and their seeds break dormancy as days grow longer and moisture accumulates. Early germination provides the best opportunity for growth, but any single rain may be followed by a long drought. Consequently, desert annuals follow a bet-hedging strategy. Only some seeds germinate in each wet spell, and if the moisture lasts, those seedlings survive and flower, but if it doesn't, then only a few seeds are lost. High variability in desert precipitation makes this strategy successful. Furthermore, unpredictability in

a

b

c

Fig. 11.9.   Spring flower show in the desert. (a) and (b) Mexican gold poppies, *Eschscholtzia mexicana,* and mixed flowers among the cactus in the Sonoran Desert (Arizona); (c) lupine and other flowers in a great basin desert (Wyoming).

rainfall leads to a higher percentage of annuals being found in the flora than where the pattern of precipitation is more predictable. An inch of soaking rain is needed to spur the abundant germination of spring annuals. Later-appearing annuals may flower after summer rains. In the most arid environments, a smaller fraction of seeds germinates with each rain, and seeds remain in the soil ready to germinate for several years: the same strategy of hedging bets, but carried over a longer term. Still, there is a greater chance of survival when growth begins early, so germination is skewed toward the beginning of the spring.

REFERENCES: FREAS & KEMP 1983; KADMON & SHMIDA 1990; FOX 1992; PHILIPPI 1993; NARITA 1998; CLAUSS & VENABLE 2000; MORIUCHI ET AL. 2000; PHILLIPS & COMUS 2000; TIELBOERGER & KADMON 2000; RAVER 2001

11.10   Nurse Plants

Known especially from arid environments, nurse plants are those that promote the growth of other plants underneath their branches. By ameliorating local conditions—providing shade from a hot sun, reducing soil temperatures, giving access to mineral nutrients, concealing seedlings from herbivores, and possibly increasing bacterial and mycorrhizal (fungal) associations— nurse plants facilitate the germination of seeds and survival of seedlings. The higher availability of nutrients under nurse plants results from their efficiency in harvesting nutrients from the surrounding soil and the deposition underneath of leaf litter, wind drift, and animal feces. Some effects are incidental, as when fallen segments from large cacti deter herbivores from finding newly germinated seedlings. Plants with distinctly clumped distributions often began life under nurse plants. The hotter and drier the environment, the greater the importance of nurse plants.

In the American Southwest, mesquite and paloverde (Fig. 11.10a) are important nurse plants, as is desert ironwood, which is known to shelter 165 species of plants and is the longest-lived tree (over eight hundred years) in the Sonoran Desert. In dry sites, ironwood increases plant diversity and abundance. Saguaro cactus, pincushion cactus, and most other desert plants require nurse plants for seedling survival. Few species can tolerate the extreme conditions of an open desert habitat, although bursage (Fig. 11.10b) and creosote bush can, thus making them critical species in the vegetation of the desert. Not all interactions with nurse plants are positive, however. Patchy and reduced light can slow seedling growth, while root overlap can lead to competition for water. The shallow roots of saguaro cactus help it collect rainwater so well that it dooms its nurse plants to accelerated death.

REFERENCES: MCAULIFFE 1984; NOBEL 1989; FRANCO & NOBEL 1989, 1990; BOWERS 1997; BOLEN 1998; FLORES ET AL. 1998; MARTINEZ & MORENO 1998; RAFFAELE & VEBLEN 1998; LEIRANA & PARRA 1999; CAZON ET AL. 2000; HOLMGREN ET AL. 2000; PHILLIPS & COMUS 2000; TIELBOERGER & KADMON 2000; TEWKSBURY & LLOYD 2001

b

a

Fig. 11.10.   Nurse plants of giant saguaro, *Carnegiea gigantea*, under: (a) foothill paloverde, *Cercidium microphyllum*; (b) bursage, *Ambrosia* sp.

11.11 Sagebrush Variation

The widespread and familiar plant of western prairies, big sagebrush (*Artemisia tridentata*), is represented by three genetically distinguishable varieties: Wyoming big sagebrush (less than 2 feet tall) throughout low, arid intermountain basins; basin big sagebrush (up to 6 feet tall) in intermediate zones; and mountain big sagebrush (3 feet tall) on foothills and at higher, moister elevations. Wyoming big sagebrush can tolerate habitats that are more arid because it produces smaller aboveground parts combined with longer roots. Sagebrush has expanded throughout western states over the past 150 years as perennial grasses have declined from overgrazing. Its pungent fragrance, widely known as the distinctive smell of the West, derives from aromatic plant chemicals called terpenes (some of which make up the paint solvent turpentine).

Sagebrush grows in deep, well-drained soils, with roots spreading up to 5 feet out and sometimes reaching 20 feet down to take up rain and snowmelt. Individual shrubs may live more than a century. The size of an individual shrub reflects both its genetic heritage (the different varieties) and the conditions under which it grows. Where snow accumulates in ravines and on the leeward side of ridges, soil moisture is available longer into the summer, and shrubs can grow to larger sizes; size of sagebrush can indicate overall water availability (some consider the land "productively arable" if the sagebrush averages at least 3 feet tall). If sagebrush can start growing in a dry area, then wind-blown snow and silt accumulate around the shrubs and promote expansion of that patch to form a sagebrush island. Wherever sage grows, animals such as antelope and sage grouse follow for cover and winter forage.

REFERENCES: TAYLOR & VALUM 1974; MCARTHUR & WELCH 1982; WELCH & JACOBSON 1988; REYNOLDS & FRALEY 1989; KNIGHT 1994; KOLB & SPERRY 1999; REED 2002.

a

b

Fig. 11.11. Variation in size of big sagebrush, *Artemesia tridentata:* (a) small; (b) intermediate; (c) large.

c

11.12   Insect Magnets

Late summer on the western plains brings dryness and fewer flowers than could be found a month or two earlier. Among the plants that bloom late in the season are numerous species in the aster (composite) family, most of which have flowers that look like tiny yellow daisies. Insects flying in August and September congregate at these flowering sites to imbibe nectar. A prime example is the shrub rabbitbrush (genus *Chrysothamnus*, from the Greek for "golden shrub"); with a shortage of feeding stations across a broad landscape of dusty dryness, each yellow-flowered rabbitbrush is a nectar and pollen oasis to which hungry butterflies, bees, and flies are drawn (Fig. 11.12a, b). Late-flowering goldenrods are similar yellow attractants (Fig. 11.12c). The focus on feeding is so strong in the insects that human observers barely distract them. Rabbitbrush itself is widespread throughout western landscapes because of its tolerance of drought and cold, though it is more restricted to moister soils than is sagebrush. It grows rapidly until the beginning of August, when flowering begins, and experiences little herbivory because of antifeedant chemicals produced within its leaves. Rabbitbrush and goldenrod, abundant plants in western lowlands, provide a surefire way to find insects in the arid West after other plants have ceased flowering.

REFERENCES: SANKHLA ET AL. 1987; BOWERS 1993

a

Fig. 11.12.   Insect magnets: (a) rubber rabbitbrush, *Chrysothamnus nauseosus*, with fritillary butterflies, *Speyeria* sp.; (b) rabbitbrush with ruddy copper butterfly, *Lycaena rubidus*; (c) goldenrod, *Solidago* sp., with small wood-nymph, *Cercyonis oetus*, butterflies.

b

c

11.13 Tumble Plants

In open and windy habitats, the wind can disperse not just individual seeds but sometimes entire dried, dead, seed-bearing parent plants, which scatter their seeds as they roll. Native tumble mustards (genus *Sisymbrium*) disperse seeds from their elongate seed pods this way, but the best-known example is the tumbleweed of the western plains. Also known as Russian thistle (*Salsola kali*), tumbleweeds are annual plants that were introduced into this country from Asia in the 1870s, probably by seeds that hitchhiked with imported grains. They show the features expected of a tumble plant: (1) a spherical form, 1 to 2 feet high, that rolls well; (2) growth as an annual so that the plants die and scatter seeds every year; and (3) flowers produced throughout the plant volume, not just on the outside, so all the seeds aren't knocked off by first contact with the soil surface.

Fig. 11.13. A characteristic sight in western North America: a tumbleweed caught in a fence.

When a tumbleweed dies in the autumn, it breaks free from its roots and then rolls freely across the windswept plains, scattering ripened seeds along the way until, typically, it is caught by a rancher's barbed wire fence. Each plant may produce 250,000 seeds. Despite their noxious attributes, tumbleweeds are not strong competitors with native plants, so they grow in disturbed soil along roads and fences and in overgrazed fields rather than in the midst of established prairie vegetation. The intensive plowing of western prairies that began in the late 1800s opened up widespread habitat for these plants to invade and become ubiquitous. With their footloose freedom, tumbleweeds have become an icon of the West.

REFERENCES: ALLEN & KNIGHT 1984; YOUNG 1991; TAYLOR 1992; WILLIAMS 2003

11.14 Chaparral Form

If sagebrush reminds one generally of the West, chaparral is reminiscent particularly of California. Chaparral, the plant community of the coastal range, consists of numerous shrubs with extensive roots, dense branching, and small, thick, tough, evergreen leaves: ceanothus, manzanita, scrub oak, chamise. The commonality of these features suggests that different species have converged in form to survive the environmental challenges of their habitat. Summer drought, especially, has guided the evolution of this plant community. Woody chaparral has low photosynthetic capacity, but by being evergreen, the shrubs can grow year round. The leaves are costly to the plants to produce because of the amount of carbon they require but are well defended against herbivory by their repellent chemistry. Chaparral is not tall, but it is nearly impenetrable; the chaps of western cowboys were designed to protect against vegetation of this kind.

Fires occur regularly in the chaparral in late summer and autumn, especially following the sweep of hot, dry winds. Older stands burn first and hotter because more fuel has accumulated there. Frequent fires keep the amount of dead wood low, reducing the likelihood of less frequent, larger fires, but human dwellings in the chaparral are threatened annually by the natural and expected occurrence of fire. Afterward, wildflowers flourish, and the shrubs regrow from roots and stumps; manzanita even requires fire for its seeds to germinate. Then the renewal process of vegetative succession leads once again back to the dominance of tough shrubs that can endure the hot, dry summers.

REFERENCES: MOONEY & MILLER 1985; DALLMAN 1998; MINNICH 2001

Fig. 11.14.   Thick shrubs of the California chaparral.

12. WATER AND WETLANDS

The presence of water in a wetland exerts as strong an effect in this habitat as does the lack of water in a desert. Wet-zone vegetation includes plants that are wetland indicators and those with specialized underwater leaves. With their abundant vegetative growth, wetlands support a wide range of animal life, including frogs, turtles, muskrats, and blackbirds. Whether the water is flowing or still, hot or cold, some living things are adapted to live in and near it, and that richness makes wetlands great places for exploration.

12.1 Wetland Indicators

Although water is necessary for growth, most plants cannot survive constant immersion. Wetlands are depressions in the landscape characterized by standing water, modified soils, and perennial soft-stemmed plants such as sedges and rushes that can tolerate being rooted under water. The transition from dry land to wetland is often conspicuous because of changes in the vegetation; goldenrods that grow outside a freshwater marsh, for example, are replaced by cattails within. Looking over a marsh, one can easily see where the soil changes from wet to dry by changes in the accompanying vegetation. Knowledge of the plant species is not necessary, for the transition is apparent simply because of differences in the shades of green. There are many different kinds of wetlands, of course, including marshes, swamps, bogs, wet meadows, and potholes, and each is characterized by different plant species. Laws about human use of wetlands require some way of recognizing their boundaries, and that is usually done by mapping the wetland plants. The easiest way to tell where there is or has been standing water is simply to look at the overall structure and color of the vegetation.

REFERENCES: MITSCH & GOSSELINK 1986; TINER 1993

Fig. 12.1. Water level at a freshwater marsh indicated by cattails (standing water) and goldenrods and trees (drier soil).

12.2 Aquatic Leaves

Depending on whether they develop at or below the water surface, the leaves of an aquatic plant may grow in two different forms despite being genetically the same. Submerged leaves are usually narrow and finely divided, whereas emergent and floating leaves are much broader, looking like more typical terrestrial leaves. Pondweeds (Fig. 12.2a) and water buttercups (Fig. 12.2b) are aquatic plants that show this pattern. The different shapes (leaf dimorphism)

Fig. 12.2. Leaf shape of aquatic leaves: (a) broad floating leaves over narrower submerged leaves of pondweed, *Potamogeton* sp.; (b) finely divided submerged leaves of water buttercup, *Ranunculus aquatilis*.

are advantageous because of the nature of the two different environments. Leaves in the air receive additional sunlight and photosynthesize more, whereas submerged leaves must endure the tearing forces of a movable viscous medium. Underwater leaves also have severely limited photosynthetic rates because of the comparatively low concentration of CO_2 in water.

The elongate shape of underwater leaves is due to the high turgor pressure (cells being full of water) found within submerged, elastic exterior cells. Aerial leaves, in contrast, have less pressure because water is lost through the leaf pores (stomates). Plant hormones can produce differently shaped leaves by effecting changes in cell pressure and elasticity that mimic the impact of air and water environments on leaf development. These examples illustrate how strongly environmental conditions may govern a developmental outcome.

REFERENCES: KANE & ALBERT 1987; RAVEN ET AL. 1999; SAND & FROST 1999

12.3   Reed Jungles

Giant reed, *Phragmites australis*, is a grasslike plant of worldwide distribution that grows in dense junglelike stands up to 14 feet tall, with feathery flowering tops that change in the fall from purple to brown. It is a memorable experience to walk through a dense patch of this plant. Not only are these reeds tall, but they persist long after death as hollow-stemmed, erect dried plants, a feature that makes them popular for household decoration. Giant reeds stabilize the soil, enhance nutrient cycling, and dry the substrate through transpirational water loss; in Europe, they are used for roof thatch and wastewater treatment. The plants can grow in oxygen-poor sites because of pressurized ventilation that forces air internally through the stems toward the roots.

But giant reeds are invasive along the edges of marshes or wherever they can gain a foothold. Where marshes are disturbed, particularly by dredging and ditching, reeds become dominant, especially where wetter and in nutrient-rich sites. While the species is native to North America, giant reeds are spreading throughout inland marshes, and there is genetic evidence that an aggressive, foreign strain is replacing a native one. The new strain is an example of a cryptic invader, one that isn't noticed or easily recognized. Giant reeds grow by rhizomes (underground stems) and runners (stems on the ground surface) in stands so thick that whatever other vegetation has been present is squeezed out, and slowly the native plants decline in abundance. A walk through a stand of these plants will convince you of their ability to compete strongly for space in a marsh.

REFERENCES: BERTNESS 1999; BARBOUR & BILLINGS 2000; VRETARE & WEISNER 2000; AILSTOCK ET AL. 2001; SALTONSTALL 2002

b

a

Fig. 12.3. Giant reed, *Phragmites australis*: (a) invasion of a wetland; (b) flowering heads.

12.4 Spring Peeping

One of the more predictable signs of spring is the sound of spring peepers singing in the early evening. Spring peepers are small tree frogs found widely in eastern North America near diverse, mostly permanent wetlands. When the temperature reaches 30°F, males start singing to attract mates, and they form lively choruses as more males join in. Females are sensitive to the sound frequencies of male calls and are drawn to the loud choruses of groups of males. Males space themselves out so that they can just hear a neighboring male's call; this spatial arrangement keeps them within the chorus but not too near a competitor. Males that sing more persistently mate more often, but it is energetically expensive to sing. So that they can sing longer, males have trunk muscles for vocalization that are five times larger relative to

Fig. 12.4. A singing male spring peeper, *Hyla crucifer*, with throat inflated.

body size than those of females. Oxidation of fats provides the energy to keep singing. Stronger and healthier males can sing more persistently within the chorus and consequently mate more often, and females that mate with these healthier males likely produce more surviving offspring. Whenever spring peepers are singing, there's courtship in the air.

REFERENCES: TAIGEN ET AL. 1985; FORESTER & HARRISON 1987; FORESTER ET AL. 1989; GERHARDT ET AL. 1989; ZIMMITTI 1999

12.5   Frog Waves

Each species of frog develops in ponds and marshes on its own schedule each year, beginning with a breeding season filled with evening serenades, through a stage of abundant tadpoles, to the final emergence of hopping adults. Males sing to advertise their presence to nearby females, and frog song is as much a part of spring's arrival as bird song. Choruses of wood frogs begin in March and April, followed closely by toads and spring peepers, with leopard and pickerel frogs singing in April and May, and finally green frogs and bullfrogs during the summer months. The actual emergence dates depend on latitude. It is thought-provoking to realize that the dates of spring emergence for some of the spring breeders have become measurably earlier over the past century because of global warming.

The earliest singers reproduce mostly or exclusively in temporary vernal pools, so they breed quickly and explosively, and their young grow rapidly in these food-rich habitats. Summer breeders, in contrast, require permanent water; bullfrogs and green frogs (Fig. 12.5a), the last waves, make use of prolonged breeding periods, and their young develop more slowly. The advantage of slower emergence is that the tadpoles of these species metamorphose into larger froglets, with a lower risk of predation. Tadpoles of different species mature in the same sequence in which the adults appeared during the breeding season, with young wood frogs and spring peepers reaching adulthood in midsummer, green frogs waiting until the following year, and bullfrogs maturing two years later.

REFERENCES: TYLER 1994; TYNING 1990; GIBBS & BREISCH 2001; SKELLY 1997

a   b

Fig. 12.5.   Green frogs, *Rana clamitans*, one of the late-emerging frog species: (a) adult; (b) tadpole.

12.6 Beaver Meadows

Beavers alter the landscape more than any other animal except humans. Efficient wetland engineers, they are the largest rodents in North America (up to 80 pounds; the next largest rodent is the porcupine, at 30 pounds). Being more adept in water than on land, they actively build dams along shallow-gradient streams where they seek broad areas with high grass, sedge, shrub cover, and proximity to the aspen, cottonwoods, willows, alders, and birch that they like to eat. Here they construct dams by first felling untrimmed trees to catch on the stream bottom and then adding mud and rocks to the base, followed by branches and mud along the inside wall. Maintenance of a dam requires continual surveillance and plugging of leaks. All of this beaver activity creates shallow wetlands that provide homes for many aquatic plants, frogs, turtles, fish, ducks, wading birds, mink, and insects that would otherwise be excluded. Their dams also control erosion, retard flooding, recharge groundwater reservoirs, and reduce siltation downstream. Water that flows down a stream in a day will take a week to pass through a beaver meadow. Through their characteristic eagerness and activity, beavers create their own environment.

Fig. 12.6. Meadow and wetland formed from water drainage being restricted by dams made by beavers, *Castor canadensis*.

Several generations of beavers may build a series of dams along a stream, forming terraced wetlands with lodges made from accumulated sticks. As a pond fills with sediment, or after all nearby trees have been cut (they eat 2 pounds of bark per day, and it takes them only five minutes to cut through a 5-inch-diameter tree), beavers abandon the dam and build a new one elsewhere. Leaks then enlarge in the abandoned dam, which eventually fails, sending a flood wave downstream. But rich, wet beaver meadows are left behind as signs of what the beavers accomplished.

REFERENCES: SUZUKI & MCCOMB 1998; MARCHAND 2001A; JACKSON & DECKER 2002; SNELL 2002; VANCE 2002; WILKINSON 2003

12.7 Muskrat Lodges

Harvesting a wide range of plants from the surrounding marsh, muskrats form their lodges by building mounds of torn vegetation that rise 2 or 3 feet above the water level. The density of these lodges across a marsh gives a good indication of the size of the local muskrat population. As marsh specialists, muskrats are widespread in North America and are our most frequently trapped furbearer; some speak of them as aquatic mice. The entrances to their lodges are underwater, and a single family occupies each, though other organisms make use of these structures, too. Ducks, herons, gulls, and turtles rest or feed on the lodges, while

Fig. 12.7. Muskrat, *Ondatra zibethicus*, nest from a pile of vegetation.

red-winged blackbirds use them for territorial displays. Because lodges and feeding shelters emerge above the water, plant species intolerant of standing water can grow on top, such as jewelweed (*Impatiens* spp.), which makes the mounds in late summer appear from a distance like polka dots of pale green against a darker background of reeds and sedges. One can almost map the location of muskrat lodges by observing the shades of green seen across a late summer marsh.

REFERENCE: WELLER 1981

12.8   Blackbird Zones

Blackbirds breed in freshwater marshes, where they divide up the nesting habitat into concentric circles surrounding the open water. Yellow-headed blackbirds (Fig. 12.8a) are the largest blackbirds, taking over cattails and other emergent vegetation closest to open water in highly productive marshes of central and western states. Red-winged blackbirds (Fig. 12.8b), which are abundant throughout North America, settle around the edges of the marsh, while Brewer's blackbirds (Fig. 12.8c) occupy land farther from the water. It is with these birds that the names of different bird species are the most logical, and one doesn't have to be a birder to match the species names to the males: the first has a yellow head with white wing patches, while the second has red wing patches. The separate zones result from interspecific competition among the birds for the richest, most protected breeding habitat, and the replacement sequence from the water outward reflects the individual dominance of yellow-headed blackbirds as well as the adaptations each species has for different parts of the marsh. Brewer's blackbirds have longer legs, for example, so they are better able to forage in the grasses surrounding the marsh. Males of redwings and yellowheads are both highly territorial; they return to the breeding ground each year before the females, and their success in breeding depends on choosing productive, high-quality territories. Through their behavioral interactions, the birds superimpose discrete zonation on more gradual changes in the marsh vegetation across the gradient from open water toward land.

REFERENCES: ORIANS 1980; WELLER 1981

Fig. 12.8. Blackbirds from distinct zones around western lake edges: (a) yellow-headed blackbird, *Xanthocephalus xanthocephalus*; (b) red-winged blackbird, *Agelaius phoeniceus*; (c) Brewer's blackbird, *Euphagus cyanocephalus*.

12.9   Turtle Nests

A summer walk down a wetland trail sometimes reveals the perils of nesting on the ground. After mating earlier in the spring, painted and snapping turtles crawl out of the water in June to dig nests in higher, sandy soil, where they lay ping-pong-ball-shaped eggs. Nesting in higher ground provides a warmer, drier environment, which accelerates egg development while ensuring that the nest won't be flooded. But there is a price to pay for this choice of

sites. Lured most likely by odors of egg laying, hungry predators such as raccoons, skunks, and foxes are drawn to a breakfast of fresh eggs. Few nests escape these perceptive consumers; studies have reported that 80 percent of most turtle nests are predated. You can tell that the nest was destroyed by the scattered broken pieces of leathery eggshell that surround the excavated, bowl-shaped nesting depressions; the shells of eggs that hatch successfully, in contrast, remain within the soil that the mother scraped over her nest.

Fig. 12.9.   Turtle nest, likely snapping turtle, *Chelydra serpentina,* in the dry soil surrounding a freshwater marsh, dug up by an egg predator.

One can distinguish snapping turtle nests from those of painted turtles most easily by size; snappers lay twenty to forty eggs per nest, whereas painted turtles lay four to eight eggs. The few nests that do survive yield hatchlings two or three months later, in the fall, and the babies must then run a gauntlet of other predators—herons, crows, snakes, and more raccoons—to reach the safety of water. It is remarkable that enough young turtles survive to continue the cycle; the hazards they face are made obvious in the destroyed nests we see.

REFERENCES: BURKE ET AL. 1998; THREE TEACHERS SOFTWARE 2000; MARCHAND 2001B; CHESAPEAKE BAY PROGRAM 2002; DAWSON 2002

12.10   Riffle Insects

Among rocks in the shallow and fast-flowing riffles of a stream (Fig. 12.10a) lives a diverse and abundant community of small, bottom-dwelling invertebrates. Most people think the slower, calmer water of deeper pools would support more living organisms, but that expectation is misguided. Living conditions are good in a riffle: organic matter washes in continually to provide food for filterers and collectors, oxygen levels are high from churning of the water, high light penetrates shallow water to promote plant growth, solid rock surfaces are available for attachment, and spaces among the rocks provide refuges from predators. All that's needed for an aquatic insect such as a mayfly or caddisfly to live in a riffle is a streamlined shape and an ability to hold on to a rock surface or to settle among the rocks (Fig. 12.10b).

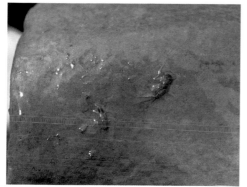

Fig. 12.10. Streams and their insects (unidentified species): (a) a riffle; (b) mayfly nymphs on a turned over rock; (c) stream invertebrates from a riffle, including caddisfly, stonefly, and fishfly nymphs, as well as an annelid worm.

Pools, in contrast, offer an unstable, silty substrate without the advantages of fast, shallow water for food and gas exchange. The more uniform bottom provides little escape from roaming predators, too. Though preferring riffles, some invertebrates are washed into pools by the faster current upstream. Riffles may have ten times the number of juvenile insects as pools (Fig. 12.10c); the evidence is right before you if you turn over rocks in each of these stream habitats.

REFERENCES: BORROR ET AL. 1989; BROWN & BRUSSOCK 1991; DEGANI ET AL. 1993

12.11   Water Walkers

Water striders don't need ice to go skating. In pools or slow-flowing streams, these intriguing little insects skitter over the water's surface while searching for food and mates. They can walk on water because of their small size (high surface-to-volume ratio) and physical properties of the exposed surface of liquids.

Tension develops within the surface layer of water because of its cohesive properties. Water molecules attract each other through hydrogen bonding, and molecules that are under the surface cohere in all directions with the surrounding water molecules. Those molecules at the surface have nothing to cohere with immediately above them, however, so more of the attractive forces point toward the water molecules at their sides. This stronger coherence in the uppermost layer creates surface tension; the water acts as if covered by a thin membrane.

Cloaked with small hairs, the feet of water striders are hydrophobic (repel water). The insect weighs enough to press down on the surface of the water but not enough to break the surface tension, so downward dimples form wherever its feet touch the surface. Their elongate middle legs provide rowing power to skate across the water at a speed of up to 5 feet per second, but the power to move comes when their feet push against the sloped surface of the dimples, creating vortices in the subsurface water. That lets them glide ahead, while they use their long third pair of legs for steering. Living on the surface tension makes water striders exceptionally sensitive to surface vibrations, which they use to communicate among themselves and to detect small insect prey trapped at the surface.

REFERENCES: TENENBAUM 2002; HU ET AL. 2003

a   b

Fig. 12.11.   Water striders, *Gerris* sp., (a) and (b), on the surface of a stream.

12.12   Water Clarity

You can tell whether fish, particularly trout, are present in a high mountain lake simply by looking at the clarity of the water. This surprising result is due to the effect of fish on the rest of the biological community. As visual predators, trout eat the largest zooplankton—tiny shrimplike crustaceans—that predominate in mountain lakes and ponds, while the zooplankton in turn feed on algae in the water. The effects of trout as top-level predators cascade down through the food web; with trout present, zooplankton abundance is depressed, and with fewer herbivorous zooplankton, more algal cells accumulate in what looks like greener, more turbid water (Fig. 12.12a). In contrast, fishless waters contain more zooplankton herbivores, less algae, and more transparent water (Fig. 12.12b). This example shows clearly (in more than one way) how a top-level predator may affect the rest of the biological community so strongly that it is a key to which species can coexist.

Fig. 12.12. Zooplankton of high elevation ponds: (a) smaller, transparent zooplankton of a lake with fish; (b) large, pigmented zooplankton of a fishless pond at the same concentration and magnification as in (a) (in petri dishes); (c) a subalpine pond without inlet or outlet and without fish.

a

b

c

In transparent alpine waters, the zooplankton are conspicuous because of their deep colors, which shield against the intense ultraviolet radiation of high elevations. The cascading effects of predators, illustrated so well in alpine ponds, are more apparent in aquatic than terrestrial food webs because of homogeneity of the water column, the small individual size of the algae and herbivores, and the simplicity of the food webs. Fishing in mountain lakes with transparent water is good outdoors recreation, but it won't fill the creel.

REFERENCES: WILLIAMS 1976; ZARET 1980; KERFOOT & SIH 1987; CHASE 2000; SOMMARUGA 2001

12.13 Colorful Hot Pools

Rainbow-like bands of brilliant colors surround the steaming hot pools and their outflow channels in geologically active thermal regions such as Yellowstone National Park. Living organisms are the sources of these colors; it is astonishing that microorganisms can tolerate the scalding high temperatures enough to grow, but they do. While the most important pigments are green, photosynthetic chlorophylls, other pigments are also present, especially carotenoids, which produce yellows, oranges, and reds. In many photosynthetic cells, carotenoids help harvest energy from sunlight, but these pigments also serve as sunscreens to reduce high levels of damaging sunlight.

The pattern of bands around a hot pool show that color follows temperature gradients of the water. The middle of the pool is deep blue from the physical properties of light passing through water; toward the edges, white then dominates because no pigmented bacteria can grow in the hottest temperatures (above 160°F). Outside the white zone, orange bacterial mats develop. Different shades of tan, yellow, orange, and pink form in subsequent outer, shallower, and cooler bands, with the color of the zone determined by the relative balance of chlorophylls and carotenoids and the matlike growth of algae and bacteria. In cooler areas, especially during the winter, when sunlight is less intense, chlorophylls dominate, and algal mats appear green. In the hostile environment of a hot pool, color serves as an indicator of temperature gradients and of single-celled organisms adapted to function under extreme conditions.

REFERENCE: BROCK 1999

a

b

Fig. 12.13. Hot pool algae: (a) algal bands showing different temperatures in a hot pool runoff; (b) color bands at the edge of a hot pool, with a carotenoid zone (orange and hotter) and a chlorophyll zone (green and cooler); (c) hot water flowing from thermal features into the Firehole River in Yellowstone National Park (Wyoming), where color bands are readily seen.

c

13. COASTS

The habitats of coastal margins include marshes, estuaries, mud flats, sand dunes, rocky shores, and coastal forests, all of which are influenced by salt spray and the rising and falling of tidal waters. The intertidal gradient from high and dry to continuously submerged strongly affects plants and animals because the physical conditions for life change so dramatically over such a short distance. A number of the observations described in this chapter reflect the differences across the intertidal zone.

13.1 Intertidal Zonation

The vertical layering that is so apparent in the intertidal zone—bands of species growing at different heights above the low-tide level—results from the response of attached organisms to differences in exposure. Dampened by ocean spray but infrequently covered by water, organisms that live high in the rocky intertidal are exposed to heat, freezing, and desiccation. These environmental factors override all others in determining what marine life lives in the high zone. Lower in the intertidal gradient, more frequent and longer immersion ameliorates the physical stresses of exposure and allows more organisms to attach and grow. Here, space to attach on rocks may be in short supply because of the denser growth, and mobile predators such as starfish and dogwhelks roam about feeding, reducing the abundance of their prey.

Barnacles, which can withstand desiccation by closing up, occupy the highest intertidal zone, with rocks in the middle covered by mussels and algae. The lowest zone is dominated by kelps, a group of brown algae; nutrients are so abundant here that the kelps grow faster than grazers can eat them. The distribution of living organisms reflects the gradient in the intertidal zone from physical stresses up high to the biological stresses of predation and competition down lower. The gradient is steep, too, which is why the bands of different species stand out so discretely to our eyes.

REFERENCES: HAWKINS & JONES 1992; BERTNESS 1999

Fig. 13.1. A rocky intertidal zone (Massachusetts), showing zones of different marine life at different heights above the water (the brown seaweed is Irish moss, *Chondrus crispus*, below a zone of paler rockweed, *Fucus* sp.).

13.2   Exposure Gradient

In addition to the vertical layering of the rocky intertidal zone—a product of drought and varying temperature at the highest level and predation and competition down lower (see 13.1)—a horizontal gradient exists from shores exposed to the open ocean to those that are sheltered in bays. The intertidal zones spread out vertically in distinct bands on exposed shores, where salt spray raises the upper limits to marine life by moistening higher rocks (Fig. 13.2a). Wave action on open shores also limits the spread of algae (seaweeds) by tearing at their attachments; instead, filter feeders and grazers that can hold on strongly, typically barnacles, mussels, and limpets, are more abundant.

At the other end of the exposure scale, reduced water movement on sheltered shores leads to more silting, reduced settlement of larvae, and a vertically compressed intertidal gradient whose zones are less distinct (Fig. 13.2b). In addition, seaweeds dominate because mobile predators are more active here, reducing the numbers of herbivores. The amount of wave action determines where the balance falls between filter-feeders and seaweeds. As one would expect, organisms in the intertidal zone change with the physical conditions that surround them.

REFERENCES: LUBCHENCO & MENGE 1978; HAWKINS & JONES 1992; BERTNESS 1999

Fig. 13.2.   Intertidal gradients (Massachusetts): (a) exposed coast, with the intertidal zones spread out vertically (a wide barnacle zone above a zone of rockweed, *Fucus* sp.); (b) protected coast, with the bands collapsed together (the seaweed is knotted wrack, *Ascophyllum nodosum*).

13.3   Tide Pool Variability

Tide pools on rocky shores provide a refuge to many marine organisms, including those that prefer continuous submersion. As tides recede along these coasts, rock depressions and crevices remain filled with water and samples of ocean creatures. Tide pools differ, however, from coastal waters; tide pools warm under the sun, increase in salinity as water evaporates, decrease in salinity when it rains, and vary enough over time in CO_2 concentration to raise or lower the pH. Shallower tide pools and those higher in the intertidal zone experience greater environmental variation and stresses, limiting the diversity of organisms that can occupy them but still providing oases for survival among exposed expanses of rock (Fig. 13.3a). Low, large tide pools, in contrast, are rich, diverse marine aquaria that more closely resemble what is found in the open ocean (Fig. 13.3c).

Biological interactions also play an important role in the variability of tide pools. Green algae such as sea lettuce dominate some tide pools, but where herbivorous periwinkle snails (*Littorina* spp.) are numerous, green algae are replaced by herbivore-resistant, calcium-infused algal species. There's another factor, too. Crabs may lurk underneath the algal canopy of tide pools where green algae dominate, preying on and excluding herbivorous periwinkles and thus maintaining the dense growth of algae. In tide pools, as elsewhere in nature, the biological communities we see are strongly affected by who's eating whom.

REFERENCES: LUBCHENKO 1978; BERTNESS 1999; SMITH & SMITH 2001

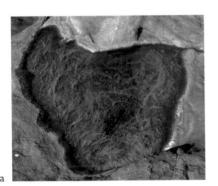

a

b

Fig. 13.3.   Tide pools (Maine and Massachusetts): (a) a high tide pool (with the seaweed *Enteromorpha* sp.); (b) an intermediate-height tide pool (the deep green is sea lettuce, *Ulva* sp.); (c) a diverse, low tide pool.

c

13.4   Fouling Communities

Much of the year, ocean waters are teeming with the young of invertebrate animals in search of hard substrates on which to settle. More than 80 percent of marine organisms release free-swimming larvae that disperse to new places to grow. Any hard surface can serve for settlement, so whatever humans leave in the water, such as dock pilings and boat bottoms, can over time become covered with attached marine life: algae, barnacles, mussels, marine worms, and less familiar forms such as bryozoans and tunicates. These creatures form crusts on hard surfaces but are "fouling" only in the sense that they interfere with the activities of humans, who sometimes use toxic paints to prevent the settlement of such organisms or periodically scrape them away. Boats and docks in partially closed harbors have higher rates of fouling than those in more open harbors because of slowed water currents.

The living communities on these substrates change over time. A thin bacterial film quickly coats any clean surface immersed in the water, and the substrate is subsequently colonized by whatever animals are reproducing heavily at that moment. Additional larvae of the same species that settled initially may follow chemical cues from their relatives and settle nearby. Larvae of other species may be attracted to the early colonizing community or repelled by the defensive abilities of the organisms already settled. The local environmental conditions and availability of food and space also contribute to speeding up or slowing down the process of change over time.

Fig. 13.4.   The fouling community of an exposed pier piling; barnacles are most visible.

REFERENCES: RICKETTS ET AL. 1985; BERTNESS 1999; FLOERL & INGLIS 2003

13.5   Dune Zonation

Wind, salt spray, dryness, and instability of the sand provide challenges to the growth of plants on open sand dunes. Only a few species can grow under these conditions; the first colonizing plants, such as beach grass, are stress-tolerant and characterized by small leaves, deep roots, low stature, growth by roots and runners (spreading stems) to form clones, and an ability to store or reduce the loss of water. As the first plants gain footholds on a dune, their roots and rhizomes (underground stems) help stabilize the sand, while decaying leaves contribute nutrients and water-holding capacity to the developing soil. Amelioration of the harsh dune conditions allows other species to invade, so over time the colonizing plants are replaced by larger, less exposure-tolerant species.

Because new dunes form near the water as sand accumulates, the differences seen along a transect running inland from the ocean mirrors the changes that occur on a single dune over

a

b

Fig. 13.5. Sand dunes (Massachusetts): (a) the newest dunes, nearest the water, stabilized with beach grass, *Ammophila* sp.; (b) older dunes supporting a more diverse, woody vegetation.

time. Pioneer plants on dunes near the water (Fig. 13.5a) are replaced by shrubs and vines such as bayberry and nitrogen-fixing beach pea, which add nutrients to the developing soil. Farther inland lies a thicket zone, where larger shrubs and trees, dwarfed and sculpted by blowing salt spray, grow on enriched soil (Fig. 13.5b). Occasionally, the wind produces a blowout by gouging out the vegetation of a high dune, returning the site to open, eroding sand. The change in the vegetation across sand dunes reflects a gradient in the conditions for growth, which are harshest at the water's edge.

REFERENCE: BERTNESS 1999

13.6   Sand Life

High wave energy and instability of sand particles make it too difficult for most species to live on sandy beaches, but a few small organisms are abundant near the water. Egg-shaped mole crabs, also known as sand crabs, move up and down the beach with the tides in order to stay in the wash zone, where waves break; they burrow quickly in the wet sand and extend their feathery antennae to filter food particles from the water flowing above them. These are the animals seen most often on sandy beaches, but little clams—coquinas and bean clams—live there, too. The presence of small invertebrate animals is revealed by trails in the sand (Fig. 13.6a) and by the foraging of some birds. Sanderlings are small, light-colored sandpipers that run down to the water and back up just as a wave comes in, actively searching for prey with their beaks while seeming to chase the waves (Fig. 13.6b). Probing half an inch down in the wet sand and tasting it for the presence of food, they grasp the largest prey items they can find. To discover where beach invertebrates are abundant, all you have to do is watch where the sanderlings run and feed.

REFERENCES: KOZLOFF 1973; MYERS ET AL. 1980; LEBER 1982; VAN HEEZIK ET AL. 1983; RICKETTS ET AL. 1985; CASTRO ET AL. 1992; BERTNESS 1999; SMITH & SMITH 2001

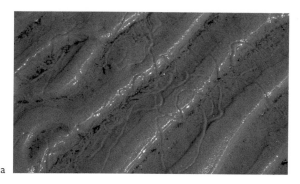

a

b

Fig. 13.6.   Beach sand with: (a) trails of invertebrate animals; (b) a sanderling, *Calidris alba*, feeding near the water's edge.

13.7   Mudflat Burrows and Casts

Holes and casts are evidence of the abundant life of mudflats, where more animals live within the soft sediments (infauna) than on the surface (epifauna). Hidden down in the burrows are filter feeders, including numerous species of clams, that poke up above the surface to take in food. Deposit feeders such as mud snails and many species of worms, ingest mud for its accumulated bacteria and organic compounds; some, such as lugworms, leave behind coiled and conical castings of the sediments they have processed. The algae-rich surface of mudflats is also crossed by the trails of surface-feeding snails and fiddler crabs. All these signals point to a three-dimensional community within the mud that, by feeding and burrowing, reworks the sediments: sorting and oxygenating them, processing dead and living organic materials that wash in from elsewhere, and returning nutrients to the water. Trails, burrows, and casts are visual recordings of this abundant activity.

REFERENCES: KOZLOFF 1973; RICKETTS ET AL. 1985; BERTNESS 1999; SMITH & SMITH 2001

Fig. 13.7.
Mudflat with
snails, snail trails,
and burrows
(Massachusetts).

13.8   Mudflat Odors

On shores with low wave energy, silt accumulates to form coastal mudflats. The surface of a mudflat is well oxygenated from exposure at low tide and the rise and fall of tidal waters, but the denseness of the sediment slows the downward diffusion of oxygen, and organisms burrowing in the mud use up what limited oxygen diffuses there. The result is an abrupt transition to anoxic conditions, sometimes only a fraction of an inch below the surface, where bacteria that can grow in the absence of oxygen (anaerobes) release sulfurous compounds that turn the mud black (iron sulfides) and form rotten-egg odors (hydrogen sulfide). The transition to the anoxic zone is up to a foot deep where less organic material is deposited and, because water drains better through sand than silt, where the particle size of the sediments is larger. Deposit-feeding animals alter the chemistry of the sediments by turning the mud over and feeding on organic material, and their burrows improve drainage and aeration. It is the anaerobic bacteria, however, that create the very noticeable odor of disturbed mudflats.

Fig. 13.8.   Mudflat with a boot print exposing the black anaerobic sediment beneath the surface.

REFERENCE: BERTNESS 1999

13.9   Marsh Zonation

The flat landscape of a salt marsh, the marsh platform, is found at a level near the average high tide. Although the gradient across a salt marsh from water to land is more gradual than it is across a rocky coast, rising and falling tidal waters lead to different species of plants dominating on slightly higher and slightly lower marsh sediments. Two zones are most noticeable in North Atlantic salt marshes: high marsh with shorter salt-meadow hay, and low marsh with taller cordgrass. Salt-meadow hay (*Spartina patens*) competitively dominates the high marsh with its dense roots and stems. Closer to the water, cordgrass (*Spartina alterniflora*) grows with hollow stems that can carry oxygen down to its roots, so it tolerates longer immersion. It is found in wide expanses and is tallest closer to open water, where the soil drains better.

Both grasses must spend energy to cope with the saline environment. They minimize the uptake of salt but accumulate organic compounds within their cells to provide osmotic protection against the loss of water that occurs when living things are immersed in salt water. Cordgrass also has salt-secreting cells. Fiddler crabs (see 13.12) and mussels are more common in the lower cordgrass zone, where mussels entwined with cordgrass stems help resist uprooting from storms and movement from wintertime ice sheets. The separation of the high marsh and low marsh results from a gradient in tidal conditions and competition between the two grass species. As elsewhere, however, humans are having an impact on the natural zonation of marshes; the lower zone is shifting higher because of anthropogenically increased nitrogen favoring the stress-tolerant cordgrass, while giant reeds (see 12.3) are invading marsh edges.

REFERENCES: BERTNESS 1992, 1999; KOCSIS & HANSON 2000; EMERY ET AL. 2001; BERTNESS ET AL. 2002; MORRIS ET AL. 2002

Fig. 13.9. A shallow spatial gradient in the plants of a salt marsh, mostly cordgrass, *Spartina alterniflora* (Massachusetts).

13.10 Salt Pans

The level topography of a salt marsh is broken occasionally by gentle depressions where sediments drain less well and where evaporation under a hot sun leads to an accumulation of salt. These altered conditions give a competitive edge to plants more tolerant of high salinity, such as glassworts (*Salicornia* spp.), which are thick-stemmed succulents characteristic of salty conditions. Glassworts store excess sodium in fluid-filled organelles (vacuoles) within their cells, and these vacuoles absorb water to keep the internal salt concentration tolerable. Although the middle of a salt pan may lack plants completely, the gradient of decreasing salinity that runs outward from the center produces concentric rings of plant species with different abilities to cope with salt. Some clonal plants such as spikegrass, *Distichlis spicata,* can invade the margins

a

Fig. 13.10. Salt pan: (a) a low area with glasswort, *Salicornia* sp.; (b) closer view of glasswort.

b

of a salt pan with runners or rhizomes, provided that colonizing parts remain connected to leafy stems outside the salt-stressed area. Because of seasonal differences, southern salt pans are more permanent than northern ones, which form anew each summer. Salt pans provide another example of variation across the coastal landscape.

REFERENCES: DOWNTON & MILLHOUSE 1985; LARCHER 1995; BOLEN 1998; BERTNESS 1999

13.11   Eat-outs and Cowlicks

Patches of disturbance are often visible within wide stands of salt marsh grasses. Wind blowing on marsh grasses knocks over clusters of stems in a dominolike fashion that produces cowlicks, swirled mats of flattened vegetation in the marsh. Cowlicks are widespread by late summer.

Though less common, another kind of disturbance is created when feeding herbivores are abundant enough to denude a single spot. Such patches are sometimes known, aptly, as eat-outs. Muskrats make extensive use of marsh grasses for lodge construction as well as for food, and they can produce noticeable eat-outs where they are abundant. When feeding is more spread out, as with nutrias in southern marshes, eat-outs are less frequent. An abundance of gregariously feeding snow geese can significantly reduce a patch of marsh vegetation by feeding heavily on roots and rhizomes, slowing regrowth of the vegetation the following year; however, the mobility of geese usually means that the damaging effects of their feeding are less concentrated. Recovery by seed germination or regrowth from rhizomes is usually slow, but the rate depends on how destructive the feeding has been. Disturbances such as these are quite visible in marshes because marsh vegetation grows in such uniform expanses.

REFERENCES: SMITH & ODUM 1981; CHABRECK 1988; BOLEN 1998; SMITH & SMITH 2001

Fig. 13.11.   A cowlick in salt marsh grasses, *Spartina* sp.

13.12   Marsh Crabs

Running over the muddy surfaces of salt marshes with their large claws held high, fiddler crabs are conspicuous and abundant components of the marsh community. Holes in the mud mark their burrows, which can be deep as well as numerous. They feed at low tide on the detrital remains of dead plants, selectively ingesting organic particles from the mud they scoop with their claws. Their presence is often characterized by balls of processed sediment that they leave behind in piles on the mud surface. Males feed with only the smaller of their two claws, keeping the major claw for fighting with other males and for standing tall and waving to females in courtship displays. If a female responds, he'll run to lure her to his burrow. In some species of fiddler crabs, males have either left-handed or right-handed major claws, but even in the world of fiddler crabs, right-handed individuals predominate. There is a cost to having a large claw, however: bird predators preferentially attack the more conspicuous males rather than the less obvious females. Foraging fiddler crabs prowl the marsh away from their burrows, except when hiding from predators or during high tides or wintry temperatures. When a predator approaches fiddler crabs out on the sediment surface, they run toward each other for group defense. The feeding and burrowing activities of fiddler crabs improve the growth of marsh grasses by mixing the muddy sediments and promoting drainage and decomposition. Thus, these intriguing little animals produce benefits in the marsh just like earthworms in upland areas.

REFERENCES: BERTNESS 1999; KOGA ET AL. 2001; ROSENBERG 2002; VISCIDIO & WETHEY 2002

Fig. 13.12.   Fiddler crabs, *Uca* sp., on a mudflat (North Carolina).

13.13   Sculptured Forest

Salt spray creates smooth contours on coastal trees. As the wind blows droplets of ocean water inland, the high salt concentration kills buds on the windward side of growing tips of the coastal vegetation, but buds on the leeward side are sheltered. As the first stems survive, they block the salt spray, allowing the next stems and trees downwind to grow a little higher. In this manner, the edge of maritime forests develops a sculpted shape, with the canopy being lowest near the water and higher farther inland. The shape of the undulating plant canopy gives evidence about the patterns of wind flow over the coast.

Fig. 13.13. Sculptured maritime forests: (a) North Carolina; (b) Oregon; (c) Massachusetts.

a

b

c

On nutrient-poor sandy soils, salt spray provides some benefit as well as harm by depositing calcium and other mineral nutrients needed for growth. Live oaks in dwarfed coastal form are characteristic of southeastern maritime forests; the thick cuticle and leaf wax of their tough leaves provide partial protection from salt spray, and they stabilize the dunes and serve as windbreaks for other plants. Their smoothly sculpted canopy is often so dense that plants underneath are protected from salt spray.

REFERENCES: BOLEN 1998; WALKER 1999

13.14 Kelp and Sea Otters

Extensive stands of large brown kelp grow in patches just off the Pacific coast. Kelp are algae (seaweeds), sometimes more than 100 feet in length, that attach to the seafloor with structures known as holdfasts, while gas-filled floats lift their flattened blades upward. A kelp forest results when the blades reach the surface, spread out, and form a canopy over the water. Although few herbivores feed on kelp, sea urchins do, and urchins can be so numerous that they dramatically lower the abundance of these brown seaweeds.

Living near kelp forests, sea otters feed voraciously on sea urchins, in addition to other foods such as abalones, and therein lies an ecological tale. Several lines of evidence point to a cascade of effects running through this food web. Where sea otters are present, they reduce the number of sea urchins so much so that kelp flourishes; in contrast, sea urchins dominate where sea otters are absent, and feeding by urchins then reduces the amount of kelp. Hungry orcas (killer whales), whose seal and sea lion prey have declined in abundance in recent years, have recently reversed the outcome in some coastal areas by eating sea otters, leading to increased numbers of sea urchins, which in turn mow down the kelp beds. Food webs really are webs of interactions, and top-level predators are often keys to their structure.

REFERENCES: ESTES ET AL. 1998; BOLEN 1998

Fig 13.14. Sea otter, *Enhydra lutris*, in a kelp bed, *Macrocystis pyrifera*.

14. GLOBAL PATTERNS

This final chapter presents key observations seen over very broad spatial and temporal scales. The first three are readily observable, at least in the right geographic areas, but the last two—species and area and latitudinal gradient—are simply the two broadest patterns in the distribution of life on earth. Though not immediately observable, they help one understand nature a little better. And that is the overall goal of this book.

14.1   Green World

Green is a predominant color in nature because, despite variation in temperature and precipitation, most land is covered with green plants. The sunlight that strikes living vegetation has wavelengths representing all colors of the spectrum, but plants appear green because their most abundant pigments, chlorophylls, absorb light with longer (red) and shorter (blue) wavelengths but absorb less of intermediate (green) wavelengths. The unabsorbed green light is reflected from the leaves or transmitted through them, giving plants their characteristic green color. Carotenoids and other photosynthetic pigments capture light energy for photosynthesis, too, and different combinations of other pigments with chlorophyll produce the different shades of green we see in terrestrial vegetation.

Although some bacteria harvest light with other pigments, most land plants have chlorophyll. The light absorption spectrum of chlorophyll provides efficient harvesting of the sun's energy, but some researchers have proposed another advantage to chlorophyll. Photosynthetic pathways are partially inhibited by intense sunlight. Under such conditions, the less-absorbed green light is able to penetrate deeper within the leaf, where it can continue to drive some photosynthesis under the reduced light levels. Thus, green-reflecting chlorophyll serves land plants quite well for light absorbance under varying light intensities, and, as a result, we see the world through what seem to be green-tinted glasses.

Some researchers have proposed that the greenness of terrestrial habitats indicates that herbivores have so much food that their abundance can't be food-limited. But plants have evolved numerous protective defenses, including many chemical poisons, and as a result, the greenness of nature says little about how much food is available for plant eaters. It says a lot, on the other hand, about the abundance of chlorophyll.

REFERENCES: GOLDSWORTHY 1987; POLIS 1999; NISHIO 2000

Fig. 14.1.   The world is predominantly green (New York).

14.2 Dynamic Nature

The temporal scale of most human experience makes us think that nature is static: a large oak we saw at the edge of a field last year is still there this year. But the landscape changes continuously—sometimes dramatically, as when fire sweeps through a forest, and sometimes barely perceptibly, as in the midst of global climate warming. Disturbances occur on many different temporal and spatial scales. And there is no simple balance of nature; what we see at any one time is the outcome of many interactions, with the outcome tilting in one direction or another as the contributing factors vary in intensity.

The dynamism of nature is typified by the landscape in Yellowstone National Park, where extensive fires raged in the hot, dry year of 1988 (see 9.8). Before that smoke-filled summer, many people thought that Yellowstone had been cloaked forever with a green pine forest and would continue forever to be so; once it burned, they thought that the park would remain blackened from that time on. Living things take advantage of new opportunities, however, and fire is a natural form of disturbance. The fires recycled nutrients from fallen timbers to spur new growth in sunlit areas. Grasslands have recovered fully, aspen have resprouted vigorously, lodgepole pine seeds have germinated abundantly in even the most severely burned areas, and wildflowers have bloomed abundantly. Recovery of sagebrush, streams, and forest cover is taking more time, but the mosaic of vegetational patches produced by the fires has created diverse habitats for many different species. The same cycle of infrequent severe fires has occurred in the park for thousands of years. Here, as elsewhere, change and renewal are inevitable.

REFERENCES: KRICHER 1998; BASKIN 1999; TURNER ET AL. 2003

Fig. 14.2.   The changing vegetation of a fire-burned landscape (Yellowstone National Park, Wyoming).

14.3   Rain Shadows

Often one side of a mountain or island is wetter than the other side, and therein lies a clue about the direction of prevailing winds. Air masses rise as they flow over a mountain, and because of greater distance from the center of the earth, the air masses experience less gravity and expand. As they expand, they cool.[1] Because cool air holds less moisture than warm air (think of condensation on the outside of an ice-filled glass), the water vapor in a rising air mass condenses and falls on the upslope as rain or snow. Wherever winds ascend higher elevations after crossing lakes or oceans, precipitation is abundant.

The opposite effect takes place on the other side; after crossing the top of the mountain, air masses descend, condense, warm, and absorb moisture from the landscape. This process produces a rain shadow on the downwind side wherever the wind flows consistently over a mountain in the same direction. Deep snow piles up on the western slope of the Sierra Nevada Mountains, for example, as water is squeezed out of the rising air, whereas arid basins and deserts are found on the eastern slope, often receiving less than 4 inches of precipitation annually.

REFERENCE: SMITH & SMITH 2001

Fig. 14.3.   A rain shadow: the dry landscape east of the Sierra Mountains (California).

---

[1]The cooling of an expanding air mass is called adiabatic cooling (cooling without the transfer of heat). One explanation for this cooling is that some energy is used in accomplishing the work of pushing the air mass boundary outward. Another explanation is based on temperature being a measure of molecular motion. When an air mass stays the same size (i.e., the boundaries are stationary), molecules of the air mass move about, retaining the same energy they started with; but if the boundaries begin to recede, as when the air mass expands, molecules reflect back from the boundary with less energy than they started with. The same effect occurs when bunting a baseball; the bat is held loosely and pulled back so that the pitched ball bounces off with less energy and drops in front of the plate. With a gas molecule, less energy gives a lower temperature.

14.4   Species and Area

Larger geographic areas generally house more species than smaller areas. This simple observation is the most basic pattern in the distribution of living things on the earth's surface. The relationship between geographic area and the number of species yields an easy rule of thumb: a tenfold increase in area supports approximately twice as many species.[2] Two factors produce this fundamental relationship: larger areas support rare species by including greater abundances of all organisms, and larger areas include greater diversity of habitats. The effect of abundance is apparent because geographic islands have fewer species than equivalently sized areas of a mainland; the difference is that islands include only those species abundant enough to maintain breeding populations within the island boundaries. The global relationship of species and area is so pervasive that it's visible on very local scales as well as continental ones. In nearby fields and forests, you can find a longer list of species and more morphological forms as the square footage you look at increases (Fig. 14.4).

REFERENCES: HORN 1993; BROWN AND LOMOLINO 1998; HAWKINS 2001

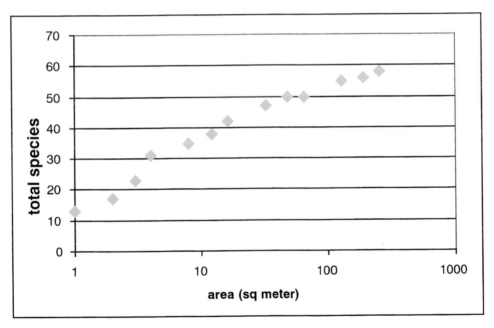

Fig. 14.4.   A plant species-area curve from counts in study plots of different sizes in an alpine meadow (unpublished data; Wyoming). For readability, only the x-axis is logarithmic in this figure.

---

[2]This result is best understood using a quantitative approach. Species-area relationships are often written as $S = cA^z$, with the number of species S dependent on area A, a constant c that varies with different kinds of organisms and geographic areas, and an exponent z that reflects how rapidly the number of species increases with area. Actual z values hover around 0.3, an exponent that, as long as the c values are constant, gives a doubling of species for each tenfold increase in area. Different relationships result when c values vary.

14.5   Latitudinal Gradient

The second broadest pattern of life on earth (see 14.4 for the first) is that the number of resident species increases from the poles to the equator, a gradient repeated in nearly all groups of living organisms. From the northern tip of North America down to Panama, for example, the number of species of birds and mammals increases tenfold. Simply put, there are more species in the tropics, a pattern first recognized in the early 1800s.

There are several reasons for this conspicuous pattern. (1) An important factor is that more solar energy enters the food web near the equator, spurring greater plant productivity, leading to more animal biomass and increased opportunities for specialization. (2) Environmental stresses dominate in polar regions, whereas the biological interactions of competition and predation, both of which promote diversity by limiting the range and abundance of individual species, are more influential in the less seasonal, more benign tropics. At higher latitudes, species must cope with a wider range of climatic conditions as well as much shorter growing seasons (only ten weeks in the subarctic). (3) Long-term climatic stability in tropical areas (e.g., the lack of glaciation) has provided additional time and space for the processes of speciation. (4) Greater contiguous surface area in a region of uniform climate has also promoted specialization and speciation. As a result of these primary factors, tropical forests and coral reefs are the most species-rich habitats on earth.

REFERENCES: BROWN AND LOMOLINO 1998; CHOWN AND GASTON 2000; KORNER 2000; HAWKINS 2001

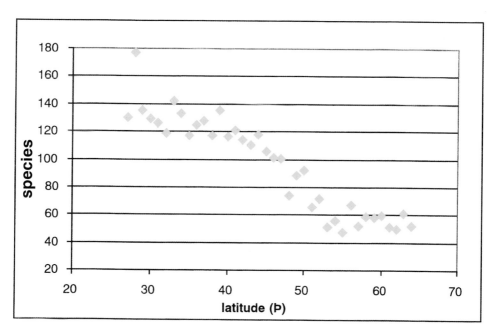

Fig. 14.5.   Latitudinal gradient in butterfly species diversity from Canada to Mexico. Each symbol marks the average number of species found within 170 mi × 170 mi squares of land area at each degree of latitude (data calculated from Pearson and Cassola 1992).

Epilogue

The pages of this book describe more than two hundred patterns and behaviors that one can observe in nature, and while that may seem like a lot—certainly enough for one book—countless more remain. Any watcher of nature knows there are many more observations to make and many more stories to learn, in part because nature is so remarkably diverse.

That diversity has come about through the adaptations of living things to our complex world. Just skim quickly through the preceding pages to catch a glimpse of the range of different kinds of organisms and different kinds of solutions to the problems of life. More than 1.6 million species have been described thus far, and although no one is sure how many more are yet to be named, a currently popular number for the earth's total is about 10 million species. With that many species, how many more interactions are there? How many more solutions exist to the challenges of life?

I can imagine a giant data table to be filled in with details of each of these many species, although we don't even know the size of the table. With a little careful observation, each one of us can supplement the descriptions in this book, filling in part of that enormous table, and independently expand our own understanding of the world around us.

The world is changing rapidly due to the effects of a continually growing human population that uses more and more land and natural resources. If anything, the increasingly detrimental impact around us should help us realize how much beauty and complexity remain in nature. Enjoy that diversity, for it supplies endless fascination. The future is uncertain, though; we need to plan and act appropriately so that much will remain for the generations that follow. They, too, have the right to see, enjoy, and be inspired by all there is in the natural world.

References

Because a large number of references were used in the research for this book, the sources are listed on a Web page rather than here in print. The references noted at the end of each of the separate descriptions in the book may be found on the Web page, and I invite you to look through them for whatever interests you. The sources shown for each topic provide access to some of the original scientific literature as well as first-rate texts and popular articles. The full list of references may be found at:

http://academics.hamilton.edu/biology/ewilliam/naturehandbook/

Some works are so helpful and stimulating that I want to call attention to them here, too. These are good reads, for both enjoyment and enlightenment; they are well written and filled with fascinating information.

Berenbaum, M. R. 1993. *Ninety-nine More Maggots, Mites, and Munchers*. University of Illinois Press, Urbana.

Bertness, M. D. 1999. *The Ecology of Atlantic Shorelines*. Sinauer Assoc., Sunderland, MA.

Ehrlich, P. R., D. S. Dobkin, and D. Wheye. 1988. *The Birder's Handbook*. Fireside Books, Simon & Schuster, Inc., New York.

Hoyt, E., and T. Schultz. 1999. *Insect Lives.* Harvard University Press, Cambridge, MA.

Marchant, P. J. 1987. *North Woods.* Appalachian Mountain Club Books, Boston.

Phillips, S. J., and P. W. Comus. 2000. *A Natural History of the Sonoran Desert.* Arizona-Sonora Desert Museum Press, Tucson.

Stokes, D. W. 1981. *The Natural History of Wild Shrubs and Vines.* Harper & Row, New York.

Thomas, P. 2000. *Trees: Their Natural History.* Cambridge University Press, Cambridge.

Wood, G. L. 1982. *The Guinness Book of Animals Facts and Feats*, 3rd ed. Guinness Superlatives, Ltd., Enfield, UK

Zwinger, A. H., and B. E. Willard. 1972. *Land Above the Trees: A Guide to American Alpine Tundra.* Harper & Row, New York.

Index

Notes

Notes

Notes

Notes

Notes

Notes

Notes